Handbook of Mobility
DATA MINING

VOLUME TWO

HANDBOOK OF MOBILITY
DATA MINING
MOBILITY ANALYTICS AND PREDICTION

Edited by

HAORAN ZHANG

School of Urban Planning and Design, Peking University, Shenzhen, China

ELSEVIER

Elsevier
Radarweg 29, PO Box 211, 1000 AE Amsterdam, Netherlands
The Boulevard, Langford Lane, Kidlington, Oxford OX5 1GB, United Kingdom
50 Hampshire Street, 5th Floor, Cambridge, MA 02139, United States

Notices
Knowledge and best practice in this field are constantly changing. As new research and experience broaden our understanding, changes in research methods, professional practices, or medical treatment may become necessary.

Practitioners and researchers must always rely on their own experience and knowledge in evaluating and using any information, methods, compounds, or experiments described herein. In using such information or methods they should be mindful of their own safety and the safety of others, including parties for whom they have a professional responsibility.

To the fullest extent of the law, neither the Publisher nor the authors, contributors, or editors, assume any liability for any injury and/or damage to persons or property as a matter of products liability, negligence or otherwise, or from any use or operation of any methods, products, instructions, or ideas contained in the material herein.

ISBN: 978-0-443-18424-6

For information on all Elsevier publications visit our website at https://www.elsevier.com/books-and-journals

Publisher: Joseph P. Hayton
Acquisitions Editor: Kathryn Eryilmaz
Editorial Project Manager: Ali Afzal-Khan
Production Project Manager: Swapna Srinivasan
Cover Designer: Greg Harris

Typeset by TNQ Technologies

Working together to grow libraries in developing countries

www.elsevier.com • www.bookaid.org

Contents

List of contributors

Jinyu Chen
Center for Spatial Information Science, The University of Tokyo, Kashiwa-shi, Chiba, Japan

Zhiling Guo
Center for Spatial Information Science, The University of Tokyo, Kashiwa-shi, Chiba, Japan

Dou Huang
Center for Spatial Information Science, The University of Tokyo, Kashiwa-shi, Chiba, Japan

Renhe Jiang
Information Technology Center, The University of Tokyo, Kashiwa-shi, Chiba, Japan

Wenxiao Jiang
Center for Spatial Information Science, The University of Tokyo, Kashiwa-shi, Chiba, Japan

Hill Hiroki Kobayashi
Center for Spatial Information Science, The University of Tokyo, Kashiwa-shi, Chiba, Japan; Information Technology Center, The University of Tokyo, Kashiwa-shi, Chiba, Japan

Peiran Li
Center for Spatial Information Science, The University of Tokyo, Kashiwa-shi, Chiba, Japan

Wenjing Li
Center for Spatial Information Science, The University of Tokyo, Kashiwa-shi, Chiba, Japan; Information Technology Center, The University of Tokyo, Kashiwa-shi, Chiba, Japan

Lifeng Lin
Graduate School of Interdisciplinary Information Studies, The University of Tokyo, Bunkyo, Tokyo, Japan; Center for Spatial Information Science, The University of Tokyo, Kashiwa-shi, Chiba, Japan

Kai Mao
Center for Spatial Information Science, The University of Tokyo, Kashiwa-shi, Chiba, Japan

Xiaowei Shao
Center for Spatial Information Science, The University of Tokyo, Kashiwa-shi, Chiba, Japan; Earth Observation Data Integration and Fusion Research Initiative, The University of Tokyo, Kashiwa-shi, Chiba, Japan

Xiaodan Shi
Center for Spatial Information Science, The University of Tokyo, Kashiwa-shi, Chiba, Japan

Ryosuke Shibasaki
Center for Spatial Information Science, The University of Tokyo, Kashiwa-shi, Chiba, Japan

Xuan Song
Center for Spatial Information Science, The University of Tokyo, Kashiwa-shi, Chiba, Japan; Southern University of Science and Technology-University of Tokyo Joint Research Center for Super Smart Cities, Department of Computer and Engineering, Southern University of Science and Technology, Shenzhen, Guangdong, China

Guangming Wu
Center for Spatial Information Science, The University of Tokyo, Kashiwa-shi, Chiba, Japan

Haoran Zhang
School of Urban Planning and Design, Peking University, Shenzhen, China

Junxiang Zhang
Southern University of Science and Technology-University of Tokyo Joint Research Center for Super Smart Cities, Department of Computer and Engineering, Southern University of Science and Technology, Shenzhen, Guangdong, China

Preface

In recent times, the smartphone is becoming more and more potent in both computing and storage aspects. The data generated by the smartphone provide a means to get new knowledge about various aspects like usage, movement of the user, etc. Increasingly, application and service providers collect data through sensors embedded in smartphones, such as GPS receivers, while mobile operators collect them through the cellular infrastructure. This information is precious for marketing applications and has an incredible potential to benefit society.

Mobility Data Mining (MDM) is a novel research and business field supported by the growth in smartphone use. MDM can help breed new digital, data–driven services that use several technological capabilities associated with intelligent mobility innovation. It relies on building an ecosystem of stakeholders that agree to manage the supply and demand of the services that travelers want, such as intelligent transportation systems, smart emergency management, sustainability development innovates, etc.

MDM is an emerging topic both in academic and industrial aspects. Currently, all studies about mobile big data mining are fragmented. Few works have summarized the systemic knowledge on this field. Specifically, there is no book focusing on introducing how to screen and process the potential value from "deluge" of unverified, noisy, and sometimes incomplete information of mobile big data. Also, few works comprehensively summarized frontier applications of MDM technologies. However, the above knowledge is significant for stakeholders, such as researchers, engineers, operators, company administrators, and policymakers in related fields, to comprehensively understand current technologies' infra-knowledge structure and limitations. Therefore, we planned to write a series of books mainly focusing on these issues.

The readers of this book can find the knowledge of how to preprocess mobile big data, visualize urban mobility, simulate and predict human travel behavior, and assess the urban mobility characteristics and their matching performance as conditions and constraints in transport, emergency management, and sustainability development systems that are undergoing automation and are highly dependent on software, navigation systems, and connectivity. Further, this book will focus on introducing how to design MDM platforms that adapt to the evolving mobility environment, new types of transportation, and users based on an integrated solution that utilizes the sensing and communication capabilities to tackle the significant challenges that the MDM field faces.

The handbook includes three volumes:

Volume 1: *Data Preprocessing and Visualization* focuses on how to efficiently preprocess mobility big data to extract and utilize critical feature information of high-dimensional city people flow. It first provides a conceptual theory and framework, then goes on to discuss data sources, trajectory map matching, noise filtering, trajectory data segmentation, data quality assessment, and more. It concludes with a chapter on mobility big data visualization.

Volume 2: *Mobility Analytics and Prediction* provides a basis for how to simulate and predict mobility data. After an introductory theory chapter, it then covers crucial topics such as long-term mobility pattern analytics, mobility data generators, user information inference, grid-based population density prediction, and more. It concludes with a chapter on graph-based mobility data analytics.

Volume 3: *Mobility Data-driven Applications* looks at various case studies to illustrate and explore the methods introduced in the first two volumes. It begins with a set of chapters on intelligent transportation management, using cases of bicycle-sharing, ride-hailing, travel time prediction, railway usage analysis, mobility data-driven service, and dynamic road pricing. It concludes with chapters on urban sustainability development, including road emission and living environment inequity analysis.

To help to utilize book outcomes by fellow researchers and developers, all book outcomes will be offered as Open Source Code. Please see the open project, OpenMob, https://github.com/openmob/openmob.

Acknowledgments

I want to thank all lab team members: Zhiling Guo, Dou Huang, Xiaodan Shi, Peiran Li, Jinyu Chen, Yuhao Yao, Qing Yu, Wenjing Li, Zhiheng Chen, Xudong Shen, Wenyi Lu, and Ning Xu, for their efforts, and would also like to thank lab leaders Prof. Ryosuke Shibasaki and Prof. Xuan Song for their support for this book.

CHAPTER ONE

Multi-data-based travel behavior analysis and prediction

Kai Mao

Center for Spatial Information Science, The University of Tokyo, Kashiwa-shi, Chiba, Japan

1. Introduction

In the context of the rapid development of the Internet, people are used to interacting with mobile intelligent devices anytime and anywhere. Among them, devices with location services are operating all the time, recording and displaying users' mobile information in real time. This kind of information not only includes users' travel location coordinates, mobility trajectories, specific travel time, and stay time but also shows users' travel mode selection, user labels, and other information. Collecting and analyzing the mobile data of massive users constitute the subject of mobility big data.

The beginning of the problem is about the acquisition of mobility big data. A global positioning system (GPS) is a radio navigation positioning system based on artificial earth satellites. It can provide the accurate geographic location, vehicle speed, and accurate time information anywhere in the world. With its high-precision, all-weather, global coverage, convenience, and flexibility, GPS technology is more and more widely used in the field of transportation, and the provision of location-based services based on GPS data is also emerging rapidly. At present, the acquisition methods of mobility big data are expanding. The traditional mobile data acquisition methods based on Bluetooth, WiFi signal, and video recognition are developing in specific fields due to the limitations of application scenarios. However, the emerging location-based service using GPS and Point of Interest (POI) data is widely applied in transportation, urban construction, commerce, and advertising industries with its advantages of accuracy, real-time, wide coverage, ease to be used, and analysis in deep learning.

The topics widely concerned include mobile trajectory analysis and prediction, travel behavior description and speculation, travel destination and travel route selection, etc. The study focuses on how to mine potential patterns, rules, and other knowledge from the travel trajectory information

Handbook of Mobility Data Mining, Volume 2
ISBN: 978-0-443-18424-6
https://doi.org/10.1016/B978-0-443-18424-6.00005-2
1

with spatial-temporal characteristics, analyze the location relationship between user objects as well as the hidden value between users and the environment, so as to provide personalized services.

First of all, GPS data can draw high-resolution pictures to express the stay or movement of the research object, and it contains time and space information; however, the feature extraction of travel information by this method is a very complicated process, and the features of travel information are not included [1]. In travel research, we generally focus on the mode of transportation and the purpose of the trip. There are relatively few studies on travel purposes [2]. At present, there are no existing imputation methods for travel purpose research on GPS data, but more focus on the comparison between data, mining, and method evaluation.

2. Description of mobility big data and travel behavior

2.1 Mobility data mining methods based on heterogenyeousmeans

2.1.1 Based on Bluetooth, WiFi, video detection

At present, the widely used monitoring method is to install cameras for shooting, but the storage of video images is huge. For hospitals, factories, schools, and other places with general infrastructure, there is no large server to store and process these video data, and there is no sufficient security team to conduct 24 hours continuous monitoring. Therefore, if the video shooting method is used alone, the work efficiency is exceptionally low, and it is prone to false alarms and omissions in emergency situations.

Bluetooth technology is an open global specification for wireless data and voice communication. It is a special short-range wireless technology connection based on a low-cost, short-range wireless connection to establish a communication environment for fixed and mobile devices. Like Bluetooth technology, Wireless Fidelity (WiFi) is also a technology used in offices and homes, which can connect personal computers, handheld devices (such as PDAs, mobile phones), and other terminals to each other wirelessly. It consists of access points (AP) and a wireless network card and uses RSSI technology to achieve location acquisition.

WIFI and Bluetooth wireless positioning can solve the limitations of video surveillance, such as the inability to shoot people in dim environments and the inability to work in bad weather conditions. As long as wireless LAN devices are installed in public places, ordinary users can connect to the devices in the area, participate in communications, and share the investment in video equipment, saving a lot of capital and labor costs.

The observed value of the method discussed in this section is mainly received signal strength (received signal strength indication, RSSI). There are two general methods for positioning using RSSI [1]: Convert RSSI to distance by using the signal propagation model and perform distance intersection [2]; Use the precollected signal strength background field to perform spatial matching. Its positioning accuracy depends on stable and reliable signal strength values. Due to the complex and changeable indoor environment and serious signal attenuation, RSSI is unstable, so filtering is needed to solve this problem. Including filtering the positioning coordinates.

However, these positioning methods have certain limitations. Positioning based on Bluetooth and WiFi requires the intensive deployment of detection equipment, so it is mostly used in indoor scenarios. In open areas such as nonurban areas, the cost will increase, and the positioning accuracy will decrease. Secondly, this method requires that the access device has WiFi or Bluetooth capabilities and remains connected to the Internet. Otherwise, it will not work.

Therefore, we need to use more efficient and convenient GPS and POIs data to carry out mobility big data mining.

2.1.2 Based on GPS and POI

Based on the above shortcomings, now we use GPS and POI data to obtain location data. GPS data is mainly collected by the GPS module, and the general GPS module reports its own position (longitude and latitude) through serial communication, basically following the NMEA-0183 protocol. In addition, in a geographic information system, a POI can be a house, a shop, a mailbox, a bus stop, and so on. POI data is the core data of location-based services and has a wide range of application scenarios, such as viewing nearby restaurants and bus stops. It plays a very important role in urban planning research, preresearch and policy design of commercial real estate, and investment promotion and operation. For example, analyzing the composition and distribution of surrounding business formats, mining the aggregated traffic of sellers/the value of business district locations, etc.

In some scenarios, users may need real-time POI recommendations. For example, when using food delivery applications, users need to recommend suitable restaurants at a specific moment. Therefore, how to mine users' lifestyles and current preferences becomes an important issue for real-time POI recommendations. To address the above issues, we propose an LSTM-based real-time preference mining model (RTPM) to recommend the next POI with time constraints.

A huge volume of data generated from LBSNs opens up a new avenue of research that gives birth to a new subfield of recommendation systems, known as POI recommendation. A POI recommendation technique essentially exploits users' historical check-ins and other multi-modal information such as POI attributes and friendship networks to recommend the next set of POIs suitable for a user. Our work categorizes and critically analyzes the recent POI recommendation works based on different deep learning paradigms and other relevant features. This review can be considered a cookbook for researchers or practitioners working in the area of POI recommendations.

2.2 Definition and description of travel behavior

Travel behavior theory is one of the most important theories in traffic planning and even traffic management and control. Strengthening the analysis of travel behavior can organically combine qualitative analysis and quantitative analysis to more effectively analyze and predict traffic demand and formulate more effective policies and measures for traffic construction, management, and control.

The theoretical study of travel behavior analysis, especially the study of individual travel behavior, has become the focus. It involves four important aspects: one is the attributes that individuals consider when making demand selection; the other is the specific choice described by the model, including the type of choice (way, destination), and the time of travel research (day, month, year, etc.) and the nature of the set of possible choices; the third is the decision rule (complementarity, rejection, etc.), and the fourth is the assumption of the information available to the decision-maker (including information acquisition and use).

The study of travel behavior is an important part of traffic planning. Whether it is the investigation of basic travel data or the determination of the objective function in the process of traffic distribution, the development of this field is involved. In fact, most travel demand matrices are implicitly or explicitly based on individual utility maximization assumptions. Such models include a series of neoclassical consumer behavior economic models, discrete choice models, and research mechanisms related to transportation in markets and psychology. The reason why the utility maximization hypothesis is widely used is that it is easy to handle, and the analysis results are easy to obtain, especially when it is assumed that multi-attribute (such as transportation, etc.) service decisions can be reduced to subindex optimization.

As a behavioral theory, many of the goals of utility maximization can be achieved by modifying other assumptions in the neoclassical economic model. For example, psychologists argue that when faced with multiple options, subjectivity depends on the "sacrifice" rule. Therefore, individuals will choose the plan that satisfies the upper and lower limits of their attributes rather than the plan that combines the nondegrading attributes into one form of compensation. This behavior seems to have a fixed desire by decision-makers, which can be approximated by a utility-maximizing individual who is faced with many solutions at a certain event, and each of the considered solutions has a searching bag associated with its cost. Although the model obtained in this way deviates a bit from the assumption of utility maximization, it can generate a behavioral individual inspection plan until a plan with all attributes above a certain lower limit is found. Examples of this type appear primarily in the statistical decision theory literature and have recently been extended to more fields by Weibull, Hall, Jones, Harata, Heidemann, and others.

There are many factors that affect the traveler's travel behavior, among which the individual factors of the traveler mainly include psychological factors, personal factors, and situational and environmental factors. Psychological factors mainly include needs and motivations, feelings and perceptions, learning and memory, beliefs and attitudes; personal factors mainly refer to demographic factors such as age, gender, occupation, education level, as well as personality, and lifestyle. Situational and environmental factors include culture, social class, social group, family, economic environment, and so on.

3. Travel behavior analysis based on mobility big data

3.1 Mobility data processing

There are four types of common trajectory data, namely human trajectory, vehicle trajectory, animal trajectory, and natural phenomenon on trajectories.

Human trajectories are divided into two categories, one is passively recorded trajectory data, and the other is actively recorded trajectory data. Every time the mobile phone receives a signal, the server of the telecom operator will record the location of the mobile phone. In this case, it is generally not that the user actively wants to record the location, so this type of track data is passively recorded. Actively recorded trajectory data. For example, some people share their daily activities on social platforms with location information, then this type of actively recorded trajectory data.

The vehicle trajectory data is the data recorded by in-vehicle navigation equipment or mobile phone navigation. Vehicle trajectory data can be used to improve transportation networks, such as using trajectory data to generate road information. Vehicle trajectory data can also be used for resource allocation, such as predicting vehicle demand in a certain area, so that platforms such as Uber can schedule idle vehicles in advance. Vehicle trajectory data can also be used for traffic analysis, such as using trajectory data to discover congested roads or detect road damage.

Animal trajectories are used to study animal migration patterns and habitat characteristics.

Trajectories of natural phenomena can help capture changes in the environment and climate, helping humans better protect the environment and resist natural disasters.

3.1.1 Trajectory noise data processing

Data preprocessing mainly includes three parts, which are trajectory data noise processing, stay point detection, and trajectory map matching. First, the first point is introduced, the noise processing of moving trajectory data.

With the rapid development of machine learning and the increasing replacement of data processing technologies, we have been able to obtain massive amounts of travel trajectory-related information more effectively. In this process, the accuracy of data has become more important. Accurate data constitutes a prerequisite for research.

Machine learning and data processing involves not only the mathematical analysis of the relevant parameters but also the necessary statistical principles. Therefore, accurate and complete data is very important, and data noise will have a serious impact on research, which will not only bring errors to model development but also affect the feasibility and authenticity of the final output results.

In the field of traffic data processing, based on the foregoing, information can be obtained in various ways, including but not limited to Bluetooth, Wi-Fi, video monitoring, and GPS methods. However, the original trajectory data obtained by the above method may show different advantages, disadvantages, and accuracy levels due to factors such as equipment failure and poor signal. At the same time, no matter how the above tools are selected in the experiment, the data we collect is at risk. That is, it may have a noise level that exceeds the threshold set by the project, which requires necessary measures to denoise the data [3]. In the early 1960s, R. E. Kalman and R. S. Bucy (a new achievement of linear filtering and prediction theory) proposed a new linear filtering and prediction theory called Kalman filter. The characteristic is to process the noisy input and observation signals on the basis of linear state space representation and obtain the system state or real signal.

Data filtering is a data processing technique that removes noise and restores real data. Kalman filtering can estimate the state of a dynamic system from a series of data with measurement noise when the measurement variance is known. Because it is convenient for computer programming and can update and process the data collected on-site in real-time, Kalman filtering is the most widely used filtering method at present and has been well applied in many fields such as communication, navigation, guidance, and control [4].

3.1.2 Analysis of stay point detection

In the acquired trajectory data, the stay points include important semantic information. For some application scenarios, it is very important to discover the stop points in the trajectory. For example, in the trajectories of tourists, the stop point is very likely to be a scenic spot. Determining the stop points in a trajectory is a crucial procedure in trajectory data mining and analysis. The current method of judging the presence of lingering behavior of an object generally requires the operator to set an appropriate threshold in advance, and this method will cause quite obvious errors in the recognition result. And on the other hand, the setting of these thresholds often takes empirical methods and lacks support at the mathematical and physical levels. There are many types of moving objects, such as cars, cargo ships, airplanes, people, and animals. These moving objects have their own properties, such as different geometric/physical properties, or the navigation environment, which will lead to obvious differences in the trajectory data of these moving objects. Therefore, it is impossible to set an appropriate threshold for the identification process.

There are many main stop point detection methods currently in existence, which are mainly divided into four categories [5, 6] : Based on geographic information, stay point information is further integrated, and eigenvalue derivation is adopted for object-based trajectory information, density-based clustering methods, and step-by-step merging methods. The current stop point identification is applied in the following fields: (1) The existing methods usually set a threshold and use this threshold as a standard for defining stop points. The choice of this threshold has a decisive impact on the quality and quantity of the result. Ref. [7] shows a method for stay point detection. For this task, parameter sensitivity tests were performed. Increasing the time threshold significantly changes the number of identified steps. Few tracks have multiple stops if the time exceeds 300 s. This means that many breakpoints are lost. A small-time threshold may result in many stopovers being misidentified or splitting a large stopover into several smaller stopovers. An analogous situation exists for distance thresholds. (2) Most of the existing threshold determination research is based on user experience and pays little attention to parameter selection. Even inexperienced and unprofessional users can quickly determine parameters for different purposes (calling, pausing, getting on and off, blocking roads, etc.) and different moving objects (cargo ships, small fishing boats, city taxis, etc.). Outside the city, etc.) cannot be targeted. long-distance) car) is exceedingly difficult. In practice, the threshold selection is closely related to a specific application, and the user must set a custom threshold for that specific application. Therefore, the contribution of this paper is to provide a new interactive visualization method for fast threshold setting. This is of great benefit to the user and improves track stop detection performance [8].

3.1.3 Map matching

The map-matching of the trajectory is a very important link. On the one hand, it can correct the accuracy of the trajectory data, and on the other hand, it can extract key features from it, such as judging the congestion of a certain road. This part of the content is aimed at the vehicle trajectory data because, generally, only the vehicle trajectory is driving on the map road, so map matching needs to be done.

Map matching algorithms can be divided into two types according to the processing time of the data [9]. If the algorithm is implemented during exercise, it is named "online algorithm." Otherwise, it is called an "offline algorithm." The reasons for dividing the algorithm into two are:

Map-matching algorithms have improved significantly over the past 3 decades. In the past, we mostly used simple point-to-point matching, which was inefficient and inaccurate. Now we can use a variety of fuzzy logic theories and other relatively general and advanced methods to experiment. Specifically, the "point-to-point" algorithm, as the name implies, is to match a point to the road closest to it, which is an intuitive method, so it is also the simplest and most natural [10]. Its opposite method is called the "curve to curve" matching method. The advantage of this method is that it uses the law of ordered points to form linear curves. These linear curves have piecewise characteristics, and finally, this method will be based on the curve. The distance between them is calculated, and the average value is calculated to realize the identification of the road [10]. The characteristic of these algorithms is to obtain the mapped matching points based on the similarity of geometric features between these points or lines. However, these methods have two disadvantages. First, when the number of points increases, the accuracy will show a sharp drop. This phenomenon is because the vehicle trajectory may have a complex shape that crisscrosses in reality, making it difficult to draw the road. Secondly, there are also special vehicles on the road, and the trajectory information of these special vehicles, such as U-turns, emergency stops, or waiting at the intersection, may lead to relatively inaccurate results [10].

Since then, a variety of advanced methods have emerged, among which Kalman analysis [11], fuzzy logistic models [12, 13], Hidden Markov Models, and other simple methods using systems machines and probability theory method.

3.2 Analysis and prediction of travel behavior

In traffic research, neural network models have been gradually used in various research in recent years. For example, Liu et al. constructed a pedestrian traffic prediction model using an auto-encoding neural network [14], constructed a traffic accident prediction model using a recurrent neural network [15], and Liu et al. [14]. proposed driving behavior based on auto-encoding neural network. Visualization technologyLiu et al. [16] used a recurrent neural network to simulate the acceleration distribution of the car following model [17].

3.2.1 Machine learning applications in activity-travel behavior research

Machine learning is a branch of artificial intelligence. The basic concepts in machine learning are shown below.

1. Eigenvalue: The result of expressing entity features numerically is the eigenvalue of the data.
2. Training data: The training data includes the data of all the features of the entity and the classification results of the data. The training data is the basic data used to train the model.
3. Test data: The test data includes the data of all the features of the entity and the classification results of the data. The test data is used to test whether the data model meets the requirements.

4. Fitting: Accumulate experience through the training set, and use the test set to test the experience, and the matching degree of the obtained model and data, such as Fig. 1.1, put the data into the plane rectangular coordinate system, and use the function to represent the data distribution, This function representing the distribution of the data is the fit of this set of data using machine learning.

5. Underfitting: The fitting of the model and training data is too low, resulting in data with less commonality.

It can conform to the existing model and reduce the accuracy of the model prediction (As shown in Fig. 1.1).

6. Overfitting: The model and the training data fit too high, resulting in excessive special data being included in the existing model, which reduces the accuracy of the model prediction (As shown in Fig. 1.1).

In recent years, there has been an endless stream of mobile and predictive models dedicated to the study of human beings [18]. Gonzalez et al. [19] analyzed the call detail records (Call Details Records, CDRs) of 100,000 users and found that the movement trajectories of individuals have a high distribution pattern in time and space and tend to be replicable. space pattern. These findings change the general understanding of the randomness of human movement behavior. Through their research, they found that people often travel to and from several fixed locations in the city, and occasionally go to unfamiliar locations for other activities, and their travel behavior follows a certain fixed distribution. By analyzing spatiotemporal data from a large number of mobile phones, Candia et al. [20] investigated both group-level average behavior and individual-level behavior patterns, which are of immense help in understanding the diffusion phenomenon

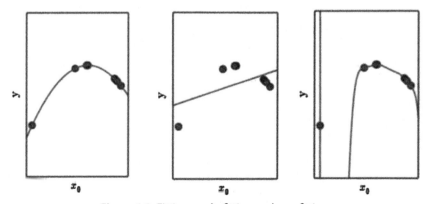

Figure 1.1 Fitting, underfitting and overfitting.

of human dynamics. To avoid building a complex urban traffic model through tedious and expensive travel surveys. Jiang et al. [21] proposed a TimeGeo urban mobility model with high resolution in time and space. After obtaining the urban structure and travel distance, personal trajectories generated from communication devices can be used to build an urban mobility model. Due to the rapid development of deep learning methods in recent years, many scholars also use deep learning methods to explore human travel behavior. Song et al. [22] collected users' Global Positioning System (GPS) records and transportation network data, and established an intelligent system based on Long Short-term Memory (LSTM) network architecture, which can be used in urban areas. However, this model does not study the travel behavior of users with sparse trajectories. Network embedding can effectively represent network features [23], Khoshraftar et al. [24] established a dynamic network embedding system based on LSTM for link prediction, but the historical step size of its training model is static. Chen et al. [25] proposed a new deep learning encoder model to predict end-to-end dynamic network links. Zhang et al. [26] took advantage of the new development of deep neural networks and proposed a new auxiliary supervised deep travel model, which can automatically and effectively extract different features and make full use of the time labels of trajectory data, which improves the prediction accuracy of the model. Rate. Yin et al. [27] proposed a hidden Markov model based on input and output, which infers the traveler's action pattern from CDRs data, and provides end-users to the traveler in the form of a modular and interpretable activity-travel demand model end-to-end solution. The goal of this model is to provide traffic assessment and decision support for traffic schedulers. Rawal and Swain [28] proposed a Hidden Markov travel prediction framework that can run on real-time and large-scale telephony communication data and can predict the movement trajectories of human beings in cities in real-time. Cui et al. [29] used social data and Google Maps data to solve the next trip prediction problem. By matching points of interest and Twitter historical data, a Bayesian network was established to predict an individual's daily travel location and purpose.

Due to the high prediction accuracy of the neural network model, many scholars also use neural networks for traffic data prediction. Liu et al. [30] proposed an end-to-end deep learning architecture, called Deep Passenger Flow, to predict passenger flow in and out of subway stations. This model enables the integration and modeling of external environmental factors, time dependencies, spatial characteristics, and subway operational characteristics in short-term subway passenger flow forecasting. Jiang et al. [31] constructed an online system called DeepUrbanMomentum to make predictions of the next short-term movement using human movement data with limited steps observed. A deep learning architecture is designed using recurrent neural networks to efficiently model these highly complex sequence data in a huge urban area. Other scholars deal with spatial information by expanding graph convolution. Sun et al. [32] proposed to use of spatial graph convolution to build a multi-view graph convolution network to solve the crowd flow prediction problem, where different views can capture different factors. Ke et al. [33] proposed a fusion of convolutional long and short-term memory networks to solve the problem of spatially dependent, temporally dependent, and externally dependent short-term passenger flow prediction. Yao et al. [34] proposed a multi-view spatiotemporal network framework for modeling spatiotemporal relationships to solve the taxi demand prediction problem. Chen et al. [35] proposed to use a residual recurrent graph neural network to jointly capture graph-based spatial correlation and temporal dynamics for traffic prediction, which effectively improved the accuracy of the model for spatiotemporal prediction. Zhang et al. [36] proposed a spatiotemporal neural network architecture specifically designed for accurate network-wide mobile traffic prediction, uniquely combining STN predictions with historical statistics to make reliable long-term mobile traffic predictions. Li et al. [37] proposed a diffuse convolutional recurrent neural network that fuses the spatiotemporal dependencies of traffic flow, which models the traffic flow process on a directed graph. Geng et al. [38] proposed spatiotemporal multi-graph convolutional networks, a novel deep learning model for car-hailing demand forecasting. Since the convolutional graph network can better manage the spatial correlation of the data, the prediction accuracy of the traffic model is further improved.

References

[1] J. Du, L. Aultman-Hall, Increasing the accuracy of trip rate information from passive multi-day GPS travel datasets: automatic trip end identification issues, Transportation Research Part A: Policy and Practice 41 (3) (2007) 220–232.

[2] A. Ermagun, Y. Fan, J. Wolfson, G. Adomavicius, K. Das, Real-time trip purpose prediction using online location-based search and discovery services, Transportation Research Part C: Emerging Technologies 77 (2017) 96–112.

[3] Q. Gao, F.L. Zhang, R.J. Wang, et al., Trajectory big data: a review of key technologies in data processing, Journal of Software 28 (4) (2017) 959–992.

[4] A. G, B. Ca, C. Is, A method for the treatment of pedestrian trajectory data noise, Transportation Research Procedia 41 (2019) 782–798.

[5] X. Longgang, S. Xiaotian, Visualization and extraction of trajectory stops based on kernel-density, Acta Geodaetica et Cartographica Sinica 45 (9) (2016) 1122–1131.

[6] Z. Zheng, Z. Zhao, G. Wang, et al., Ship trajectory extraction method for port parking area identification, Journal of Computer Applications (2019).

[7] L.H. Tran, Q.V. Nguyen, N.H. Do, Z. Yan, et al., Robust and hierarchical stop discovery in sparse and diverse trajectories, Epfl (2011).

[8] Y. Zhang, Y. Lin, An interactive method for identifying the stay points of the trajectory of moving objects, Journal of Visual Communication and Image Representation 59 (FEB) (2019) 387−392.

[9] T. Miwa, D. Kiuchi, T. Yamamoto, et al., Development of map matching algorithm for low frequency probe data, Transportation Research Part C: Emerging Technologies 22 (5) (2012) 132−145.

[10] D. Bernstein, A. Kornhauser, An introduction to map matching for personal navigation assistants, Geometric Distributions 122 (7) (1998) 1082−1083.

[11] H. Xu, H. Liu, C.W. Tan, Y. Bao, et al., Development and application of an enhanced kalman filter and global positioning system error-correction approach for improved map-matching, Journal of Intelligent Transportation Systems 14 (1) (2010) 27−36.

[12] M.A. Quddus, R.B. Noland, W.Y. Ochieng, A High Accuracy Fuzzy Logic Based Map Matching Algorithm for Road Transport.

[13] D. Yang, T. Zhang, J. Li, et al., Synthetic Fuzzy Evaluation Method of Trajectory Similarity in Map-Matching.

[14] L. Liu, R.C. Chen, A novel passenger flow prediction model using deep learning methods, Transportation Research Part C: Emerging Technologies 84 (nov) (2017) 74−91.

[15] M. Zhou, X. Qu, X. Li, A recurrent neural network based microscopic car following model to predict traffic oscillation, Transportation Research Part C: Emerging Technologies 84 (2017) 245−264.

[16] H.L. Liu, T. Taniguchi, Y. Tanaka, et al., Visualization of driving behavior based on hidden feature extraction by using deep learning, IEEE Transactions on Intelligent Transportation Systems (2017) 1−13 (9).

[17] J. Morton, T.A. Wheeler, M.J. Kochenderfer, Analysis of recurrent neural networks for probabilistic modeling of driver behavior, IEEE Transactions on Intelligent Transportation Systems 18 (5) (2017) 1289−1298.

[18] L. Alessandretti, P. Sapiezynski, V. Sekara, et al., Evidence for a conserved quantity in human mobility, arXiv 2 (7) (2016) 485−491.

[19] M.C. González, C.A. Hidalgo, B. AL, Understanding individual human mobility patterns, Nature 458 (7235) (2009), 238−238.

[20] J. Candia, M.C. González, P. Wang, et al., Uncovering individual and collective human dynamics from mobile phone records, Journal of Physics 41 (22) (2007).

[21] S. Jiang, Y. Yang, S. Gupta, et al., The TimeGeo modeling framework for urban motility without travel surveys, Proceedings of the National Academy of Sciences of the United States of America (2016) E5370.

[22] X. Song, H. Kanasugi, R. Shibasaki, Deeptransport: Prediction and Simulation of Human Mobility and Transportation Mode at a Citywide Level, 2016.

[23] C. Peng, X. Wang, J. Pei, et al., A survey on network embedding, IEEE Transactions on Knowledge and Data Engineering (2017). PP (99):1−1.

[24] S. Khoshraftar, S. Mahdavi, A. An, et al., Dynamic graph embedding via LSTM history tracking, in: 2019 IEEE International Conference on Data Science and Advanced Analytics (DSAA), 2019.

[25] Chen J, Zhang J, Xu X, et al. E-LSTM-D: A deep learning framework for dynamic network link prediction. IEEE Transactions on Systems, Man, and Cybernetics: Systems, PP(99):1−14.

[26] H. Zhang, W. Hao, W. Sun, et al., Deeptravel: a neural network based travel time estimation model with auxiliary supervision, in: Twenty-Seventh International Joint Conference on Artificial Intelligence IJCAI-18, 2018.

[27] M. Yin, M. Sheehan, S. Feygin, et al., A generative model of urban activities from cellular data, IEEE Transactions on Intelligent Transportation Systems (2016) 1682–1696.

[28] A. Rawal, P. Swain, Prediction of Human Mobility Using Mobile Traffic Dataset with Hmm.

[29] C. Yu, C. Meng, Q. He, et al., Forecasting current and next trip purpose with social media data and Google Places, Transportation Research 97 (DEC) (2018) 159–174.

[30] Y. Liu, Z. Liu, R. Jia, DeepPF: a deep learning based architecture for metro passenger flow prediction, Transportation Research Part C: Emerging Technologies 101 (APR) (2019) 18–34.

[31] R. Jiang, X. Song, Z. Fan, et al., DeepUrbanMomentum: An Online Deep-Learning System for Short-Term Urban Mobility Prediction AAAI2018, 2019.

[32] J. Sun, J. Zhang, Q. Li, et al., Predicting citywide crowd flows in irregular regions using multi-view graph convolutional networks, IEEE Transactions on Knowledge and Data Engineering (2020). PP(99):1–1.

[33] J. Ke, H. Zheng, H. Yang, et al., Short-term forecasting of passenger demand under on-demand ride services: a spatio-temporal deep learning approach, Transportation Research 85c (dec) (2017) 591–608.

[34] H. Yao, W. Fei, J. Ke, et al., Deep Multi-View Spatial-Temporal Network for Taxi Demand Prediction, eprint arXiv:1802.08714, 2018.

[35] C. Chen, K. Li, S.G. Teo, et al., Gated residual recurrent graph neural networks for traffic prediction, Proceedings of the AAAI Conference on Artificial Intelligence 33 (2019) 485–492.

[36] C. Zhang, P. Patras, Long-Term Mobile Traffic Forecasting Using Deep Spatio-Temporal Neural Networks, 2018, pp. 231–240.

[37] Y. Li, R. Yu, C. Shahabi, et al., Diffusion Convolutional Recurrent Neural Network: Data-Driven Traffic Forecasting, 2017.

[38] X. Geng, Y. Li, L. Wang, et al., Spatiotemporal multi-graph convolution network for ride-hailing demand forecasting, Proceedings of the AAAI Conference on Artificial Intelligence 33 (2019) 3656–3663.

CHAPTER TWO

Mining individual significant places from historical trajectory data

Wenjing Li[1,3], Haoran Zhang[2], Ryosuke Shibasaki[1], Jinyu Chen[1], Hill Hiroki Kobayashi[1,3]

[1]Center for Spatial Information Science, The University of Tokyo, Kashiwa-shi, Chiba, Japan
[2]School of Urban Planning and Design, Peking University, Shenzhen, China
[3]Information Technology Center, The University of Tokyo, Kashiwa-shi, Chiba, Japan

1. Background

With the development of information and communication technologies, big data with location provide a new horizon to human mobility. The mobility of individuals is closely related to the place. People move from place to place to perform various activities driven by their daily routine or interests. Human mobility shows a high degree of temporal and spatial regularity. People have a significant tendency to return to places they frequently visit. Significant places refer to the places that people frequently visit. Significant places are important to a user and carry rich semantic meaning, such as "the place of living," "the place of work," or "favorite park." Significant places are crucial for a better understanding of human mobility. Significant place mining techniques have been widely used in the studies of urban sciences, urban computing, smart transportation, and the application such as location recommender systems, precise advertising, and personalized route arrangement.

2. Related work

In this section, we review the previous work about mining individual significant places from historical mobility data. Two main techniques have been used in the current research: location-based methods and time-based methods [1,2].

Location-based methods are popular. K-Means and DBSCAN are the most widely used methods. Ashbrook and Starner [3] utilized KMeans to identify the home location of the users. Li et al. [4] used DBSCAN methods to identify the home, work and other significant places of individuals. Bogorny et al. [5] integrated background geographical information into trajectories to extract the semantics of potential significant places. Xiao et al. [6] modeled a user's GPS trajectories with semantic location history, including shopping malls, restaurants, cinemas, etc. They considered the uncertainty of possible POI categories that are assigned to the region. Spinsanti et al. [7] proposed a location-based method that used the aggregate probabilities to assign possible POI categories to each significant place to identify the semantics.

Some used time-based methods. Kang et al. [8] utilized WiFi network data to capture the users' location on campus. They developed a time-based clustering algorithm to extract significant places taking advantage of the continuity of the WiFiI positioning. Andrienko et al. [9] created "temporal signatures" that characterized the temporal distribution of a person's presence at each POI to mine the individuals' significant places.

Some research combined these two methods together. Zhou et al. [2] proposed a two-step approach that discretized continuous GPS data into places and learned important places from the place features. Shen and Cheng [10] implemented the ST-DBSCAN framework to detect spatio-temporal features of the significant places. Siła-Nowicka et al. [11] proposed a new framework for significant places mining and spatio-temporal analysis. Using the relational Markov networks (RMN) model, Liao et al. [12] identified the significant place from GPS trajectories records according to temporal information such as date, day of week and stay duration, speed information such as average speed between two GPS records, and other geographic information such as whether it is on a bus route or not, etc. Phithakkitnukoon, Horanont [13] trained a Random Forest model which can identify the tourist home and workplace by 10 spatial-temporal features.

3. Methodology

The individual significant places mining method has been widely used in human mobility-related research [14]. In general, most work includes at least three steps: stay location extraction, spatial clustering of stay location, and significant places identification. Here, we will introduce the basic method.

3.1 Stay location extraction

The first step is to extract the *stay location* of the individual's raw human trajectory. The *stay location* of an individual's raw mobility trajectory is a series of consecutive points that represent the user staying at a location, while the moving location represents the user moving. The stay locations represent the places where a user spends a considerable amount of time. Here, let u denote the user index, N_u denote the number of all users. If $X_u = \{x_{t1}, x_{t2}, ..., x_{ti}, ...\}$ denotes a set of GPS locations (Fig. 2.1A) of user u where x_{ti} is the location at time ti, $\{x_{ti}, x_{ti+1}, x_{ti+2}, ..., x_{tm}, ...\}$ that are within the distance Δl and $x_{tm} - x_{ti} \leq$ time span Δt are grouped as a stop (Fig. 2.1B). The ones which are greater than the threshold are identified as moving segments. The noise points are removed according to the mean and standard deviation of Gaussian distribution. By implementing this process, we can obtain $S_u = \{S_1, S_2, S_3, ..., S_i\}$ that represents the user u's stay location history. Each stay point S_i retains the arrival time (*S.arvt*) and the leaving time (*S.levt*) which, respectively, equal to the timestamp of the first and last GPS point constructing this stay point (Fig. 2.1C).

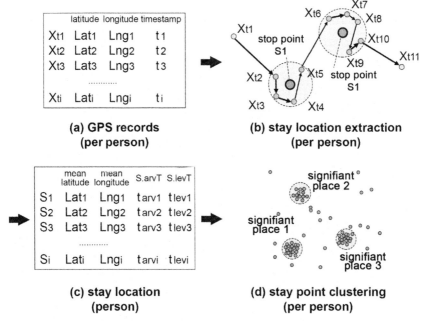

(a) GPS records
(per person)

(b) stay location extraction
(per person)

(c) stay location
(person)

(d) stay point clustering
(per person)

Figure 2.1 The illustration of the significant places detection. (a) raw GPS records; (b) stay location extraction; (c) example of the stay location records; (d) stay points clustering.

3.2 Spatial clustering of stay location

The second step is the spatial clustering of stay location to group different stay points with the same semantic meaning (Fig. 2.1D). Due to the uncertainty of human movements, two stay points in the same places may have different spatial coordinates. Thus we need to conduct spatial clustering methods to group different stay points with the same semantic meaning. The centroid of the cluster is considered as a significant place (e.g., home, workplace, other) which represents the individual's typical activity [14]. Here, Density-Based Spatial Clustering of Applications with Noise (DBSCAN) is a highly popular clustering method. DBSCAN has been wildly utilized in determining the zones regularly visited by individuals ([15,16]) and has been proved to have a good performance among other techniques [13]. Two parameters are required in the DBSCAN method: the minimum number of points that can form a cluster (*minpts*) and the maximum distance within which two points belong to a cluster (*eps*). Points with a neighborhood *eps* more than *minpts* are categorized as core points, and points reachable by a core point are border points of the cluster. Both core points and border points are considered as clustered points. Points not within the *eps* search radius of any core point are treated as noise [17].

3.3 Identify the semanteme of the significant places

The last step is to identify the semanteme of the significant places. The homes and workplaces are commonly identified [13], other places include tourist attractions [13], shopping [18], and catering [19] also be subdivided in some studies.

Several metrics has been used in the current research to identify the semanteme of the significant places, including but not limited to:

Categories	Metrics	Explanations
Human movement	Cluster ranking	Top ranked clusters can be indicative of home and workplace locations
	Portion of stops in the cluster	The importance of places because people tend to visit important places, such as home and work more frequently than others
	Hours of stops	The hours of the day where clustered stops appeared
	Days of stops	The number of days where clustered stops were observed

—cont'd

Categories	Metrics	Explanations
	Inactive hours	The hours where a number of GPS locations are less than the average for consecutive hours
	Day-hour stops	Day hours that stops were observed
	Night-hour stops	Night hours that stops were observed
	Max stop duration	The maximum value of stop duration
	Min stop duration	The minimum value of stop duration
	Avg. Stop duration	The average value of stop duration
Urban context	Land use	The use of land. It represents the economic and cultural activities at a specific place.
	POI types	Such as parks, bus stops, train stations, a grocery store
	POI density	The density and complexity of the POI

4. Application

4.1 Preliminary setting

Here, we use two cases to show the application of the significant place mining: analysis of life pattern changes in the Great Tokyo Area [4] and analysis of population changes after the Fukushima earthquake.

Dataset. We utilized GPS records from "Konzatsu-Tokei (R)" as the dataset. "Konzatsu-Tokei (R)" is an individual location dataset collected from mobile phones with enabled AUTO-GPS function through the "Docomo Map Navi" service provided by NTT DOCOMO, INC. The mobile phone users had agreed to the terms and conditions for using the services provided by the network operator in order that their communications may be recorded and analyzed. The dataset was preprocessed by another company on behalf of the network provider before releasing this data to the authors. The preprocessing ensured that no connection could be made between the data and the individual mobile phone users. It does not include specific individual information such as name, age, or gender. The dataset we utilized in this research contains 11.67 billion GPS records collected from about 2.35 million mobile-phone users throughout Japan. Original GPS location data (latitude, longitude, timestamp) are sent in about every minimum period of 5 min.

Computation environment. The data are processed through python in Anaconda environment. The libraries we used include Pandas, Geopandas, Matplotlib, and DBSCAN module of Sklearn.

Parameter setting for DBSCAN. In this study, we set $eps = 30$m and $minpt = 10$ for DBSCAN method. These parameters approximate to the uncertainty in GPS positioning. They are recommended in related references ([20–24]) and proved to be effective in detecting the significant places of individuals.

Condition hypothesis for significant places identification. We assume that every person has his/her own home and most people return homes at the end of the day. Although there are exceptions in the real world, this assumption simplifies the way we identify the significant places from unlabeled GPS data and allows us to estimate places. We classify the significant places into five groups—home(H), other frequently visited nighttime spots (N), workplaces (W), other frequently visited daytime spots (D), and other significant places (O). Within each cluster, we extract the stay points which meet the following conditions as candidate points of nighttime spots or daytime spots: (1) candidates points of nighttime spots: between 8.pm to 6.am, the duration is larger than 1.5 h, more than 10 day's records within one cluster; (2) candidates points of daytime spots: between 9.am to 7.pm in the workday, the duration is larger than 1.5 h, more than 10 day's record within one cluster. Then, we compare the day of stop and the total stop duration for daytime spot candidates and nighttime spot candidates within each cluster to determine the semantic meaning. The clusters whose stop days and stops duration of nighttime spot candidates are highest are identified as H, and the clusters whose stop days and stops duration of daytime spot candidates are highest are identified as W. Other clusters that contain daytime spot candidates or nighttime spot candidates are identified as N or D. The clusters without daytime spot candidates or nighttime spot candidates that meet the conditions are identified as other significant places.

4.2 Case one: analysis of life pattern changes in the Great Tokyo area

The Great Tokyo area (Fig. 2.2) includes Tokyo Metropolis and the surrounding area of prefecture Chiba, Ibaraki, Kana-gawa, Saitama, Gunma, Yamanashi, and Tochigi. Both metropolitan areas and rural areas are included in the study area. The GPS records from 2013 January 1st to 2013 July 31st is extracted for this analysis. There are totally 74,693 users

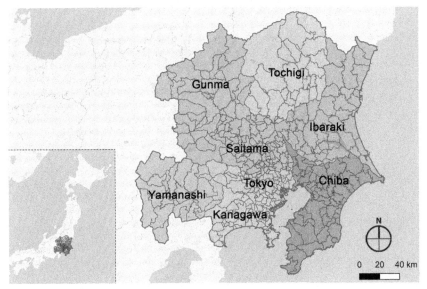

Figure 2.2 Study area.

who can be clearly detected the home location. There are totally 74,693 home places, 17,033 other frequently visited nighttime spots, 50,125 workplaces, 63,183 other frequently visited daytime spots, and 266,895 other significant places detected for the raw GPS records. Fig. 2.3 shows the spatial distribution of significant places.

(a) total significant places: total clusters that the uses frequently visit;

(b) home: clusters with the longest period GPS records between 8.pm to 6.am and the duration is larger than 1.5 h;

(c) nighttime spot: other clusters with GPS records between 8.pm to 6.am and the duration is larger than 1.5 h;

(d) work: clusters with the longest period GPS records between 9.am to 7.pm in the workday and the duration is larger than 1.5 h;

(e) daytime spot: other clusters with GPS records between 9.am to 7.pm in the workday and the duration is larger than 1.5 h;

(f) other significant places: other clusters that the users frequently visit

Then, by applying the metagraph-based life pattern clustering methods developed by Li et al. [4], the users can be classified into seven groups. The standard deviation of the population percentage of seven groups can be visualized according to their home location to explore the spatial distribution characteristics of different life patterns (Fig. 2.4).

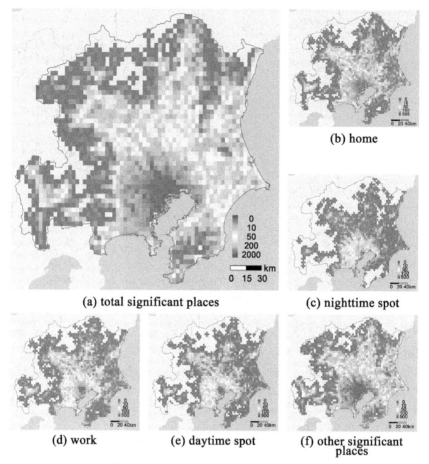

Figure 2.3 Heatmap of significant places.

We can see that the standard deviation of the population percentage of the seven groups in metropolitan areas is small, while the standard deviation in the outlying area is high. This indicates that the types of life patterns in the metropolitan area are more diverse and the one in the outlying area is relatively single. This could be due to the demographic composition in metropolitan areas is more even and the demographic composition in the outlying area is more imbalanced, so the standard deviation of population percentage of life pattern could be higher.

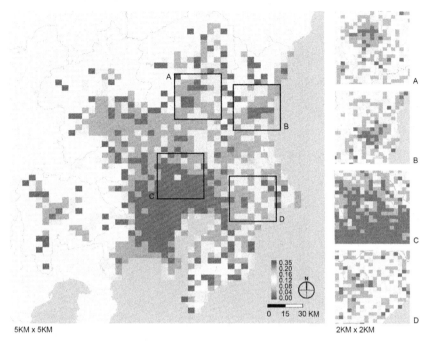

Figure 2.4 The standard deviation of population percentage of seven groups.

4.3 Case two: analysis of population changes after the fukushima earthquake

On 2011 March 11, Japan experienced the strongest earthquake in its recorded history. The earthquake caused widespread damage on land and initiated a series of large tsunami waves that devastated many coastal areas, especially the Fukushima area. With detailed GPS records, we can analyze how the population changed after the Fukushima earthquake. By the significant place detection methods introduced above, we can identify each user's home and work location. The changes in home location and work location after the Fukushima earthquake can also be detected. The results are shown in Figs. 2.5 and 2.6.

4.4 Case three: analysis of the residential location of the park visitors in Tokyo and the surrounding area

Parks are important places for human—nature interaction in the urban area. Parks provide opportunities for city dwellers to experience nature, and bring environmental, social, and economic benefits in numerous ways. Since

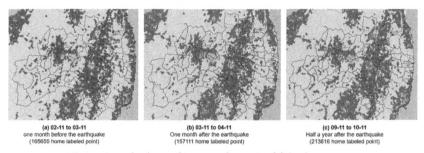

(a) 02-11 to 03-11
one month before the earthquake
(165655 home labeled point)

(b) 03-11 to 04-11
One month after the earthquake
(157111 home labeled point)

(c) 09-11 to 10-11
Half a year after the earthquake
(213616 home labeled point)

Figure 2.5 The home location changes of fukushima area.

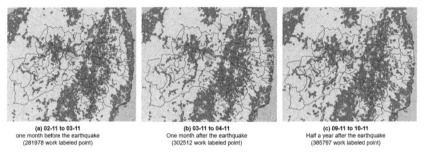

(a) 02-11 to 03-11
one month before the earthquake
(281978 work labeled point)

(b) 03-11 to 04-11
One month after the earthquake
(302512 work labeled point)

(c) 09-11 to 10-11
Half a year after the earthquake
(385797 work labeled point)

Figure 2.6 The work location changes in the fukushima area.

many benefits of parks can only be realized by active usage, it is important to understand how parks are being used. With detailed GPS records, we can analyze how citizens are using the parks. One important topic is the residential location of the park visitors. We can identify each visitor's home by the significant place detection methods introduced above. The relationship between the distance from home to the park and the park visitation behavior can be further analyzed. The results are shown in Fig.7.

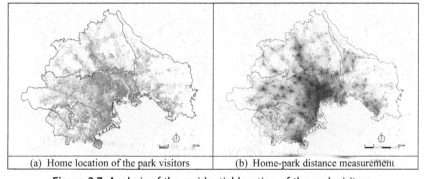

(a) Home location of the park visitors	(b) Home-park distance measurement

Figure 2.7 Analysis of the residential location of the park visitors.

References

[1] M. Yang, C. Cheng, B. Chen, Mining individual similarity by assessing interactions with personally significant places from GPS trajectories, ISPRS International Journal of Geo-Information. 7 (2018) 126.

[2] C. Zhou, N. Bhatnagar, S. Shekhar, L. Terveen, Mining personally important places from GPS tracks, in: 2007 IEEE 23rd International Conference on Data Engineering Workshop, IEEE, 2007, pp. 517—526.

[3] D. Ashbrook, T. Starner, Using GPS to learn significant locations and predict movement across multiple users, Personal and Ubiquitous Computing 7 (2003) 275—286.

[4] W. Li, H. Zhang, J. Chen, P. Li, Y. Yao, X. Shi, et al., Metagraph-based life pattern clustering with big human mobility data, IEEE Transactions on Big Data (2022), https://doi.org/10.1109/TBDATA.2022.3155752.

[5] V. Bogorny, B. Kuijpers, L.O. Alvares, ST-DMQL: a semantic trajectory data mining query language, International Journal of Geographical Information Science 23 (2009) 1245—1276.

[6] X. Xiao, Y. Zheng, Q. Luo, X. Xie, Finding similar users using category-based location history, in: Proceedings of the 18th SIGSPATIAL International Conference on Advances in Geographic Information Systems, 2010, pp. 442—445.

[7] L. Spinsanti, F. Celli, C. Renso, Where you stop is who you are: understanding people's activities by places visited, in: The Proceedings of Behaviour Monitoring and Interpretation (BMI) Workshop, 2010.

[8] J.H. Kang, W. Welbourne, B. Stewart, G. Borriello, Extracting places from traces of locations, ACM Sigmobile Mobile Computing and Communications Review 9 (2005) 58—68.

[9] G.L. Andrienko, N.V. Andrienko, G. Fuchs, A.-M.O. Raimond, J. Symanzik, C. Ziemlicki, Extracting Semantics of Individual Places from Movement data by Analyzing Temporal Patterns of Visits, 2013, pp. 9—15. COMP@ SIGSPATIAL.

[10] J. Shen, T. Cheng, A framework for identifying activity groups from individual space-time profiles, International Journal of Geographical Information Science 30 (2016) 1785—1805.

[11] K. Siła-Nowicka, J. Vandrol, T. Oshan, J.A. Long, U. Demšar, A.S. Fotheringham, Analysis of human mobility patterns from GPS trajectories and contextual information, International Journal of Geographical Information Science 30 (2016) 881—906.

[12] L. Liao, D. Fox, H. Kautz, Location-based activity recognition, Advances in Neural Information Processing Systems 18 (2005).

[13] S. Phithakkitnukoon, T. Horanont, A. Witayangkurn, R. Siri, Y. Sekimoto, R. Shibasaki, Understanding tourist behavior using large-scale mobile sensing approach: a case study of mobile phone users in Japan, Pervasive and Mobile Computing 18 (2015) 18—39.

[14] Y. Ye, Y. Zheng, Y. Chen, J. Feng, X. Xie, Mining individual life pattern based on location history, in: 2009 Tenth International Conference on Mobile Data Management: Systems, Services and Middleware, IEEE, 2009, pp. 1—10.

[15] X. Liu, Q. Huang, S. Gao, Exploring the uncertainty of activity zone detection using digital footprints with multi-scaled DBSCAN, International Journal of Geographical Information Science 33 (2019) 1196—1223.

[16] C. Comito, D. Falcone, D. Talia, Mining human mobility patterns from social geotagged data, Pervasive and Mobile Computing 33 (2016) 91—107.

[17] K. Khan, S.U. Rehman, K. Aziz, S. Fong, S. Sarasvady, DBSCAN: past, present and future, in: The Fifth International Conference on the Applications of Digital Information and Web Technologies (ICADIWT 2014), IEEE, 2014, pp. 232—238.

[18] T. Hu, R. Song, Y. Wang, X. Xie, J. Luo, Mining shopping patterns for divergent urban regions by incorporating mobility data, in: Proceedings of the 25th ACM International on Conference on Information and Knowledge Management, 2016, pp. 569–578.

[19] F. Zhang, N.J. Yuan, K. Zheng, D. Lian, X. Xie, Y. Rui, Exploiting dining preference for restaurant recommendation, in: Proceedings of the 25th International Conference on World Wide Web, 2016, pp. 725–735.

[20] S. Kisilevich, F. Mansmann, D. Keim, P.- DBSCAN, A density based clustering algorithm for exploration and analysis of attractive areas using collections of geo-tagged photos, in: Proceedings of the 1st International Conference and Exhibition on Computing for Geospatial Research & Application, 2010, pp. 1–4.

[21] I.K. Savvas, D. Tselios, Parallelizing DBSCAN algorithm using MPI, in: 2016 IEEE 25th International Conference on Enabling Technologies: Infrastructure for Collaborative Enterprises (WETICE), IEEE, 2016, pp. 77–82.

[22] P. Viswanath, R. Pinkesh, l-dbscan, A fast hybrid density based clustering method, in: 18th International Conference on Pattern Recognition (ICPR'06), IEEE, 2006, pp. 912–915.

[23] J. Tang, F. Liu, Y. Wang, H. Wang, Uncovering urban human mobility from large scale taxi GPS data, Physica A: Statistical Mechanics and Its Applications 438 (2015) 140–153.

[24] D. Huang, Y. Chen, X. Pan, Optimal model of locating charging stations with massive urban trajectories, in: IOP Conference Series: Materials Science and Engineering, IOP Publishing, 2020, p. 012009.

CHAPTER THREE

Mobility pattern clustering with big human mobility data

Wenjing Li[1,3], Haoran Zhang[2], Ryosuke Shibasaki[1], Jinyu Chen[1], Hill Hiroki Kobayashi[1,3]

[1]Center for Spatial Information Science, The University of Tokyo, Kashiwa-shi, Chiba, Japan
[2]School of Urban Planning and Design, Peking University, Shenzhen, China
[3]Information Technology Center, The University of Tokyo, Kashiwa-shi, Chiba, Japan

1. Introduction

"Mobility patterns" refers to individual general mobility regularity and activity style. Despite some degree of change and spontaneity, human mobility shows a high degree of temporal and spatial regularity [1]. This inherent regularity enables us to summarize the reproducible patterns of an individual's mobility in the long term. There are some similarities in daily activity patterns within the group of people [2]. For example, a typical mobility pattern of office employees on workdays is that they go to work in the morning and return home in the evening. A homemaker may usually stay home all day. Abstracting the group's characteristics of mobility patterns from diverse individual cases is essential for urban infrastructure improvement and policy making toward multiple types of citizens. Mobility pattern clustering is the core of abstracting the group's characteristics of mobility patterns.

In the past, mobility pattern-related studies were mainly based on the statistics results from official records or questionnaire surveys([3,4]). However, the relatively small sampling data would bring bias in representing all characteristics of the overall research population [5]. They are not enough to reveal group's characteristics of mobility patterns on a large scale. The similarity and differences of mobility patterns remain to be further quantified. Recently, with the development of information and communication technologies, big data with location provide a new horizon to mobility patterns for urban research. Smart card data [6], Wi-Fi data [7], call detail record data [8] and mobile phone data [9] have been utilized to capture individual activity-based behavior and mobility patterns on a large scale. Many insightful works have been done in the field of mobility pattern clustering([10−13]). The complexity, diversity and data amount of big data place challenges to large-scale mobility pattern clustering.

S refers to a set of significant places for all users. m refers to the index of the day. Nm refers the total number of days. $L_{(m,u)} = \{L_m^0, L_m^1, L_m^2, ..., L_m^{23} \mid L_m^h \in S\}$ denotes the location of an individual u in 24 h of day m. $L_u = \{L_{(0,u)}, L_{(2,u)}, L_{(3,u)}, ..., L_{(m,u)} \mid m \in \{0, ..., Nm-1\}\}$ denotes the long-term mobility patterns of individual u during Nm days period. L denotes the long-term mobility patterns of multiple users. $L_u \in L$. The mobility pattern clustering task is described as:

Input: L.

Output: users with cluster memberships in L.

2. Related works

Similarity measurement between different mobility patterns is the core problem for mobility pattern clustering-related research. From the aspect of the similarity metric, the current methods can be categorized as the following:

(1) **Consider the mobility relationship between different stops, such as stop-stop or stop-stop-stop.** Schneider, Belik [13] utilized the concept of motifs from network theory, their work extracted 17 unique networks that are present in daily mobility and these patterns follow a universal law. These works discard the additional information about the purpose of the activity, the travel time, and the activity duration as well as the distances and the number of trips between the visited locations. If we want to consider these more refined spatial-temporal coupled features, the problem would be more high-dimensional.

(2) **Measure the similarity from statistical features mining from trip data.** With a fixed number of clusters, Ordóñez Medina and Erath [14] categorized workers and their daily work activities according to start time and duration. El Mahrsi, Côme [15] recognized weekly traveling patterns of public transport users and clustered passengers based on temporal profiles. Ma, Wu [16] represented the regularity of users by four features: number of travel days, number of similar first boarding times, number of similar route sequences and number of similar stop ID sequences. Medina [17] utilized 14 features to summarize the user's primary activity patterns and applied the DBSCAN algorithm for user clustering. As the number of measure metrics is preset and limited,

they are not enough to reflect the temporal modes of mobility patterns between different groups. Besides, they cannot describe the coupled relationship between space and temporality.

(3) **Cluster mobility patterns share similar locations with high frequency.** Lee, Han [18] proposed a clustering algorithm that grouped similar trajectories as a whole. Yang, Cheng [19] utilized GPS data to mine the individual similarity with common significant places. This work emphasized the spatial-temporal similarity between individuals and their personally significant places. The people with closer trajectories in geolocation and time have similar mobility behavior. However, the sequential properties are ignored, and they could not measure the temporal contextual similarities.

(4) **Some focus on semantic sequential relations.** Zheng, Zhang [20] proposed a clustering method considering the sequence of movements, the hierarchical properties of the geographic space, and the popularity of the visited places. Based on threeGPS datasets, Xu, Xia [21] proposed a method that captures the semantic features to detect the popular temporal modes. This method considers the contextual similarities and enables the individuals with similar temporal modes yet have a large spatial distance to own similar representations. But some information which is important when regarding the mobility pattern in long term, such as prior probability, frequency of travel at different time, are missing during the aggregation process.

Table 3.1 gives an overview of similarity measurement of mobility pattern clustering in related literature studies.

3. Methods

In this section, we will introduce different methods of the currently published papers about mobility pattern clustering. These methods represent the mobility patterns information with different data structures. The metagraph-based clustering method proposed by Li et al. [24] will be introduced in detail. Other methods will be introduced succinctly. Once the geodesic distance is defined by different presenting methods, Euclidean distance can be introduced to measure the mobility pattern similarities. Traditional clustering methods such as K-means can also be incorporated into the specific data structures for mobility pattern clustering.

Table 3.1 An overview of similarity measurement of mobility pattern clustering in related works.

Similarity measurement	References	Dataset type	Study area	User scale	Duration	Clustering features	Temporal metric for handling long-term data	Data structure
Mobility relationship between stops	Schneider et al. [13]	Surveys and mobile phone billing data	Paris, Chicago	23,764 and 23,429 weekdays of people	Six month	Weekday, duration, location, reason for and mode of trip	Pattern similarity between stays	Network
Aggregate statistical features	Ordóñez Medina and Erath [14]	Household interview transport survey	Singapore	23,900 users	One week	Start time and duration of work	The duration of staying at the places	Vector
	El Mahrsi et al. [15]	Smart card data	Rennes, France	53,100 users	One month	The number of trips that the user took over each hour of each day of the week and the probability	Average days that the user travel	Matrix
	Ma et al. [16]	Smart cards	Beijing, China	Unknown	One week	Number of travel days, number of similar first boarding times, number of similar route sequences, number of similar stop ID sequences	Total number of travel days	Vector

Reference	Objective	Data	Study area	Data size	Duration	Feature	Similarity/method	Data representation
Medina [17]	Cluster mobility patterns that share similar geolocation with high frequency	Household interview transport survey and smart card data	Singapore	Unknown	One week	The start time and the duration of the activity of each day over a week	The duration of the activity of each day over a week	Vector
Lee et al. [18]		Trajectory data sets include timestamp, longitude and latitude	Atlantic	570 trajectories; 65 trajectories	Unknown	Graphic similarity of trajectory	Graphic similarity	Vector
Yang et al. [19]		GPS data	Beijing, China	182 users	Five years	Share common significant places	Geolocation similarity	Vector
Zheng et al. [20]	The temporal sequential similarities	GPS data	Beijing, China	75 users	One year	The hierarchical properties of the geographic space, the sequence of movements, the popularity of the visited places	The sequence of movements	Matrix
Ying et al. [22]		GPS data	Cambridge, USA	106 mobile users	One year	Semantic tags and sequential relations	The contextual temporal modes	Matrix
Xu et al. [21]		GPS data	Shanghai, China	10,000 mobile users	44 days	The contextual temporal modes	The contextual temporal modes	Matrix

(Continued)

Table 3.1 An overview of similarity measurement of mobility pattern clustering in related works.—cont'd

Similarity measurement References	Dataset type	Study area	User scale	Duration	Clustering features	Temporal metric for handling long-term data	Data structure
Widhalm et al. [23]	CDRs	Vienna, Boston	600,000 users	2 weeks	Semantic tags and sequential relations	The contextual temporal modes	Network
Li et al. [24]	GPS data	The Great Tokyo	74,693 users	Half a year	Significant places semantics, time-sequential properties, duration, frequency, and prior probability	The contextual temporal modes	Graph

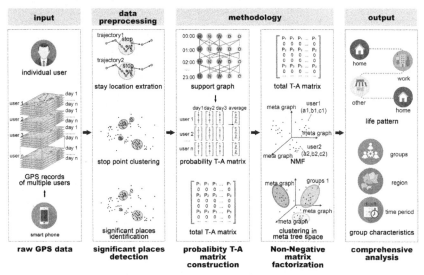

Figure 3.1 Methodology framework.

3.1 Metagraph-based clustering method

In the research of Li et al. [24], a metagraph-based data structure is proposed for presenting the diverse mobility pattern. Spatial-temporal similarity includes significant places semantics, time-sequential properties and frequency are integrated into this data structure, which captures the uncertainty of an individual and the diversities between individuals. Nonnegative-factorization-based method is utilized for reducing the dimension.

The methodology includes two subsystems: probability T-A matrix construction and matrix factorization. The whole process of the methodology is shown in Fig. 3.1.

3.1.1 Support graph and topology-attribute matrix construction

For each user, a graph is first built to represent his/her location of each hour within one day, which we call it *individual graph*. One edge of the individual graph represents 1 h movement. One node of the graph represents one significant place where the user stays within the corresponding hour. For users who stay at multiple significant places within 1 h, we select the one with the longest duration. As the time sequence of the movement in one day is always from 0:00 to 23:00, the graph is unidirectional. There is only one edge between the same source and target nodes. The direction of the edge is always from the node of the last hour to the node of the next hour. Fig. 3.2A illustrates the construction of the individual graph based on four individuals.

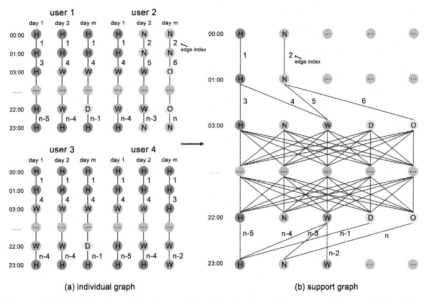

(a) individual graph   (b) support graph

Figure 3.2 Individual graph construction, support graph construction and the edge indexing strategy based on a population of four individuals. *m*, the index of a day; *n*, the unique edge index; *u*: user index.

Secondly, a graph is constructed in the way that any of the individual graphs can always be found to have the same topology. This graph is called as support graph. In the support graph, each edge is assigned a unique index. Here, an ascending manner in chronological order is assigned. Let Nn denote the total number of edges in the support graph, n denote the unique index of all the edges in the support graph. The edge index of the support graph will be assigned from 1 to n. Then, the edges of the individual graph will be respectively assigned one index which corresponds to the index of the edges with the same topology in the support graph by definition. Fig. 3.2B illustrates the construction of the support graph and the edge indexing strategy based on four individuals.

Then, T-A matrix is used to represent the graphs. The T-A matrix of one user one day $T_{(m,u)}$ will be generated with its row number being equal to the total index number of the support graph edges n. In other words, $T_{(m,u)}$ is a matrix with the size of n × 1. The first row of the T-A matrix corresponds to the first edge of the support graph, the second row to the second edge, and so forth. For individuals each day, the element in the n-th row is assigned the value 1 if the n-th edge of the support graph is also contained in the individual graph; otherwise, 0 is assigned to the element in the n-th

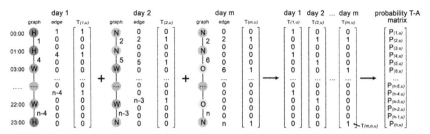

Figure 3.3 T-A matrix generation based on user 2. m, the index of a day; n, the unique edge index; u, user index (here $u = 2$).

row. Let $T_u = \{T_{(1,u)}, T_{(2,u)}, \ldots, T_{(m,u)}\}$ corresponding to all T-A matrix of user u of total days. By computing the average value of T_u, the average probability matrix $P_{average\ u} = \{P_{(1,u)}, P_{(2,u)}, \ldots, P_{(n,u)}\}$ of user u within m days can be computed. Fig. 3.3 is an illustration of the T-A matrix generation based on User 2.

3.1.2 Structure constrained NMF and meta-graph space

For a population of average probability T-A matrix $P = \{P_{average\ 1}, P_{average\ 2}, \ldots, P_{average\ u}\}$, Nn denotes the number of edges of the support graph, Nu denotes the number of users. A total T-A matrix $T_{Nn \times Nu}$ can be constructed for the total graph. With this representation, the graph can be mapped into a matrix space by applying matrix factorization, and we can conduct clustering in the matrix space. M represents the mapping matrix space. Once the mapping function is identified, which is the bases of M, each $P_{average\ u}$ can be decomposed into a linear combination of these bases. Then, the similarity between a pair of graphs can be defined based on the linear combination coefficients. Considering that the value of individual graph edges and the value of probability T-A matrix are all nonnegative, it is natural to consider the nonnegative matrix factorization (NMF) [25] when identifying the bases of M. Two more reasons to use NMF: (1) NMF does not make the orthogonality assumption, thus it adapts to a wide range of matrix manifolds [26]; (2) the bases obtained from NMF have physical meanings [27]. Li et al. [24] call the mapping matrix space of NMF as metagraph *space*. The mapping function, which is also the basis for factorization and the axis of metagraph space, is called as *metagraph*. NMF decomposes the total T-A matrix as $T_{Nn \times Nu} \approx W_{Nn \times k} \cdot H_{k \times Nu}$. Note that the columns of W are actually the metagraphs and the axis of the metagraph space M. The columns of H are the corresponding coefficients of the linear combination of these metagraphs for the corresponding users, also can be seen as the corresponding coordinate point of the corresponding individual graph in the metagraph space M. The origin of the metagraph is an empty graph. Fig. 3.4 is an illustration of the NMF process.

Here is the pseudocode for the whole process of individual graph construction, support graph construction, edge indexing, T-A matrix construction and NMF:

```
Support graph node ← {H, W, O, D, N … }
    Support graph Edge ← unique (life pattern set(hour, location1, location2))
    location1, location2 ∈{H, W, O, D, N … }}
    for user in user set:
    for day in dataset time span:
    T-A matrixuser(edge index, day) = 1 if user has corresponding edge in his
life pattern set else 0.
    T-A matrix = sum(T-A matrixuser for user in user set)
    T-A matrix probability.
    ← {column vector/sum of column vector for column in T-A matrix}
    Basis, user coordinate matrix = NMF (T-A matrix probability)
```

3.2 Other methods

Table 3.2 introduces other mobility pattern clustering methods.

Preliminary definition

- A_0^u, A_1^u, A_2^u, A_3^u, A_4^u, A_5^u, respectively, denote the matrix of one user u that input to the K-means clustering algorithm in the metagraph based method, other method 1, other method 2, other method 3, other method 4 and other method 5.

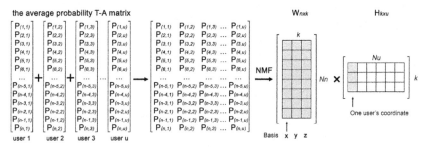

Figure 3.4 The NMF process based on T-A matrix. k, dimension of NMF; m, the index of a day; n, the unique edge index; Nn, the number of edges in the support graph; Nu, the number of users.

Table 3.2 Methods for mobility pattern clustering.

Methodology	Feature capturing					Data structures to represent an individual's mobility pattern
	Significant places semantics	Time-sequential properties	Time duration	Frequency	Prior probability information	
Metagraph based method	√	√	√	√	√	Construct a matrix A_0^u of dimension 1×3 as the figure shows. $P_0^u(1,j) \in A_0^u.$ $j \in \{1, 2, \ldots, k\}$ $P_0^u(1,j) =$ the user u's coordinate on the j axis of the metagraph space
Other method 1	√	√	√	√	√	Construct a matrix A_1^u of dimension $Nn \times 1$ as the figure shows. $P_1^u(i,1) \in A_1^u.$ n ∈ unique (mobility pattern set) (hour, location1, location2) $i \in \{1, 2, 3, \ldots, Nn\}$ $P_1^u(i,1) =$ The probability that user u moves following the

$$
\begin{bmatrix}
P_{(1,1)} & P_{(1,2)} & P_{(1,3)} & \cdots & P_{(1,u)} \\
P_{(2,1)} & P_{(2,2)} & P_{(2,3)} & \cdots & P_{(2,u)} \\
P_{(3,1)} & P_{(3,2)} & P_{(3,3)} & \cdots & P_{(3,u)} \\
P_{(4,1)} & P_{(4,2)} & P_{(4,3)} & \cdots & P_{(4,u)} \\
\vdots & & & & \\
P_{(n-3,1)} & P_{(n-3,2)} & P_{(n-3,3)} & \cdots & P_{(n-3,u)} \\
P_{(n-2,1)} & P_{(n-2,2)} & P_{(n-2,3)} & \cdots & P_{(n-2,u)} \\
P_{(n-1,1)} & P_{(n-1,2)} & P_{(n-1,3)} & \cdots & P_{(n-1,u)} \\
P_{(n,1)} & P_{(n,2)} & P_{(n,3)} & \cdots & P_{(n,u)}
\end{bmatrix}
\xrightarrow{\text{NMF}}
W_{xu} \text{ (Basis)} \times H_{xu}\ (Nu \times k)
$$

One user's coordinate $A_0^u = (x, y, z)$

average probability T-A matrix
$$
A_1^u = \begin{bmatrix}
P_{(1,u)} \\
P_{(2,u)} \\
P_{(3,u)} \\
P_{(4,u)} \\
\vdots \\
P_{(n-3,u)} \\
P_{(n-2,u)} \\
P_{(n-1,u)} \\
P_{(n,u)}
\end{bmatrix} \Bigg\} Nn
$$

(Continued)

Table 3.2 Methods for mobility pattern clustering.—cont'd

| | Feature capturing | | | | | Data structures to represent an individual's mobility pattern |
Methodology	Significant places semantics	Time-sequential properties	Time duration	Frequency	Prior probability information	information
						pattern that edges n represent (move from location 1 to location 2 at the corresponding hour) This baseline aims to examine the performance of NMF process. 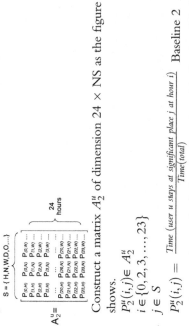 Construct a matrix A_2^u of dimension $24 \times NS$ as the figure shows. $P_2^u(i,j) \in A_2^u$ $i \in \{0,2,3,\ldots,23\}$ $j \in S$ $P_2^u(i,j) = \dfrac{Time\ (user\ u\ stays\ at\ significant\ place\ j\ at\ hour\ i\ )}{Time(total)}$ Baseline 2 represents the methods that we mentioned in Section 2.3 that use the matrix data structure to represent the mobility pattern features.
Other method 2 √		√		√		
Other method 3 √		√				

S = {H,N,W,D,O....}

$$\overbrace{}^{\text{24 hours}}$$

$$A_3^u = \begin{bmatrix} 1 & 0 & 0 & 0 & \cdots & 0 & 0 & 0 & 0 \\ 0 & 0 & 0 & 1 & \cdots & 0 & 0 & 0 & 0 \\ 0 & 0 & 1 & 0 & \cdots & 0 & 0 & 0 & 0 \\ 0 & 1 & 0 & 0 & \cdots & 1 & 0 & 0 & 0 \end{bmatrix}$$

Construct a matrix A_3^u of dimension 24 × NS as the figure shows.

$P_3^u(i,j) \in A_3^u$

$P_3^u(i,j) \in \{0, 1\}$

$i \in \{0, 2, 3, \ldots, 23\}$

$P_3^u(i,:) \in softmax(P_2^u(i,:))$

Baseline 3 also uses matrix data structure to represent the mobility pattern features. However, it only presents the movement of the highest probability. Other movements of lower probability are ignored.

$$B = \left\{ \begin{matrix} H \leftrightarrow H & H \leftrightarrow H & H \leftrightarrow H & H \leftrightarrow H \\ \downarrow_W & \downarrow_O & \downarrow_W & \downarrow_O \\ W \neq O \end{matrix} \cdots \right\}$$

$A_4^u = [P_{pattern1}\ P_{pattern2}\ P_{pattern3}\ P_{pattern4}\ \cdots]$

Construct a matrix A_4^u of dimension 1 × NB as the figure shows.

$P_4^u(1,j) \in A_4^u$

$j \in B$

$P_4^u(1,j) = \dfrac{Time(\text{user } u \text{ moves following the pattern } j)}{Time(total)}$

Baseline 4 is an improvement from Ref. [13]. Schneider et al. [13] considered the sequence relationship between different stops. Besides sequential order, Baseline 4 also considers the significant places semantics.

Other method 4 √   √

Baseline 5   √   √

(Continued)

Table 3.2 Methods for mobility pattern clustering.—cont'd

	Feature capturing					Data structures to represent an individual's mobility pattern information
Methodology	Significant places semantics	Time-sequential properties	Time duration	Frequency	Prior probability	
						$S = \{H, N, W, D, O, ...\}$ $A_3^u = \begin{bmatrix} p_H & p_N & p_W & p_D & ... \end{bmatrix}$ Construct a matrix A_5^u of dimension $1 \times NS$ as the figure shows. $P_5^u(1,j) \in A_5^u$ $j \in S$ $P_5^u(1,j) = $ *total time that user u spend at significant j* Baseline 5 represents the methods that we mentioned in Section 2.3 that use aggregate statistical features and vector data structure for clustering.

- $P(i,j)$ refers to the entry of a matrix A. $P(i,j) \in A$.
- $S = \{H, W, N, D, O, \ldots\}$ refers to a set of all significant places of all users that were detected from raw GPS data. NS refers to the number of elements in S.
- $B = \{B_1, B_2, B_3, \ldots, B_b\}$ refers to a set of all user's mobility patterns of each day. B_b only considers the significant places semantics and sequential order, such as $H-W-H$, $H-O-H$, $H-W-O-H$ et al. NB refers to the number of elements in B.
- n denotes the unique index of all the edges in the support graph. Nn denotes the total number of edges in the support graph.
- u denotes the user index, Nu denotes the number of all users.
- k denotes the dimension of NMF.

4. Application

4.1 Application case

Here, the Great Tokyo area is chosen as the application to show how to conduct mobility pattern clustering (Fig. 3.5). The dataset used is the same as Chapter 2.

Based on the generation principle we introduce in section3, the high-dimension mobility pattern data are transformed to one point in the metagraph space. Then, traditional clustering methods K-means can be introduced to measure the similarities between the points of this metagraph space. Here, the distortion elbow method is used for determining the optimal value of k in K-Means which is introduced in the metagraph space. It is calculated as the

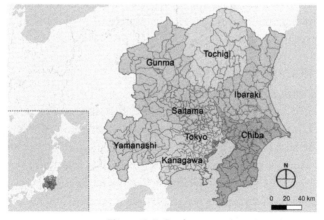

Figure 3.5 Study area.

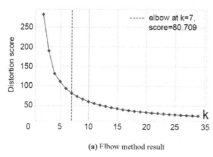
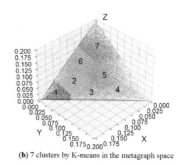

(a) Elbow method result

(b) 7 clusters by K-means in the metagraph space

Figure 3.6 Determine the number of clusters in kmeans by elbow method. (A) Elbow method result. (B) 7 clusters by K-means in the metagraph space.

average of the squared distances from the cluster centers of the respective clusters. As seven is the point of inflection on the curve (Fig. 3.6), all the users are classified into seven groups.

Table 3.3 shows the mobility pattern characteristics of the central point of each group and gives a general description of the mobility patterns of each group. The X-axis refers to 24 h of a day. Each block refers to one node in the support graph, that is, one significant place of each hour. The height of the block in the Y-axis direction refers to the probability of which the users stay in the corresponding significant place. Here, only the blocks whose probability is larger than 1% are visualized. We can see that the users who have larger X values in the metagraph space tend to have a higher probability of staying at home. The users who have a larger Y value in the metagraph space tend to have a higher probability to stay at the other significant places. The users who have a larger Z value in the metagraph space tend to have a higher probability of staying at the workplace. The users whose corresponding points in the metagraph space are closer tend to have a more similar mobility pattern.

4.2 Algorithm performances
4.2.1 *The computation efficiency*
Li, Zhang [24] compared the computation efficiency of different methods (Fig. 3.7). Under the same computation environment, the metagraph-based method shows more advantages in computation efficiency than other methods. Besides, as the number of clusters increases, the computation tasks for other methods become heavier and heavier, and the multiples of computation efficiency between the metagraph-based method and other methods become larger. However, the metagraph-based method can easily handle the clustering tasks of massive groups with as many users.

Table 3.3 Mobility pattern characteristics of each group.

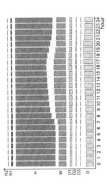

Group 1. Home stayer: 85% stay-at-home

The users of this group spent most of their time at home. They almost have no workplace and seldom go to other places. This group may refer to the old people or homemakers who stay at home all day.

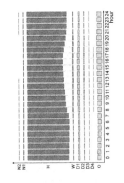

Group 3. Home stayer: 50%-stay-at-home and 40%-stay at-other

The users of this group spend most of their time in the home or other places. They almost have no workplace

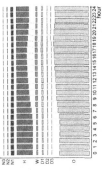

Group 2. Home stayer: 60%-stay-at-home

The users of this group have clear workplaces but they don't go to the workplaces often. This group may refer to the people who telework at home and go to the company sometimes.

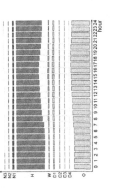

Group 4. Traveler: 70%-stay-at-other

The users of this group spend most of their time in multiple other significant places.

(Continued)

Table 3.3 Mobility pattern characteristics of each group.—cont'd

Group 5. Work-life balance

The users of this group spend roughly equal time at home, work and other places. Their working times are relatively short and they have much leisure time to go to other places.

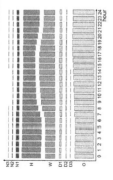

Group 7. Workaholics

The users of this group have high-intensity work and spend most of their time in the workplace. The time spent in the home and other places is rare.

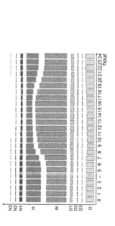

Group 6. Regular office workers

The users of this group usually stay at home at nighttime and go to work in the daytime. They are typical office workers and have regular schedules. Little leisure time is spent in other places.

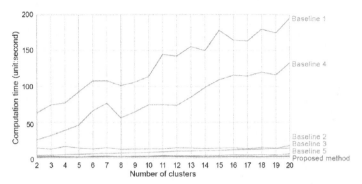

Figure 3.7 The computation efficiency comparison.

4.2.2 The representational capacity to the mobility pattern differences

Li et al. [24] further evaluate the representational capacities to the mobility pattern differences of different methods. $L_{(m, u)} = \{L_m^0, L_m^1, L_m^2, ..., L_m^{23} \mid L_m^h \in \{H_u, W_u, O_u, N_u, D_u\}\}$ denotes the location of an individual u in 24 h of day m. $L_u = \{L_{(1,u)}, L_{(2,u)}, L_{(3,u)}, ..., L_{(m,u)} \mid m \in \{0, ..., Nm - 1\}\}$ denotes the long-term mobility patterns of individual u during Nm days period. They randomly change activities in L_u and the new mobility patterns of individual u is assigned as Q_u. Let $L = \{L_1, L_2, L_3, ..., L_u\}$ and $Q = \{Q_1, Q_2, Q_3, ..., Q_u\}$. Six methods introduced above are applied to the union set of L and Q. Then, they find the point Q_u's neighbors in L and the neighbors are sorted in descending order by their normalized distance. R_u refers to the ranking of point L_u to point Q_u. If the activities do not change, ideally L_u should the nearest point for Q_u in L. Table 3.4 shows

Table 3.4 The representational capacity comparison.

	Change percent	Mean ranking	Std	Min ranking	25% ranking	50% ranking	75% ranking	Max ranking
Proposed method	1% change	50.71	93.53	1	2	5	40	581
	5% change	468.80	576.96	1	103	227	561	2924
	10% change	1775.83	1516.26	1	662	1379	2371	7303
Other method 1	1% change	1.39	3.07	1	1	1	1	62
	5% change	62.44	258.87	1	1	1	1	1431
	10% change	199.04	722.48	1	1	1	21.5	4363

(Continued)

Table 3.4 The representational capacity comparison.—cont'd

	Change percent	Mean ranking	Std	Min ranking	25% ranking	50% ranking	75% ranking	Max ranking
Other	1% change	1.05	0.49	1	1	1	1	23
method 2	5% change	19.04	74.93	1	1	1	1	710
	10% change	91.49	321.20	1	1	1	2	1873
Other	1% change	1.07	0.30	1	1	1	1	7
method 3	5% change	1.20	0.56	1	1	1	1	8
	10% change	1.29	0.69	1	1	1	1	11
Other	1% change	1.08	0.87	1	1	1	1	12
method 4	5% change	11.85	51.70	1	1	1	1	97
	10% change	20.69	72.44	1	1	1	2	210
Other	1% change	1.01	0.22	1	1	1	1	2
method 5	5% change	1.06	0.31	1	1	1	1	5
	10% change	1.16	0.58	1	1	1	1	7

the validation result of the representational capacity of baselines. Here, 1%, 5% and 10% activities are randomly changed.

The result shows that the metagraph-based method has the highest representational capacity of the mobility pattern differences among the other methods. It means that small changes in the mobility patterns will be captured by the metagraph-based method and taken into consideration in similarity measurement when conducting the clustering task. The topology structure of the metagraph-based method is more sensitive to the mobility pattern changes and has stronger distinguishing ability of mobility pattern differences. The metagraph-based method can distinguish the small differences in mobility patterns.

References

[1] M.C. Gonzalez, C.A. Hidalgo, A.-L. Barabasi, Understanding individual human mobility patterns, Nature 453 (2008) 779–782.

[2] S. Phithakkitnukoon, T. Horanont, G. Di Lorenzo, R. Shibasaki, C. Ratti, Activity-aware map: identifying human daily activity pattern using mobile phone data, in: International Workshop on Human Behavior Understanding, Springer, 2010, pp. 14–25.

[3] D. Kahneman, A.B. Krueger, D.A. Schkade, N. Schwarz, A.A. Stone, A survey method for characterizing daily life experience: the day reconstruction method, Science 306 (2004) 1776–1780.

[4] C.J. Matz, D.M. Stieb, K. Davis, M. Egyed, A. Rose, B. Chou, et al., Effects of age, season, gender and urban-rural status on time-activity: Canadian Human Activity Pattern Survey 2 (CHAPS 2), International Journal of Environmental Research and Public Health 11 (2014) 2108–2124.

[5] J. Chen, W. Li, H. Zhang, W. Jiang, W. Li, Y. Sui, et al., Mining urban sustainable performance: GPS data-based spatio-temporal analysis on on-road braking emission, Journal of Cleaner Production 270 (2020) 122489.

[6] F. Devillaine, M. Munizaga, M. Trépanier, Detection of activities of public transport users by analyzing smart card data, Transportation Research Record 2276 (2012) 48–55.

[7] G. Poucin, B. Farooq, Z. Patterson, Activity patterns mining in Wi-Fi access point logs, Computers, Environment and Urban Systems 67 (2018) 55–67.

[8] S. Jiang, J. Ferreira, M.C. Gonzalez, Activity-based human mobility patterns inferred from mobile phone data: a case study of Singapore, IEEE Transactions on Big Data 3 (2017) 208–219.

[9] T. Qin, W. Shangguan, G. Song, J. Tang, Spatio-temporal routine mining on mobile phone data, ACM Transactions on Knowledge Discovery from Data (TKDD) 12 (2018) 1–24.

[10] Y. Ye, Y. Zheng, Y. Chen, J. Feng, X. Xie, Mining individual life pattern based on location history, in: 2009 Tenth International Conference on Mobile Data Management: Systems, Services and Middleware, IEEE, 2009, pp. 1–10.

[11] X. Chen, D. Shi, B. Zhao, F. Liu, Periodic pattern mining based on GPS trajectories, in: 2016 International Symposium on Advances in Electrical, Electronics and Computer Engineering, Atlantis Press, 2016.

[12] C. Li, J. Hu, Z. Dai, Z. Fan, Z. Wu, Understanding individual mobility pattern and portrait depiction based on mobile phone data, ISPRS International Journal of Geo-Information. 9 (2020) 666.

[13] C.M. Schneider, V. Belik, T. Couronné, Z. Smoreda, M.C. González, Unravelling daily human mobility motifs, Journal of The Royal Society Interface 10 (2013) 20130246.

[14] S.A. Ordóñez Medina, A. Erath, Estimating dynamic workplace capacities by means of public transport smart card data and household travel survey in Singapore, Transportation Research Record 2344 (2013) 20–30.

[15] M.K. El Mahrsi, E. Côme, J. Baro, L. Oukhellou, Understanding passenger patterns in public transit through smart card and socioeconomic data: a case study in rennes, France, in: ACM SIGKDD Workshop on Urban Computing, 2014, p. 9p.

[16] X. Ma, Y.-J. Wu, Y. Wang, F. Chen, J. Liu, Mining smart card data for transit riders' travel patterns, Transportation Research Part C: Emerging Technologies 36 (2013) 1–12.

[17] S.A.O. Medina, Inferring weekly primary activity patterns using public transport smart card data and a household travel survey, Travel Behaviour and Society 12 (2018) 93–101.

[18] J.-G. Lee, J. Han, K.-Y. Whang, Trajectory clustering: a partition-and-group framework, in: Proceedings of the 2007 ACM SIGMOD International Conference on Management of Data, 2007, pp. 593–604.

[19] M. Yang, C. Cheng, B. Chen, Mining individual similarity by assessing interactions with personally significant places from GPS trajectories, ISPRS International Journal of Geo-Information. 7 (2018) 126.

[20] Y. Zheng, L. Zhang, Z. Ma, X. Xie, W.-Y. Ma, Recommending friends and locations based on individual location history, ACM Transactions on the Web (TWEB) 5 (2011) 1–44.

[21] F. Xu, T. Xia, H. Cao, Y. Li, F. Sun, F. Meng, Detecting popular temporal modes in population-scale unlabelled trajectory data, Proceedings of the ACM on Interactive, Mobile, Wearable and Ubiquitous Technologies 2 (2018) 1–25.

[22] J.J.-C. Ying, E.H.-C. Lu, W.-C. Lee, T.-C. Weng, V.S. Tseng, Mining user similarity from semantic trajectories, in: Proceedings of the 2nd ACM SIGSPATIAL International Workshop on Location Based Social Networks, 2010, pp. 19–26.

[23] P. Widhalm, Y. Yang, M. Ulm, S. Athavale, M.C. González, Discovering urban activity patterns in cell phone data, Transportation 42 (2015) 597—623.

[24] W. Li, H. Zhang, J. Chen, P. Li, Y. Yao, X. Shi, et al., Metagraph-based life pattern clustering with big human mobility data, IEEE Transactions on Big Data (2022), https://doi.org/10.1109/TBDATA.2022.3155752.

[25] D.D. Lee, H.S. Seung, Learning the parts of objects by non-negative matrix factorization, Nature 401 (1999) 788—791.

[26] N. Lu, H. Miao, Clustering tree-structured data on manifold, IEEE Transactions on Pattern Analysis and Machine Intelligence 38 (2016) 1956—1968.

[27] D. Donoho, V. Stodden, When does non-negative matrix factorization give a correct decomposition into parts? Advances in Neural Information Processing Systems 16 (2003) 1141—1148.

CHAPTER FOUR

Change detection of travel behavior: a case study of COVID-19

Lifeng Lin[1,2]
[1]Graduate School of Interdisciplinary Information Studies, The University of Tokyo, Bunkyo, Tokyo, Japan
[2]Center for Spatial Information Science, The University of Tokyo, Kashiwa-shi, Chiba, Japan

1. Introduction

1.1 Background

Human travel behavior leads to various spatial and temporal phenomena and is thought to be the major driven force in human society. The individual consistently contributes to the shaping of an urban area by movement, such as commuting and touring [1,2]. Because of the circadian rhythm of daily life and constraints of external factors like spatial distance and economics, an individual's travel behavior usually show preferences and specific choice in various aspects, like place to visit, active time, and transportation mode, in a certain period. These preferences and stable choice in travel is called travel behavior pattern [3], and they will finally be reflected in social operation. Studying human travel behavior patterns, especially on the individual level and on a large scale, can provide us with sufficient information about how human society operates and thus help urban planning and management [4].

Although travel behavior pattern is usually stable, an individual may alter his travel preference because of changes in daily life, such as changes in home location and job. The change in travel behavior pattern is normal at the individual level. However, a large-scale and concentrated change is relatively rare and always related to a huge change in society like war and disaster. This kind of collective change started in January 2020 and is continuing at an even global level, caused by the outbreak and spread of COVID-19. To prevent the further spread of this contact infection, human society has made a series of efforts, including lockdown, quarantines, and curfew. Almost infection-preventing policies aim to restrict travel behavior

Handbook of Mobility Data Mining, Volume 2
ISBN: 978-0-443-18424-6
https://doi.org/10.1016/B978-0-443-18424-6.00009-X
49

to reduce contact between people and thus minimize the probability of disease transmission, and it leads to an irresistible change in travel behavior on a social scale. Moreover, due to the reduction of human mobility and lack of dynamics of human activities, such as tourism and transnational communication, COVID-19 also poses both social and economic shocks to many countries. According to a report by World Bank, we are experiencing the worst global economic crisis since the Great Depression, caused by the COVID-19 lockdown, which saw a stagnation of stock markets and consumer activity and other precautions. Typical evidence of an economic downturn is the unprecedented unemployment rate. The unemployment rate in America has reached its peak of 10.2% since this century, which is accompanied by a 5.6% shut-down rate in small businesses [5]. Besides restriction policies, the change in the economy and society also forces people to change their travel behaviors. For example, a salaryman will never visit his workplace again because he was fired. Therefore, research on human travel behavior change during the COVID-19 period can be potent support of decision making for fighting COVID-19 because of the strong relationship between travel behavior and infection. On the other hand, understanding travel behavior change at an individual level can also give us a thorough comprehension of how COVID-19 affected human society and identifies and help affected individuals.

Owing to the development of positioning technology and the prevalence of mobile phones, an individual's mobility can be captured in real-time by smartphones with GPS functions. Mobile phone trajectory data, generated in enormous size every day, provides strong support to study human mobility from individual level to regional level. Compared with other mobility data, mobile phone trajectory data does not require additional devices besides mobile phones. Many are using every data, which confirms the low cost of collecting data and a considerable number of users. Also, it can achieve better accuracy than other positioning techniques by mobile phones, like Call Detail Records (CDR) [6], and the accuracy is possible for further improvement combined with some augmented methods, such as Wi-Fi and Bluetooth. Due to mentioned advantages, mobile phone trajectory data have caught researchers' attention and become an important tool in fighting COVID-19.

However, it does not mean that this data resource can always be completely sufficient for the requirement of research. Data quality is still a problem in mobile phone trajectory data. On the one hand, positioning requires a sound communication environment, but in some cases, such as the user is in underground space, the GPS signal may be shielded, and real-time position cannot be updated, which leads to interruption of trajectory and "GPS drift" phenomenon. On the other hand, although positioning by mobile phone is a kind of passive positioning methodology, few users will authorize others to capture their real-time position information incessantly because of concerns about personal privacy and device battery. Consequently, the positioning function can usually be active, and position information is collected only when users are using specifically authorized smartphone applications. All of these factors result in that the sampling rate, which is determined heavily by individual users' behavior and preference, varies, and the data quality of trajectory may be very uncertain and not meet the requirements of practical applications. This defect in data quality can lead to the unreliability of analysis results. Thus, it has been the primary problem faced by any data users, also in research about mobility in the COVID-19 period.

1.2 Related works

Breaking out in January 2020, the COVID-19 was declared a public health emergency of international concern and has infected more than 180 million individuals and caused about four million deaths spreading in almost every country in the world [7]. To contain and mitigate the COVID-19 epidemic, many governments implement measures to restrict individual mobility and promote social distancing, with the aim of interrupting transmission of the SARS-CoV-2 virus [8].

Due to the natural relationship between human mobility and COVID-19 spread, mobility change in COVID-19 became a hot topic soon, and many relative works emerged trying to explain it. Wang et al. [9] used Apply COVID-19 Mobility Trends Report to analyze the different impacts of COVID-19 on human mobility patterns and observed a 2-weeks delay in mobility change after people's awareness of the situation. Morita et al. [10] discovered Apply COVID-19 Mobility Trends Report and the Google Community Mobility Reports (GCMRs) and found that regular patterns of travel behavior have been significantly disrupted by COVID-19 and the behavioral inhibition manifests differently depending on urban structure and climatic factors. The information limitation in such statistic data restricts these works can only provide us a relatively limited understanding of mobility, and it is hard to support decision-making on a large scale and individual level.

Because of sufficient mobility information contained by trajectory data, mobile phone trajectory data are seen as a powerful tool for further exploring mobility during the COVID-19 epidemic [11]. Gao et al. [12] extended the research area to county-level and mapped mobility pattern changes using smartphone location-derived aggregated mobility data. The result shows different growths in stay-at-home dwell time in different counties in the United States. Xiong et al. [13] observe dramatic changes in mobility patterns across the United States using anonymous mobile device location data from over 100 million monthly active samples. They also evaluated mobility measures by assessing the interregional mobility of the population in three phases. Engle et al. [14] employed GPS data on changes in average distance traveled by individuals at the county level to estimate the relationship between individual mobility and local disease prevalence and restriction orders to stay-at-home. Combining COVID-19 case data and other demographic information helps them distinguish the different responses and relationships in different counties. These works give us an illustration of how humans changed their travel patterns during the COVID-19 period. However, most of them did not answer the problem "what kinds of change occurred at the individual level" quantitatively. And the quality of user data is rarely mentioned, which may influence the reliability of analyzing the result. The information vacancy may be a barrier to better decision-making because of the difference in change detail and inherent reason for the change in the same result of the reduction.

There is one thing that should be noticed most current works did similar exploration focusing on COVID-19 mobility reduction. But travel behavior is more complex and spans multiple dimensions. Besides the number of travels during a certain period, an individual also shows preference in the choice of time of travel, transportation or travel, and destination of travel. And the preference in different dimensions can be independent. For example, an affected individual trips less in stay-at-home measure, but the trip by train can be stable because he needs to work, and train is the only transportation mode he relies on. Ignoring natural multi-dimensions in travel behavior poses further difficulty in understanding COVID-19 impact, and an explanation covering multi-dimensions is necessary.

1.3 Objectives

Based on the literature review in the previous section, we can find there are still some gaps in current studies, which hinder us from having a deeper understanding of human behavior change in COVID-19:

- Most works only focus on mobility reduction, and the natural feature of multi-dimensions in travel behavior is ignored. It can be a barrier to interpreting mobility change and better decision-making.
- To have a better understanding, research on an individual level and large scale are necessary. Although usage of mobile trajectory data offers the chance to do it, the usage of unassessed data can result in uncertainty and unreliability of results because the quality of mobile trajectory data is affected by positioning accuracy and sampling rate and may be various.

This chapter focuses on the individual travel behavior pattern change and hopes to provide an explanation about when, how, and why people changed their travel behavior during the COVID-19 epidemic, using big mobile phone trajectory data, and it is needed to answer the following problem.

- How to evaluate trajectory data quality and filter useable data to make results reliable.
- How to represent travel behavior and detect changes in multi-dimensions and thus give an interpretable result.

2. Methodologies

2.1 Data preprocessing

The mobile phone trajectory data used in this chapter consist of anonymous position records collected by BlogWatcher Company from about five million mobile phone users in Tokyo. The individual position record is generated and collected each time the position sharing function is active, including:

- A specific smartphone application with authorization to use position information only in use is being used.
- Specific smartphone applications with authorization to use position information always are being used or running in the background.
- Position information is being shared actively by the user.

Data collection started on January 1st, 2020, and is still undergoing. This chapter mainly used data from January 1st, 2020, to December 30th, 2020,

52 weeks in total. Over 10 billion position records are generated in the period, and each position record contains:

- User ID. Each authorized user will be allocated a secure and random id to identify the data resource, but no personal information is included and can be inferred.
- Position Information. It is organized as latitude and longitude.
- Timestamp. Time of information return.
- Accuracy. The accuracy is estimated by the GPS function of the mobile phone.
- Device Information. It includes mobile phone model information and device OS version.
- Application Information. It indicates this record is collected by which application.

In this work, we only use several attributes in the position records, including user id, position information, and timestamp. Other attributes are deleted. Although an enormous number of records has been collected, the record number of an individual user may vary significantly. For example, we can see a user has nearly 10 1000 records; however, some individuals only have records of single digits. And the bias in data size can even appear in the same user due to the data collection mechanism. Position information can only be collected when the user is using a specific application on a mobile phone, like Google Maps and Twitter. Both the number of authorized applications and application usage behaviors are quite different between such a large number of users. For instance, a salaryman has almost no time to use the smartphone during working hours, but he uses his smartphone frequently, which leads to few position records can be only collected in his leisure time. However, an unemployed person has enough personal time to use a smartphone. Thus, a large number of position records can be collected all day. This gap between individual preferences can be reflected in various sampling rates even in the same scenario. Fig. 4.1 could be evidence of this phenomenon. The uncertain and uneven sampling rate can result in unreliable analysis results. Therefore, besides traditional data preprocessing, an extra process of assessing trajectory data quality and filtering useable data should be necessary.

As described in the previous section, the raw data are constructed as a set of returned attributes and would be difficult to use directly. Therefore, an individual's trajectory needs to be reconstructed from position records. In this chapter, the trajectory reconstruction framework proposed by

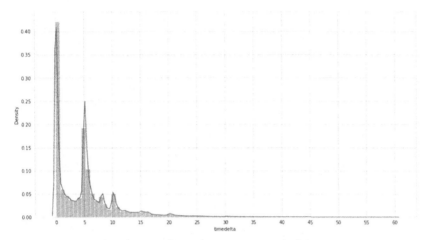

Figure 4.1 Distribution of Sampling Time Interval of Trajectories in JR.

Witayangkurn and Horannont [15] is used for data preprocessing. The overall framework is shown in Fig. 4.2.

To detect travel pattern change, the origin trajectory should be reorganized as time-series data $\{x_1, x_2, \cdots, x_n\}$. Thus, typical features need to be extracted from individual trajectories to represent travel preference and be used in further change detection. According to previous work, human travel behavior changes are generally reflected in four aspects: reduce, re-time, re-

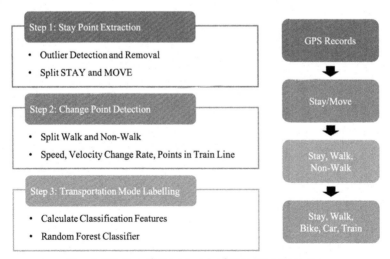

Figure 4.2 Overall Framework of Data Preprocessing.

place, and re-mode. Therefore, an individual's travel behavior is represented in four corresponding dimensions: the frequency dimension, temporal dimension, spatial dimension, and modal dimension, as shown in Fig. 4.3.

The frequency dimension indicates the preference in the number of trips and reflects whether an individual is active or not. Thus, each feature in the frequency dimension x_t can be measured by the number of trips during a timestep. An individual may travel 1 time, 2 times, or more in a certain period. We selected week as the observation period because it corresponds to the natural circadian rhythm of human society and is detailed enough. In the spatial dimension, the choice of a location to visit can also be considered a categorical variable. At every timestep, an individual may visit place A 3 times, visit place B 5 times and visit place C 10 times. Therefore, x_t can be regarded as a collection of samples drawn from a categorical distribution representing the individual preference over all locations.

Similar to the spatial dimension, x_t the temporal dimension can also be divided into someone traveling in the morning 10 times and traveling in the afternoon 20 times, which shows an individual's preference in time of traveling. There are a variety of ways to categorize time of day. One common approach is to divide it into 24 hourly bands. In this work, we assign each trip to an hour of day based on the time at the start point of the trip. Also, the representation of travel behavior in modal dimensions is alike. An individual's travel can be categorized as travel by different transportation modes, like travel by walk, travel by bike, travel by car, and travel by train. Thus, x_t in modal dimension is the number of trips by different transportation modes.

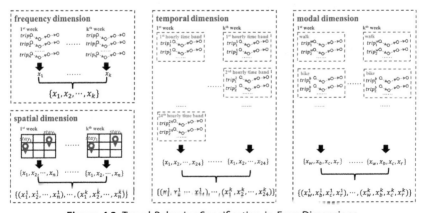

Figure 4.3 Travel Behavior Specification in Four Dimensions.

An individual's travel behavior preference, which can also be called travel pattern, will be represented in four dimensions after mentioned processing. As shown in Fig. 4.4, an individual's travel behavior can be understood easily in multiple dimensions after specification. The x-axis in all subplots represents the active sequence of weeks for the user. For the frequency dimension, it is a *1-D* frequency array of length is week number, shown as a bar plot. For the temporal, spatial, and modal dimension, it is a $M - by - T$ sparse matrix, where each cell represents the frequency of the mth outcome at week t. The y-axis represents the index of hourly time band, index of mesh, and index of transportation modes in the temporal dimension, spatial dimension, and modal dimension, respectively. The matrix is shown as a heat map, and the darkness of a cell is proportional to the value. The darker the color is, the higher this cell represents.

Travel behavior specifications can help us understand how an individual's travel preference is. Here, we choose and compare the result of two sample users to explain it. In the frequency dimension, it is obvious that user one is more active and remains similar travel frequency, while user two had many trips before but reduced travel significantly to about 50 times a week after a change occurred. For the temporal dimension, two users can be distinguished easily because user one is active all day; however, user two is used to be active only in the daytime. The fact is reflected by the even distribution of dark cells in user one and dark cells of user two concentrated in the middle of all hourly time bands. In the spatial dimension, two users have a similar preference which is visiting a few places frequently since the dark

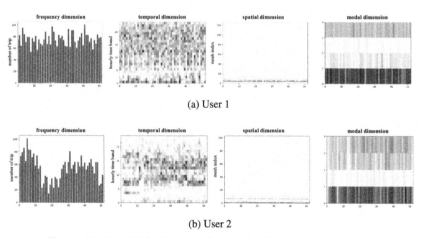

(a) User 1

(b) User 2

Figure 4.4 Travel Behavior Specification for Two Anonymous Users.

cells always concentrate at the bottom. And the similar preference also can be observed in the model dimension, with a little difference that user two travels by car more than user 1.

2.2 Travel behavior pattern change detection

In the following exposition, we formulate the change detection problem based on the online Bayesian framework proposed in Adams and MacKay [16] and the discussion of the same approach in Ranganathan [17]. We can assume that the travel pattern in the frequency dimension, which is indicated by the number of trips, follows a categorical distribution. In the spatial, temporal, and modal dimensions, the choice of a location to visit, departure time, and transportation mode can also be considered a categorical variables.

It is certain that each time point t belongs to exactly one segment that corresponds to a pattern, but the endpoint of the current segment is unknown. Taking the frequency dimension, which follows a categorical distribution, for an example, its probability mass function is given as:

$$P(x_t = b | \theta^0, \theta^1, \cdots, \theta^Q) = \theta^b$$

where b is a possible number of days with trips during a timestep ($b = 0, 1, 2, \cdots, Q$), and $\theta^0, \theta^1, ..., \theta^Q$ are parameters that specify the categorical probability distribution over all possible values of b. They change whenever a pattern change occurs. The algorithm in Fig. 4.5 detects patterns changes in the frequency dimension by assessing whether these parameter values changes.

2.3 Data grading

Due to travel behavior patterns, we need a stable observation of travel behavior in a week, and the uneven and various sampling rates can make the result incredible. For example, if an individual has recorded every day in the first week but in the next week only 2-day records were collected, it would cause the change detection model to infer there is a pattern change in the second week although the user did not have any change. Thus, a process determining which trajectory data is reliable is necessary for a trustworthy analysis. Here, we propose a data framework to conduct this mission.

For a certain model M, which requires an input of a sequence of records $\{r_1, r_2, \cdots, r_n\}$ and the time interval between two sampling records is marked as $\{t_{1,2}, t_{2,3}, \cdots, t_{n-1,n}\}$, we need to find a proper criterion of

---

Algorithm 1 Online Bayesian Changepoint Detection

1: **Initialization**

$$P(r_o) = \tilde{S}(r) \quad or \quad P(r_0 = 0) = 1$$
$$\upsilon_1^{(0)} = \upsilon_{prior}$$
$$\chi_1^{(0)} = \chi_{prior}$$

2: **Observe New Datum** x_t;

3: **Evaluate Predictive Probability**

$$\pi_t^{(r)} = P(x_t | \upsilon_t^{(r)}, \chi_t^{(r)})$$

4: **Calculate Growth Probabilities**

$$P(r_t = \tau_{t-1} + 1, x_{1:t}) = P(r_{t-1}, x_{1:t-1})\pi_t^{(r)}(1 - H(r_{t-1}))$$

5: **Calculate Changepoint Probabilities**

$$P(r_t = 0, x_{1:t}) = \sum_{r_{t-1}} P(r_{t-1}, x_{1:t-1})\pi_t^{(r)}H(r_{t-1})$$

6: **Calculate Evidence**

$$P(x_{1:t}) = \sum_{r_{t-1}} P(r_t, x_{1:t})$$

7: **Determine Run Length Distribution**

$$P(r_t = 0 | x_{1:t}) = P(r_t = 0, x_{1:t})/P(x_{1:t})$$

8: **Update Sufficient Statistics**

$$\upsilon_{t+1}^{(0)} = \upsilon_{prior}$$
$$\chi_{t+1}^{(0)} = \chi_{prior}$$
$$\upsilon_{t+1}^{(r+1)} = \upsilon_t^{(r)} + 1$$
$$\chi_{t+1}^{(r+1)} = chi_t^{(r)} + u(x_t)$$

9: **Perform Prediction**

$$P(x_{t+1} | x_{1:t}) = \sum_{r_t} P(x_{t+1} | x_t^{(r)}, r_t)P(r_t | x_{1:t})$$

10: **Return to Step 2**

Figure 4.5 Bayesian Pattern Changepoint Detection Algorithm.

sampling time interval $\{T_{g1}, T_{g2}\cdots\}$ to grade all given record sequences based on the model error.

Moreover, to solve this problem, we make the following assumption in this chapter:

- Assumption 1: for a model, there is a known optimal sampling time interval that meets all requirements of this model.} Although a smaller sampling time interval can provide us with more abundant information. It does not mean we always need a minuscule sampling time interval. A simple instance is that if we want to know which JR line a user is in from his trajectory records, we can only collect his position every 1 min because the minimum travel time between two JR stations will cost more than 1 min. Thus, a sampling time interval below 1 min can only give us redundancy information. Also, we assume this minimum sampling time interval is known or can be inferred based on background knowledge.

- Assumption 2: for a model, given input with a minimum sampling time interval (called "S-level data"), the output is always true. In most cases, we have no knowledge about the truth. Especially, travel behavior pattern is very abstract and cannot be observed directly. The truth time that a travel behavior pattern cannot even exist. However, for any question, the result which is near to the truth is most likely to be obtained from the data with adequate information, in other words, with the minimum sampling time interval. Thus, although, in some cases, the truth is impossible to be known, we assume that the true value is the output if we give the model the data with the best quality.

To solve the data grading problem, a primary target is constructing the relationship between the sampling time interval between the model error and a value that can be determined to grade data. However, this problem can be extremely hard if we try to solve it by a general dataset. Because we have no knowledge about the true value of output, it will be impossible to estimate the corresponding model error. Therefore, we implement the S-level data defined in Assumption two to deal with it.

In the simplest case, considering there is just one value g of grading criterion need to be inferred, which means the overall dataset will be divided into just two grades: a useable grade and an unusable grade. For an S-level data $S = \{r_1, r_2, \cdots, r_n\}$, the output of model input S is known, and any in its time intervals $\{t_{1,2}, t_{2,3}, \cdots, r_{n-1, n}\}$ is definitely smaller than g. If we generally delete some records from the given S-level data, some of its time intervals will be larger, and we can estimate the output error in this condition. Generally speaking, based on the knowledge about the result of S-level data, it is possible to estimate the relationship between larger sampling time intervals and model error, and how large the sampling time intervals are is related to the delete. If we consider that S-level data is a part of the model which is stable and the delete behavior as a set of variables of input, such as how many records are deleted and where the record is deleted. Thus, the problem of constructing the relationship between sampling time interval and error can be reformed as a problem about estimating the influence of a series of variables on the model output. It is a typical sensitivity analysis and can be solved using the Sobol method.

The Sobol method [18], also referred to as the variance-based sensitivity analysis, is a form of global sensitivity analysis. The basic of the method is the decomposition of the model output function $y = f(x)$ into summands of variance using a combination of input parameters in increasing dimensionality, namely:

$$f(x_1, \cdots, x_k) = f_0 + \sum_{i=1}^{k} f_i(x_i) + \sum_{1 \leq i \leq j \leq k} f_{ij}(x_i, x_j) + \cdots$$
$$+ f_{1, 2, \cdots, k}(x_1, \cdots, x_k)$$

For example, given a model with two inputs and one output, one might find that 70% of the output variance is caused by the variance in the first input, 20% by the variance in the second, and 10% due to interactions between the two. These percentages are directly interpreted as measures of sensitivity. The Sobol sensitivity indices quantify how much of the variance in the model output each uncertain parameter is responsible for. If a parameter has a low sensitivity index, variations of this parameter result in comparatively small variations in the final model output. On the other hand, if a parameter has a high sensitivity index, a change in this parameter leads to a dramatic change in the model output. And the output change or total variance D of a model function $f(x)$ is defined to be:

$$D = \int_{w^k} f^2(x) - f_0^2$$

There exist several types of Sobol indices. The first order Sobol sensitivity index S measures the direct effect each parameter has on the variance of the model:

$$S_i = \frac{E(Y|Q_i)}{V[Y]}$$

Here, $E(Y|Q_i)$ denotes the expected value of the output Y when the parameter Q_i is fixed. The first-order Sobol sensitivity index call tells us about the expected reduction in the variance of the model when we fix the parameter Q_i. Because the sum of the first-order Sobol sensitivity indices cannot exceed one, it can meet the requirement of the data quality metric proposed.

Higher-order Sobol indices also exist and give the sensitivity due to interactions between a parameter Q_i and various other parameters. The total Sobol sensitivity index S_{T_i} includes the sensitivity of both first-order effects as well as the sensitivity due to interaction between a given parameter Q_i and all other parameters. It is defined as:

$$S_{T_i} = 1 - \frac{V[E[Y|Q_{-i}]]}{V[Y]}$$

where Q_{-i} denotes all uncertain parameters except Q_i. The sum of the total Sobol sensitivity indices is equal to or greater than one. If no higher-order interactions are present, the sum of both the first and total order Sobol indices are equal to one.

For obtaining the statistical metric mentioned above, a typical way is to use the Monte Carlo method. The general idea behind the Monte Carlo method is quite simple. A set of parameters is pseudo-randomly drawn from the joint multivariate probability density function p_Q of the parameters. The model is then evaluated for the sampled parameter set. This process is repeated thousands of times, and statistical metrics such as the mean and variance are computed for the resulting series of model outputs. However, the standard Monte Carlo method is that a very high number of model evaluations is required to get reliable statistics. If the model is computationally expensive, the Monte Carlo method may require insurmountable computer power. To solve this problem, the index computing in the Sobol method is usually done by the quasi-Monte Carlo method. Quasi-Monte Carlo methods improve upon the standard Monte Carlo method by using variance reduction techniques to reduce the number of model evaluations needed. These methods are based on increasing the coverage of the sample parameter space by distributing the samples more evenly. Fewer samples are then required to get an acceptable accuracy. Instead of pseudo-randomly selecting parameters from p_Q, in the Sobol method, the samples are selected using the Sobol sequence. Sobol sequences are an example of quasi-random low-discrepancy sequences. They can offer a lower discrepancy by filling the space of possibilities more evenly and result in faster convergence and more stable estimations. And the Sobol indices can be computed by the following equations:

$$f_0 = \int f(x)dx \approx \frac{1}{N} \sum_{k=1}^{N} f(x_k)$$

$$D = \int f^2(x)dx - f_0^2 \approx \sum_{k=1}^{N} f^2(x_k) - f_0^2$$

$$D_i = D - \frac{1}{2} \int \left[f(x) - f\left(x_i, \; x'_{-1}\right) \right]^2 dx dx'_{-i}$$

$$\approx D - \frac{1}{2N} \sum_{k=1}^{N} \left[f(x_k) - f\left(x_{ik} - x'_{-ik}\right) \right]^2$$

$$D_i^{total} = \frac{1}{2} \int \left[f(x) - f\left(x_i, \; x'_{-1}\right) \right]^2 dx dx'_{-i}$$

$$\approx \frac{1}{2N} \sum_{k=1}^{N} \left[f(x_k) - f\left(x'_{ik} - x_{-ik}\right) \right]^2$$

where N is the sampling size for Monte Carlo discretization, $x_i = (x_1, \cdots, x_{i-1}, x_{i+1}, x_m)$ is the parameter combination complementary to x_i.

In summary, to calculate the Sobol indices using the quasi-Monte Carlo method, the following steps are used:

- Select the total number of simulations to be performed.
- Select the parameters of sensitivity analysis.
- Assume ranges for test variables.
- Choose a distribution for each of the parameters.
- Calculate the mean and variance of the parameters.
- Compute the first-order Sobol indices for each parameter by fixing the values of that parameter and varying the remaining parameters.
- Compute the total Sobol indices.

After the quasi-Monte Carlo method, we can get the first-order Sobol indices and the total Sobol index. Because the first order Sobol indices can be regarded as a contribution to the output, we design data defect metric U to finally measure the data quality:

$$U = \sum S_i x_i$$

Here, the data defect metric U shows how low quality the data is. The data with a higher value can be seen as lower quality. Therefore, we can use the Monte Carlo method again to explore the relationship between our data defect metric and model error, and the grading criterion can be determined (Fig. 4.6).

In this work, the target we implement the data is to detect individual travel behavior pattern changes, and the pattern is determined by observation in a week. Based on the background knowledge about travel behavior patterns and change detection methods, the individual trajectory with

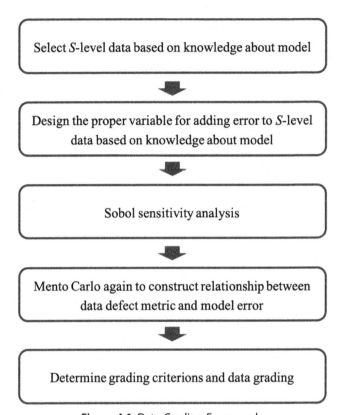

Figure 4.6 Data Grading Framework.

records every day in the data collection period is regarded as S-level data. Although it is possible that S-level data does not contain all positions the individual visit in a day, this defect is ignored in this chapter. From all 5,651,438 users, there are 69,087 users whose data meet the requirement, and thus, their trajectories are graded as S-level. After S-level data is determined, the remaining data set can be graded using the Sobol data grading framework introduced in the previous section.

Based on the knowledge about the change detection model, we define three parameters:

- Maximum Record Day Difference in Consecutive Weeks D_{max}. In the travel pattern change detection method, individual travel pattern is extracted in a weekly time window, and whether change occurs between weeks is inferred. It is obvious the model may give us an incorrect result if there are different sampling days in different weeks. For example, if an individual has a full record in the first week but no record in the second week, the model will tell us despite he did not change his behavior. In summary, this parameter measures the robustness of our model to the sampling bias in a certain period.

- Minimum Record Day in Weekday and Weekend in a Week $N_{weekday}$, $N_{weekend}$. It is also possible that some users may have similar days having records in a period. For example, a user has only records of Monday, Saturday, and Sunday in all weeks. Although the numbers of record days are the same, it may also affect model performance because Bayesian inference used in the method is hard to conduct in a small sample space. The trip number may be small in the example we mentioned before, and it is not obvious whether a change occurs if the user has three trips this week and five trips in the last week. Considering travel behavior may be the difference between weekdays and weekends, two parameters are selected Fig. 4.7.

The result of the Sobol sensitivity analysis is shown below:

Based on the result, we chose 2.45 as a criterion and evaluated the data quality metric of all individual's trajectories, as shown in Table 4.1. There are 41,758 users graded as A-level, which means their data can be reliable, and other trajectories besides S-level and $A-level were not used in the following analysis.

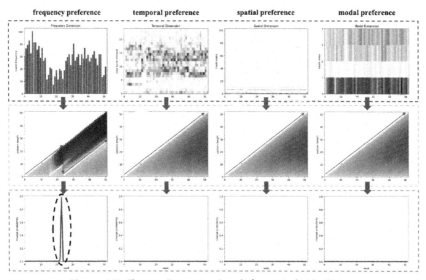

Figure 4.7 Change Detection Result for an Individual User.

Table 4.1 The first-order effects and the total order effects.

Parameters	First-order effects	Total order effects
D_{max}	0.6713	0.6694
$N_{weekday}$	0.33	0.3297
$N_{weekend}$	0.1446	0.0004

3. Results and analysis

3.1 Individual level

From the overall change, it seems that the travel pattern changes during the COVID-19 epidemic in different behavior dimensions are likely correlated to some extent. For example, someone may reduce travel frequency and places to visit simultaneously. To formally examine the correlation across dimensions, we concatenate the estimated change probability $P(\gamma_u = 1|x_{1:T})$ in each dimension over all users. Let us use p_{freq}, p_{time}, p_{space} and p_{mode} to denote the series of change probability in the frequency, temporal, spatial, and modal dimensions. Figs. 4.7 and 4.8 give samples about travel pattern detection in individual level and how a people change travel behavior during the pandemic. To quantify the degree of correlation across dimensions, the Pearson correlation coefficient (or Pearson's r) is calculated for each pair of dimensions. The result is shown in Table 4.2. We can see a strong correlation between most combinations of two dimensions, but the temporal dimension and spatial dimension do not have a relationship. It indicates when people are more likely to remain in their life cycle although they avoid or tend to visit some places.

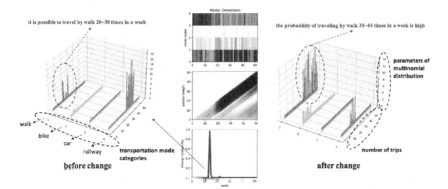

Figure 4.8 Hyperparameters Change the Result for an Individual User.

Table 4.2 Pearson's correlation coefficient among dimensions.

Pearson's r	$P_{(freq)}$	$P_{(time)}$	$P_{(space)}$	$P_{(mode)}$
$P_{(freq)}$		0.316	0.341	0.374
$P_{(time)}$	0.316		0.046	0.253
$P_{(space)}$	0.341	0.046		0.341
$P_{(mode)}$	0.374	0.253	0.341	

Pearson's r assumes a linear relationship between two continuous variables, but in reality, the correlation between dimensions may not be perfectly linear. For further exploration, we compute the expected change probability in one dimension conditional on the change probability in another. Each condition expectation takes the form of $E[A|B]$, and there are 12 possible combinations. Take $E\left[p_{freq}|p_{time}\right]$ for an example. To compute this, we first divide p_{time} Into 10 equally spaced groups between 0 and 1. Then, under the condition that p_{time} is in each of the 10 groups, we calculate the expectation of p_{freq}. Thus, each conditional expectation is a vector of 10 group averages. The result is shown in Fig. 4.9. Each of the 20 bar plots in the figure corresponds to a particular combination. If the two dimensions are significantly and positively correlated, the height of the bat should increase as the x-coordinate increases. In the frequency dimension, which has a strong correlation with the other three dimensions, it seems that the correlation with the temporal dimension may not be as strong as one would expect. When p_{freq} is above 0.9, the average p_{time} is less than 0.3. On the other hand, when p_{time} is above 0.9, the average p_{freq} is about 0.25. However, the situation is different between the frequency dimension and modal dimension. When p_{freq} is above 0.9, the average p_{mode} is above 0.4, indicating the possibility of changing preference in travel mode is relatively high in the condition someone reduces or increases the number of trips. From the viewpoint of modal dimension, it is shown that when p_{mode} is above 0.9 p_{freq} is less than 0.4, it may mean the probability an individual who has changed his behavior in frequency dimension will also change in preference in transportation mode is less than the probability he changes the trip number in the condition of change in modal dimension occur. The result between frequency dimension and spatial dimension is quite similar.

In four dimensions, the spatial dimension may be the least related one to other dimensions, especially temporal dimensions. The results of conditional

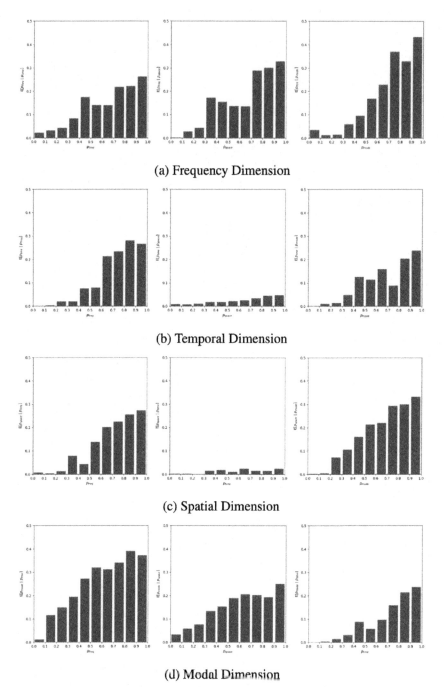

(a) Frequency Dimension

(b) Temporal Dimension

(c) Spatial Dimension

(d) Modal Dimension

Figure 4.9 Conditional Expectation of Change Probability Across Dimensions.

expectation confirm the weak correlation between them, when p_{time} is above 0.9 $E[p_{space}|p_{time}]$ is just about 0.1. It can be explained that many people inevitably need to visit someplace like workplace and supermarket, they try to alter time band to avoid crowd and infection. Another relatively weak correlation can be seen between the temporal dimension and modal dimension, the condition expectation $E[p_{mode}|p_{time}]$ 0.2 when p_{time} is above 0.9 indicate that when most people change their circadian rhythm, they tend to remain the same preference in choosing transportation modes.

3.2 Metropolitan level

Aggregating results from all individuals, a metropolitan-level analysis can be conducted. The trend of the population changing their travel behavior pattern in different dimensions during 2020 is shown in Fig. 4.10 in the form of a Theme River graph. In a Theme River graph, the "river" flows from left to right through time indicated by the x-axis, changing width to depict changes in the population whose travel behavior pattern changed in this timestep. Colored "dimensions" flowing within the river narrow or widen to indicate decreases or increases in the population change of a certain behavior dimension (Fig. 4.11).

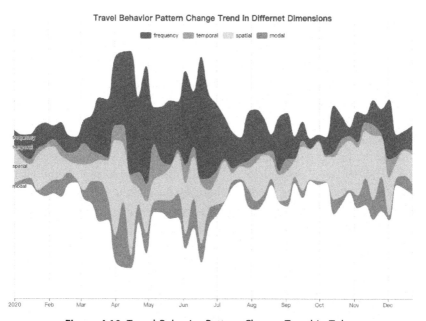

Figure 4.10 Travel Behavior Pattern Change Trend in Tokyo.

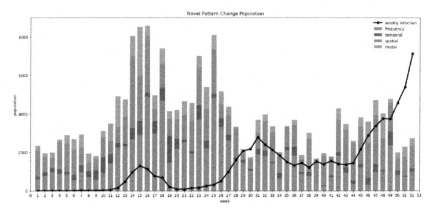

Figure 4.11 Travel Behavior Pattern Change and Infection Number in Tokyo.

From the metropolitan level result, we can identify phases of human travel behavior change:

- Phase 1 (Jan 2020 to March 2020). It is obvious that the changed population in each dimension remained stable before March 2020, when COVID-19 had not spread over Japan. The most proportion of change in this phase is made up of spatial dimension, and change in the frequency dimension is also obvious. However, few users changed in temporal and modal dimensions. This phase can be defined as a basic change pattern in the Tokyo area, associated with several daily activities such as going on a trip, going to hometown, and job shift.

- Phase 2 (March 2020 to May 2020). A remarkable change in the stable change population occurred when time went to March 2020. More and more people chose to change their travel behavior gradually when they were aware of the severity. It is a new phase caused by COVID-19 that started spreading in Japan. Changes in frequency and spatial dimensions are more significant, while still, relatively fewer people tended to change in temporal and modal dimensions. In this phase, affected by COVID-19, we can observe more and more people reduce their trip number and visit places. And the changing population reached its peak at the start of April and contained until the middle of April. On April 17th, the Japanese government announced the start of the state of emergency. It may be the fuse of such a significant change. What should be noticed is the starting of changing peak was a little early before the formal announcement of the state of emergence. It shows many people acted easier to avoid a bigger impact of this policy.

- Phase 3 (May 2020 to June 2020). After a change peak in Phase 2, the population changing travel behavior pattern decreased and returned to the stable. This stable phase can be defined as a basic change pattern in the state of emergency period. There were also many changes that occurred in the frequency dimension, while the change in the spatial dimension is smaller than before.
- Phase 4 (June 2020 to August 2020). On May 26th, the Japanese government announced the end of the state of emergency. We can see an increase again in the population changing their travel behavior pattern, especially in frequency dimension and spatial dimension. However, temporal and modal dimensions did not show significant changes. It shows that because of the end of the state of emergency, many people may try to return to daily life before COVID-19 by traveling more and visiting more places. The general decrease of changes can also be evidence because it is not necessary to change so frequently in daily life.
- Phase 5 (August 2020 to October 2020). From the middle of July, a stable phase can be observed until October. Compared with the basic change pattern, it shows a litter stronger tends to change. And another difference in this phase is the proportion of change in frequency dimension was decreasing.
- Phase 6 (October 2020 to December 2020). The change population started increasing again from the start of October. An interesting thing is the increase was mainly reflected in the change in the spatial dimension, which means people are exploring more places or controlling their outdoor activities. However, the latter should occur with the change in the frequency dimension. Thus, in this period, more people have done more tourism, and it may be affected by GoToCampaign.

The relationship between infection number and human mobility is what people are concerned about. To identify the relationship between travel behavior change and infection number, Pearson's r is also calculated in four dimensions.

From the result in Table 4.3, we can see the relationship between infection and travel behavior is minus, besides the spatial dimension.

Table 4.3 Pearson's correlation coefficient between dimension and infection number.

	Frequency	Temporal	Spatial	Modal
New infection	-0.207	-0.232	0.046	-0.059
Total infection	-0.329	-0.264	0.084	-0.174

Undoubtedly, the correlation between the frequency dimension and infection number is the strongest. On the one hand, people may avoid changes in
the total trip number, like keeping staying home, when the infection number increases. On the other hand, once the infection number decreases, people are likely to change by traveling more. It can also be interpreted that the
change in traveling less can result in a fall in infection numbers. The correlation between temporal dimension and infection is similar but weaker. In
the model dimension, it shows a very small correlation with new infection
but a stronger correlation with total infection. The correlation between
spatial dimension and infection is too small and can be negligible. It means
people are not likely to change their preference in place in any infection
number.

4. Conclusion and discussion

4.1 Summary

This work explored the human travel behavior pattern change in
Tokyo during the COVID-19 epidemic, using big mobile phone trajectory
data. To fill up the vacuum in current studies about multi-dimensions in
travel behavior, we modified an online Bayesian change detection framework to detect when, how, and why humans change their travel behavior
patterns in multidimension from trajectory data. For low-quality data problems encountered during data analysis, we design a novel Monte Carlo data
grading framework to filter useable trajectory data and thus avoid unreliable
results caused by various and low sampling rates in data collection. The analysis result shows Tokyo experienced six phases of travel behavior change
since 2020, and the change was driven by policies to some extent, especially
in the frequency dimension and spatial dimension. Also, the correlation
analysis indicates the correlation between four travel behavior dimension dimensions and the infection number. It provides us with knowledge about
how people will make a change in their travel in the COVID-19 period.

In brief, the main contribution of this work is as follows:

- A novel Monte Carlo data grading framework is proposed to assess and
grade trajectory data quality.
- An online Bayesian framework for detecting travel behavior pattern
change in multidimensions from trajectory data is proposed.
- An analysis is done to help understand when, how, and why humans
changed their travel behavior patterns during the COVID-19 epidemic.

4.2 Limitations and future direction

However, we note several limitations and improve the direction of our work:

- The data grading framework we proposed relies on the background knowledge about the model, and the data quality is only assessed based on sampling time intervals. It leads to doubt about whether this framework is universal, and more verifications in a different dataset and different models are needed.
- Although the quality of trajectory data can be assessed, corresponding data quality improvement methodology is absent. Further studies about how to scale low-quality data can be very useful.

References

[1] Y. Yue, T. Lan, A.G. Yeh, Q.-Q. Li, Zooming into individuals to understand the collective: a review of trajectory-based travel behavior studies, Travel Behaviour and Society 1 (2) (2014) 69—78.

[2] K. Liu, S. Gao, F. Lu, Identifying spatial interaction patterns of vehicle movements on urban road networks by topic modeling, Computers, Environment and Urban Systems 74 (2019) 50—61.

[3] M.C. Gonzalez, C.A. Hidalgo, A.L. Barabasi, Understanding individual human mobility patterns, Nature 453 (7196) (2008) 779—782.

[4] X. Liu, L. Gong, Y. Gong, Y. Liu, Revealing travel patterns and city structure with taxi trip data, Journal of Transport Geography 43 (2015) 78—90.

[5] W. McKibbin, R. Fernando, The economic impact of covid-19, in: R. Baldwin, B.W. di Mauro (Eds.), Economics in the Time of COVID-19, CEPR Press, London, 2020, pp. 45—51.

[6] M. Lin, W.J. Hsu, Mining GPS data for mobility patterns: a survey, Pervasive and Mobile Computing 12 (2014) 1—16.

[7] T.P. Velavan, C.G. Meyer, The covid-19 epidemic, Tropical Medicine and International Health 25 (3) (2020) 278.

[8] T. Hale, S. Webster, A. Petherick, T. Phillips, B. Kira, Oxford Covid-19 Government Response Tracker (Oxcgrt), vol 8, 2020, p. 30, last updated.

[9] S. Wang, Y. Liu, T. Hu, Examining the change of human mobility adherent to social restriction policies and its effect on covid-19 cases in Australia, International Journal of Environmental Research and Public Health 17 (21) (2020).

[10] M.U. Kraemer, C.-H. Yang, B. Gutierrez, C.-H. Wu, B. Klein, D.M. Pigott, L. Du Plessis, N.R. Faria, R. Li, W.P. Hanage, et al., The effect of human mobility and control measures on the covid-19 epidemic in China, Science 368 (6490) (2020) 493—497.

[11] E. Pepe, P. Bajardi, L. Gauvin, F. Privitera, B. Lake, C. Cattuto, M. Tizzoni, COVID-19 outbreak response, a dataset to assess mobility changes in Italy following national lock- down, Scientific Data 7 (1) (2020) 3—9.

[12] S. Gao, J. Rao, Y. Kang, Y. Liang, J. Kruse, Mapping county-level mobility pattern changes in the United States in response to covid-19, SIGSpatial Special 12 (1) (2020) 16—26.

[13] C. Xiong, S. Hu, M. Yang, W. Luo, L. Zhang, Mobile device data reveal the dynamics in a positive relationship between human mobility and covid-19 infections, Proceedings of the National Academy of Sciences 117 (44) (2020) 27087–27089.

[14] S. Engle, J. Stromme, and A. Zhou, Staying at home: mobility effects of covid-19, Available at SSRN 3565703 (2020).

[15] A. Witayangkurn, T. Horanont, N. Ono, Y. Sekimoto, R. Shibasaki, Trip reconstruction and transportation mode extraction on low data rate GPS data from mobile phone, in: Proceedings of the International Conference on Computers in Urban Planning and Urban Management (CUPUM 2013), 2013, pp. 1–19.

[16] R.P. Adams, D.J. MacKay, Bayesian online changepoint detection, arXiv preprint arXiv:0710.3742 (2007).

[17] A. Ranganathan, PLISS: labeling places using online changepoint detection, Autonomous Robots 32 (4) (2012) 351–368.

[18] X.-Y. Zhang, M.N. Trame, L.J. Lesko, S. Schmidt, Sobol sensitivity analysis: a tool to guide the development and evaluation of systems pharmacology models, CPT: Pharmacometrics & Systems Pharmacology 4 (2) (2015) 69–79.

CHAPTER FIVE

User demographic characteristics inference based on big GPS trajectory data

Peiran Li[1], Haoran Zhang[2], Wenjing Li[1], Jinyu Chen[1], Junxiang Zhang[3], Xuan Song[3], Ryosuke Shibasaki[1]

[1]Center for Spatial Information Science, The University of Tokyo, Kashiwa-shi, Chiba, Japan
[2]School of Urban Planning and Design, Peking University, Shenzhen, China
[3]Southern University of Science and Technology-University of Tokyo Joint Research Center for Super Smart Cities, Department of Computer and Engineering, Southern University of Science and Technology, Shenzhen, Guangdong, China

1. Introduction

Tracking demographic dynamics for the built environment is important in many fields, such as smart building, railway station planning, placement of commercial advertising, emergency management and so on [1,2]. As a kind of ubiquitous Internet of Things (IoT) [3,4], portable devices (e.g., mobile phones) afford a great potential to instantly track the built environment demographic dynamics, especially GPS records. To achieve this goal, two factors have to be known: population's mobility (where do people go) and the related demographic information (who are they). Many past studies have investigated the tracking of population dynamics (which only reflects people's mobility) but few of them tried tracking the corresponding demographic dynamics (which also contains people's demographic information). In this context, our study proposed a ubiquitous IoT-based trustworthy approach for user demographic characteristics inference. As Fig. 5.1 shows, the underlying problem of this study is labeling the anonymous users with demographic information (age and gender) based on GPS trajectory data and census data so that further tracking of fine-time-interval and variable-range built environment demographic dynamics could be achieved [5].

The GPS sensor on portable IoT devices could conveniently provide the mobility information but barriers were posed on how to infer the demographic information (mainly the age/gender characteristics) based on GPS trajectory data. Although there have been many GPS trajectory data-based studies, mining demographic information from GPS trajectory data

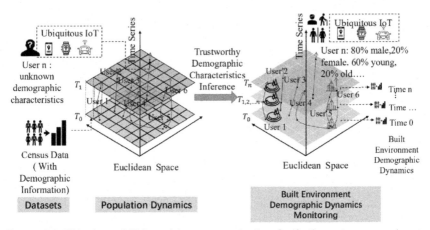

Figure 5.1 Ubiquitous IoT based instant monitoring for built environment demographic dynamics.

is not trivial since a single data source could barely afford enough information [6]. Most past studies chose to combine other types of data, such as mobile usage data [7] (e.g., social media [8]) and individual-level user profile data, to enhance the performance in data inference. However, those additional data, especially some highly sensitive data such as user profiles, is not readily accessible due to privacy risks, etc.

To address the above barriers, we proposed a trustworthy approach based on variation inference (VI) theory to perform the demographic inference with only GPS trajectory data and census data.

2. Preliminary

2.1 Definition

First, we developed the mathematical formulation of this inference problem. Suppose the number of mobile phone users is n; the number of grids obtained through dividing the target area is a; the number of time intervals obtained through dividing the period under consideration is T; the number of demographic groups is m. Define the number of ground-truth demographic samples (of an individual user) $r = a \times T$.

Definition 2.1 (Mobility Record) *A mobility record for a user is a triplet* (u, t, l)*, which denotes that user u visits location l at time t, where l stands for the gridded location (each gird is a 500m × 500m square) determined by latitude and longitude.*

Definition 2.2 (User Spatiotemporal Matrix) *The mobility sequence for a user is a vector* $\{s_0, \ldots, s_r | s \in \{0, 1\}\}$, *which indicates* u_i *is present or absent at a specific time t and location l. Then, the user spatiotemporal mobility matrix could be defined as* $S_{r \cdot n} = \left\{ \overleftarrow{s_0}, \ldots, \overleftarrow{s_n} \right\}$ *which includes all users' spatiotemporal sequence.*

Definition 2.3 (User Demographic Characteristics Matrix) *The user demographic characteristics could be defined as* $\{p_0, \ldots, p_m | p \in [0, 1]\}$, *which indicates the possibility that a user belongs to a specific age/gender group. Then, the user demographic characteristics matrix is a matrix* $A_{m \cdot n} = \left\{ \overrightarrow{p}_0, \ldots, \overrightarrow{p}_n \right\}$ *which includes all users' demographic characteristics.*

Definition 2.4 (Built Environment Demographics Matrix) *Built environment demographics is a vector* $\overrightarrow{s}a = \{sa_0, \cdots, sa_m | sa \in [0, 1]\}$ *which indicates the proportion of different demographic groups in a certain area (i.e., the built environment) at certain time. Built environment demographics matrix is a matrix* $SA_{r \cdot m} = \left\{ \overleftarrow{sa_0}, \ldots, \overleftarrow{sa_r} \right\}$ *including all areas and all time.*

Definition 2.5 (Built Environment Demographics Dynamics) *Given a built environment area (a range of location, denoted as la), and the monitoring period T, the built environment demographics dynamics is a matrix* $D_{la \cdot T} = \left\{ \overleftarrow{SA_{tstart,la}}, \ldots, \overleftarrow{SA_{tend,la}} \right\}$ *including built environment demographics in la during* $t_{start}, \ldots, t_{end}$.

2.2 Solving barriers

Thus, $SA_{r \cdot m}$ could be calculated by $A_{m \cdot n}$ and $S_{r \cdot n}$:

$$SA_{r \cdot m} = S_{r \cdot n} \cdot A_{m \cdot n}^T \tag{5.1}$$

The ground-truth demographic data can afford the exact value of $\overline{SA}_{r \cdot m}$. Left multiply the inverse matrix of $S_{r \cdot n}$ simultaneously on both sides of Eq. (5.1), we obtain:

$$A_{m \cdot n}^T = S_{r \cdot n}^{-1} \cdot \overline{SA}_{r \cdot m} \tag{5.2}$$

At first glance, $A_{m \cdot n}$ could be solved by simply utilizing Eq. (5.2); however, daunting barriers stand in the way of computing $S_{r \cdot n}^{-1}$. Specifically, the barriers embody two subproblems:

Problem 2.1 In most cases, $S_{r \cdot n}$ should be an ill-conditioned matrix that has a large condition number—most individuals' GPS information is sparsely distributed in a large spatiotemporal space. As a result, the solution could be highly unrobust due to the sensitive inverse operation of the matrix $S_{r \cdot n}$.

Problem 2.2 A purely mathematical approach limits the generality—it is prone to yield an overfitted result: solving a specific formula can well afford the demographic information of specific people within the current GPS trajectory dataset, but it may degenerate when applied with another dataset that is unseen.

Based on the above considerations, solving $A_{m \cdot n}$ through brute force should not be a good choice. Hence, our goal is redirected to find:

$$A_{opt} \Big| MAE\left(\overline{SA}_{r \cdot m}, SA_{r \cdot m} \Big| A_{opt}\right) \leq \\ MAE\left(\overline{SA}_{r \cdot m}, SA_{r \cdot m} \Big| A\right) \tag{5.3}$$

Then, the built environment demographic dynamics is:

$$D_{l \cdot T} = \left\{ S_{r \cdot n} \cdot A_{opt}^{T} \Big| \text{where } S \text{ in } T \text{ and } l \right\} \tag{5.4}$$

3. Methodology

3.1 Framework

First, users' life-pattern features were mined from heterogeneous GPS trajectory data [9]. We identified significant places (e.g., home, workplaces and others.) by clustering from trajectories for each user and generated an individual graph that reflected his/her location by each hour within 1 day. Then we constructed support trees with a uniform structure for all users - in the support graph, each edge is assigned with a unique index in an ascending manner from top to bottom and from left to right. Finally we generated a topology-attribute matrix (T-A matrix) to incorporate the user's life-pattern feature (Fig. 5.2).

Second, based on the extracted life-pattern features, a variation-inference-based demographics inference method was derived, which only requires the GPS trajectory data and census data. For each user, we reduce the dimension of the T-A matrix by NFM (Nonnegative matrix factorization) to project it into a 3-dimension space (a meta-graph space), so that the spatial locations in the meta-graph space could represent the user's life-patterns. We could assume that the possibility distribution of a certain demographic group in the meta-graph space is a Gaussian distribution (life-pattern is related to one's demographic information). Then, we employed VI theory to infer the optimal parameters of the Gaussian

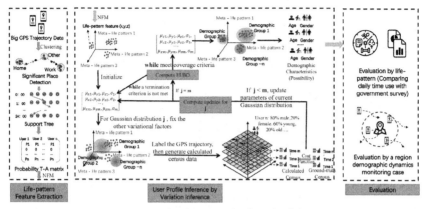

Figure 5.2 The framework of methodology.

distribution of all demographic groups. Once the parameters have been determined, we could infer each user's demographic characteristics by calculating the joint probability of all demographic Gaussian distributions.

Lastly, taking a region in Tokyo as a case study, we compared the accuracy of VI with those achieved by other baseline methods (heuristic algorithm, deep learning). Also, by comparing the daily time-use estimation from our results with survey data, and by comparing the regional demographic dynamics from our results with the ground-truth data, we evaluated the effectiveness of the VI method against other baseline methods.

3.2 Variation inference theory

In Bayesian statistics, unknown quantities inference could be considered as the calculation of posterior probabilities, which are often difficult to conduct. To tackle this problem, one of the solutions is MCMC (Markov Chain Monte Carlo), but it works slowly when confronted with a large size of data (which is expected in our task). Alternatively, VI method could serve as a powerful tool for achieving approximate possibility inference from a large size of big data [10]. The implementation of the VI method is discussed as follows.

Suppose the input observation variables are $\overrightarrow{x} = x_1, x_2, \ldots, x_n$, and the latent variables inside the model are $\overrightarrow{z} = z_1, z_2, \ldots, z_n$. Approximating a conditional density of latent variables $\overrightarrow{z}$ is the aim of VI. The basic idea of VI is to take it as an optimization problem: propose at first a family of approximate probability distribution Q which is related to latent variables $\overrightarrow{z}$, and the goal is to find a distribution among Q, which has a minimal

KL-Divergence (Kullback-Leibler Divergence) from the true posterior possibility distribution [10], that is:

$$q^*\left(\overrightarrow{z}\right) = argmin \cdot KL\left(q\left(\overrightarrow{z}\right)\middle\|p\left(\overrightarrow{z}\middle|\overrightarrow{x}\right)\right) \quad q\left(\overrightarrow{z}\right) \in Q \tag{5.5}$$

where the optimized distribution $q^*\left(\overrightarrow{z}\right)$ could be regarded as the approximate posterior possibility distribution $p\left(\overrightarrow{z}\middle|\overrightarrow{x}\right)$.

Since $KL\left(q\left(\overrightarrow{z}\right)\middle\|p\left(\overrightarrow{z}\middle|\overrightarrow{x}\right)\right)$ is difficult to compute directly, it is usually replaced by a constructed item named Evidence Lower Bound (ELBO) within the VI method:

$$ELBO = E\left[\log p\left(\overrightarrow{z}, \overrightarrow{x}\right)\right] - E\left[\log q\left(\overrightarrow{z}\right)\right] \tag{5.6}$$

It could be demonstrated that minimizing the KL-Divergence $KL\left(q\left(\overrightarrow{z}\right)\middle\|p\left(\overrightarrow{z}\middle|\overrightarrow{x}\right)\right)$ is equivalent to maximizing the ELBO. Therefore, Eq. (5.5) could be transformed to be [8]:

$$q^*\left(\overrightarrow{z}\right) = argmaxELBO(qz, pz, x)q(z) \in Q \tag{5.7}$$

Choosing an appropriate form of approximate probability distribution Q could facilitate the optimization. A common, simple and effective variational family is the *mean-field variational family* which assumes that the latent variables are independent of each other:

$$q\left(\overrightarrow{z}\right) = \prod_{j=1}^{m} q_j(z_j) \tag{5.8}$$

Based on Eqs. (5.6) and (5.8), and by combining the CAVI (Coordinate Ascent Variational Inference) method [10,11], the rule of coordinate ascent could be derived to be (the derivation is shown in Appendix):

$$q^*\left(\overleftarrow{z_k}\right) \propto e^{E_{-k}\left(\log^p\left(\overleftarrow{z_k}\middle|Z_{-k}, \overrightarrow{x}\right)\right)} \tag{5.9}$$

According to expression [12], fixing other coordinates of $\vec{z}$ allows computing the updates of current parameters, as is shown in the following procedure:

Input: A model $p(\vec{z}|\vec{x})$, observations x
Output: A variational density $q(\vec{z}) = \prod_{j=1}^{m} q_j(z_j)$
Initialize: Variational factors $q_j(z_j)$
While the ELBO do not meet the termination criterion do
    for $j \in \{1, ..., m\}$ **do**
        set $q_j(z_j) \propto e^{E_{-j}\left(\log^p(\overline{z}_j|Z_{-j},\vec{x})\right)}$
    end
    Compute $ELBO(q) = E\left(\log p(z,x)\right) - E\left(\log q(z)\right)$
end
return $q(z)$

3.3 Variation inference model construction

Parameters to be optimized. There are so numerous users that taking all users' demographic characteristics as the input parameters could be impractical. To construct an input parameter form that could be solvable, we assume that each demographic group is Gaussian distributed in the life-pattern space (as is shown in Fig. 5.2) so that only four parameters will be needed to describe each demographic group (totally $4 \times m$ parameters for m demographic groups). Once one set of Gaussian distribution parameters is determined, all users' demographic characteristics could be calculated and could then be used to iterate based on the census data to obtain a new set of Gaussian distribution parameters until the convergence of demographic characteristics.

Suppose there are m demographic groups, the parameters to be optimized could be defined as:

$$x_i = \begin{bmatrix} \mu_{x1}, \mu_{y1}, \mu_{z1}, \sigma_1, \mu_{x2}, \mu_{y2}, \mu_{z2}, \sigma_2, \\ ..., \mu_{xm}, \mu_{ym}, \mu_{zm}, \sigma_m \end{bmatrix} \tag{5.10}$$

where μ_x, μ_y, μ_z stands for the coordinate of the center of a demographic group's Gaussian distribution in the life-pattern space; σ denotes the standard error of this Gaussian distribution. Then the possibility that a specific user belongs to each demographic group could be calculated as:

$$
\vec{p}_i = \begin{bmatrix} \dfrac{1}{\sigma\sqrt{2\pi}}e^{\frac{-\left((x-\mu_{x1})^2+(y-\mu_{y1})^2+(z-\mu_{z1})^2\right)}{2\delta^2}}, \cdots, \\ \dfrac{1}{\sigma\sqrt{2\pi}}e^{\frac{-\left((x-\mu_{xm})^2+(y-\mu_{ym})^2+(z-\mu_{zm})^2\right)}{2\delta^2}} \end{bmatrix} \tag{5.11}
$$

and the demographic characteristics matrix of all users $\mathbb{U}$ should be:

$$
A = \left\{ \overleftarrow{p_0}, \ldots, \overleftarrow{p_n} \right\} \tag{5.12}
$$

Considering Eq. (5.3), we define the cost function f as:

$$
f(x_i) = MAE\left(\overline{SA}, S \cdot A^T \middle| A\right) \tag{5.13}
$$

Mathematical Derivation. Based on the VI theory and CAVI algorithm shown above, we derived the algorithm for our task as follows:

Let

$$
p(x, z) = e^{f(x,z)} \tag{5.14}
$$

where: f is the same as the cost function f in Eq. (5.13) x stands for the observations, i.e., the life–pattern coordinate (x, y, z) of each user in the life–pattern space; z stands for the parameters for mixed Gaussian distribution, which are the same as the parameters used in Eq. (5.5).where

For Eq. (5.11), let q_j stands for a Gaussian possibility density function (similar as Eq. 5.7), and m stands for the number of demographic groups. Hence, $q_j(z_j)$ should be

$$
\begin{aligned}
q_j(z_j) &\propto e^{E_{-j}\left(\log^p\left(Z_j \middle| Z_{-j}, x\right)\right)} e^{\left(E_{-j}\left[\log e^{f(x,z_j)} \middle| z_{-j}\right]\right)} \\
&= e^{\left(E_{-j}\left[f(x,z_j) \middle| z_{-j}\right]\right)} \propto E_{-j}\left[f(x, z_j) \middle| z_{-j}\right]
\end{aligned} \tag{5.15}
$$

And ELBO should be

$$
ELBO(q) = f(z, x) \tag{5.16}
$$

The overall flow is shown as below:

> **for** each particle $i = 1, \ldots, S$ **do**
> Initialize the Gaussian distributions' parameters of
> demographic groups: $\mathbf{x}_i \sim U(\mathbf{b}_{lo}, \mathbf{b}_{up})$
> Initialize the particle's best-known parameters to its
> initial parameters: $\mathbf{p}_i \leftarrow \mathbf{x}_i$
> **if** $f(\mathbf{p}_i) < f(\mathbf{g})$ **then**
>   update the swarm's best-known parameters: $\mathbf{g} \leftarrow \mathbf{p}_i$
> Initialize the particle's velocity:
> $\mathbf{v}_i \sim U(-|\mathbf{b}_{up} - \mathbf{b}_{lo}|, |\mathbf{b}_{up} - \mathbf{b}_{lo}|)$
> **while** a termination criterion is not met, **do:**
>   **for** each particle $i = 1, \ldots, S$ **do**
>   **for** each dimension $d = 1, \ldots, n$ **do**
>   Pick random numbers: $r_p, r_g \sim U(0,1)$
>   Update the particle's velocity: $\mathbf{v}_{i,d} \leftarrow \omega \mathbf{v}_{i,d} +$
> $\varphi_p r_p (\mathbf{p}_{i,d} - \mathbf{x}_{i,d}) + \varphi_g r_g (\mathbf{g}_d - \mathbf{x}_{i,d})$
>   Update the particle's parameters: $\mathbf{x}_i \leftarrow \mathbf{x}_i + \mathbf{lr}\mathbf{v}_i$
>   **if** $f(\mathbf{x}_i) < f(\mathbf{p}_i)$ **then**
>
>   Update the particle's best-known parameters:
> $\mathbf{p}_i \leftarrow \mathbf{x}_i$
>   **if** $f(\mathbf{p}_i) < f(\mathbf{g})$ **then**
>   Update the swarm's best-known parameters:
> $\mathbf{g} \leftarrow \mathbf{p}_i$

With the optimized $q(z)$, we can calculate $\mathbf{A}_{opt}$ and formulate the built environment demographic dynamics as:

$$D_{la \cdot T} = \left\{ S_{r \cdot n} \cdot A_{opt}^T \middle| \text{where } S \text{ in } T \text{ and } la \right\} \tag{5.17}$$

3.4 PSO based method (baseline method 1)

Particle swarm optimization (PSO) is a powerful optimization algorithm family, and it defines the set of candidate solutions as a swarm of particles that may flow through the parameter space, driven by their own and neighbors' best performances [13].

Basic Idea. To solve our problem by using the PSO algorithm, the definitions of "particle"——the input parameters to be optimized, and "aim"——the cost function to evaluate the input parameters should be given. In terms of input parameters, as mentioned above, there are so numerous users that we could not take all user's demographic characteristics as the input parameters. To construct a solvable input parameter form, we assume that each demographic group is Gaussian distributed in the life-pattern space (Fig. 5.3); thus, we only need four parameters to describe each demographic group (64 parameters in total for 16 demographic

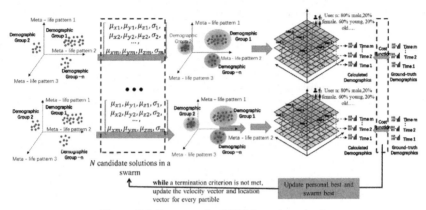

Figure 5.3 Framework of PSO-based method.

groups). Once the parameters of Gaussian distribution have been given, all users' demographic characteristics could be calculated. Through a series of iterations, we can achieve the best parameters (Fig. 5.3).

Mathematical Description. According to the PSO theory, we define our problem as follows:

Suppose there are m demographic groups, the particles could be defined as:

$$x_i = \begin{bmatrix} \mu_{x1}, \mu_{y1}, \mu_{z1}, \sigma_1, \mu_{x2}, \mu_{y2}, \mu_{z2}, \sigma_2, \ldots, \\ \mu_{xm}, \mu_{ym}, \mu_{zm}, \sigma_m \end{bmatrix} \tag{5.18}$$

where μ_x, μ_y, μ_z stands for the center coordinate of a demographic group's Gaussian distribution in the life-pattern space, σ stands for this Gaussian distribution's standard error.

And N candidate solutions constitute the swarm:

$$X = \{x_1, x_2, \ldots, x_N\} \tag{5.19}$$

Then, for each user, the demographic characteristics could be calculated as:

$$\overrightarrow{p}_i = \begin{bmatrix} \dfrac{1}{\sigma\sqrt{2\pi}} e^{\frac{-\left((x-\mu_{x1})^2 + (y-\mu_{y1})^2 + (z-\mu_{z1})^2\right)}{2\delta^2}}, \cdots, \\ \dfrac{1}{\sigma\sqrt{2\pi}} e^{\frac{-\left((x-\mu_{xm})^2 + (y-\mu_{ym})^2 + (z-\mu_{zm})^2\right)}{2\delta^2}} \end{bmatrix} \tag{5.20}$$

and the age/gender state matrix of all the users $\mathbb{U}$ should be:

$$A = \left\{ \overrightarrow{p}_0, \ldots, \overrightarrow{p}_n \right\} \tag{5.21}$$

Considering Eq. (5.20), we define the cost function f as:

$$f(x_i) = MAE\left(\overline{SA}, S \cdot A^T \middle| A\right) \tag{5.22}$$

So far, we have completed the problem construction, and the fake code is shown as follows:

Input: A model $p(\vec{z}|\vec{x})$, observations x
Output: A variational density $q(\vec{z}) = \prod_{j=1}^{m} q_j(z_j)$
Initialize: Variational factors $q_j(z_j) = \frac{1}{\sigma_j\sqrt{2\pi}} e^{\frac{-\left(\left(x-\mu_{xj}\right)^2 + \left(y-\mu_{yj}\right)^2 + \left(z-\mu_{zj}\right)^2\right)}{2\delta j^2}}$ where x, y, z
belongs to $\vec{x}$
While the ELBO do not meet the termination criterion do
    for $j \in \{1, \ldots, m\}$ **do**
        Set $q_j(z_j) \propto E_{-j}[f(x, z_j)|z_{-j}]$
    end
    Compute $ELBO(q) = f(z, x)$
end
return $q(z)$

Finally, once the optimal parameters for Gaussian distributions of all demographic groups are determined, we can calculate the demographic characteristics of all users by Eq. (5.20).

3.5 Deep learning-based method (baseline method 2)

Recent years have witnessed the magnificent booming of deep learning technology. Here, we employed an FCN and Multi-Task FCN to model the relationship between life-pattern features and users' demographic characteristics.

For FCN, we trained a model by taking life-pattern features (e.g., the x, y, z coordinates) as input and output a vector of possibilities that a user belongs to each demographic group. For Multi-Task FCN, the input is the same as FCN, but we used different output branches for different demographic groups. Each branch generates the possibility for the user to belong to the corresponding demographic group, as 0 shows Fig. 5.4.

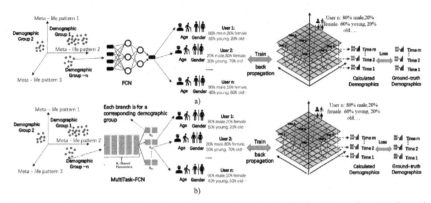

Figure 5.4 Framework of deep-learning-based method. (A) Illustrates the FCN-based method; (B) illustrates the mmultitask FCN method.

4. Case study: experiment in Tokyo, Japan

4.1 Data description

This study employed only two datasets for demographic (age/gender) inference: a large-scale GPS trajectory dataset and a census population data. In addition, a life-pattern statistical dataset is used for evaluation:

Human Mobility Data. This study employed a human mobility dataset named "Konzatsu-Tokei (R)" Data. "Konzatsu-Tokei (R)" Data refers to people flows data collected by individual location data sent from mobile phone under users' consent, through Applications provided by NTT DOCOMO, INC. Those data is processed collectively and statistically in order to obscure the private information. The original GPS data (latitude and longitude) was sent with a period of once every 5 min minimum (i.e., the minimal time interval between two continuous data uploads is 5 min) and did not include information used to specify the individual. *Some applications such as "docomo map navi" service (map navi · local guide). In this study, we selected users who passed Tokyo (23 wards) in the corresponding period with demographic dataset.

Time-series Demographics Dataset. A demographic data named "Mobaku data" was taken as the ground-truth statistical data. It is generated by the DoCoMo (i.e., NTT DoCoMo, Inc.) cell phone network - the number of cell phones can be counted and the population can be estimated considering the penetration rate of DoCoMo within each area. Since its users covered 80 million among the total of 126 million population in Japan, the estimation could achieve a significantly high statistical precision. The demographic data were selected to be consistent with the human mobility data in terms of the period as well as areas of record. As shown in Fig. 5.1, every grid (500m × 500m) contains the population of different demographic groups: male/female with age falling into eight groups: $0 \sim 15$, $15 \sim 20$, $20 \sim 30$, $30 \sim 40$, $40 \sim 50$, $50 \sim 60$, $60 \sim 70$, $70 \sim 80$.

Dataset of Time Use and Leisure Activities. To further evaluate the result of our inference, the *"Survey on Time Use and Leisure Activities"* (conducted by the Statistics Bureau of Japan) statistical data were utilized. This survey is conducted once every 5 years to observe the daily time use of different activities for Japanese people [14]. It contains the average time use in a single day on different types of activities (e.g., working, studying, sleeping and etc.) for populations with different ages (including four age groups: < 35, $35 \sim 44$, $45 \sim 64$ and > 65, male and female).

4.2 Baseline settings

For an inference problem, statistical maximum-likelihood estimation (usually a low-parameter method) and deep learning (mainly neuron network, a high-parameter method) are usually used. Among low-parameter methods, we also employed an optimization method—PSO as a baseline in addition to the proposed VI-based method in Section 3.4. Among high-parameter methods, we used a deep learning approach to fit the life-pattern feature with demographic characteristics i.e., to construct a point-to-point relationship between one's life-pattern feature and one's demographic characteristics. Specifically, we implemented two models: one was Fully Connected Neuron Network (FCN), which directly yielded demographic characteristics for each user; the other one was Multitask Fully Connected Neuron Network (Multitask FCN)—branches of different demographic groups were generated, with each branch representing the possibility for the user of belonging to that demographic group.

Base Baseline: Persistence Algorithm To further confirm the effectiveness of all inference models, we introduced a common baseline—persistence algorithm (the "naive" forecast) where regional demographics of the previous day are used for the estimation of the value of the current day.

4.3 Evaluation metrics

Evaluation by Daily Time Use. We estimated daily time use from the inferred demographic characteristics combined with human mobility data and compared the result with the statistical data *"Survey on Time Use and Leisure Activities"* (conducted by the Statistics Bureau of Japan).

First, for each demographic group (e.g., males aged 30 40), we performed min-max normalization for each demographic group aggregating all the users; then, we selected users whose normalized possibility was above 0.8 as the representatives of this demographic group. Second, we exploited the average "daily home time," "daily work time," "daily other time" for every demographic group from GPS trajectory data (we have identified users' homes, workplaces, and other significant places by clustering GPS trajectory data). Third, we counted the occurrence of the same values in the dataset *"Survey on Time Use and Leisure Activities."* Then, we resampled the results into the same age interval. Lastly, we made a regression between survey's daily time use result and our GPS-derived daily time use result. The Pearson correlation coefficient of regression was taken as the metric to evaluate the model performance.

$$r = \frac{\sum (x - m_x)(y - m_y)}{\sqrt{\sum (x - m_x)^2 \sum (y - m_y)^2}} \tag{5.23}$$

4.4 Overall results

VI achieved the highest accuracy with comparable time cost against other baselines. As Fig. 5.5 shows, VI achieved an MAE of 0.0123, while that of PSO, FCN, and Multitask-FCN are 0.013, 0.0126, and 0.0126, respectively. On the other hand, VI converged within 3000 epochs, which was close to the epoch of the deep learning approach (FCN and Multitask-FCN), and was much faster than the heuristic algorithm (PSO), which took more than 8000 epochs.

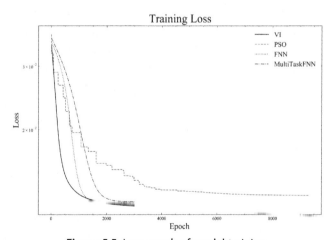

Figure 5.5 Loss-epoch of model training.

Further, we compared the relative error distribution of different demographic groups. From this aspect, VI also achieved better results compared with other baselines. Fig. 5.6 shows that all of the methods performed relatively better when inferring targets aged from 15 ~ 70, but relatively worse when the age was under 15 (the younger group) and above 70 (the elder group). The discrepancy resulted from the lower penetration of mobile phones among these two groups; as a result, their GPS trajectory data covered only a small portion of our dataset, leading to the difficulty in performing a fine fitting. Despite this obstacle, we still found the superiority of VI compared with the heuristic algorithm and deep learning model—VI inferred the younger and the elder groups far better than the other two methods even though their relative errors were similar when estimating demographic groups between 15 ~ 70-year-old.

4.5 Evaluation by time use survey data

Although results of training loss and relative errors indicated the superior performance of VI, it is yet to be demonstrated whether our method evidently reveals the underlying life pattern of different demographic groups. To quantitatively evaluate whether the estimations are consistent with the practical data or not, we compared the daily time use data derived

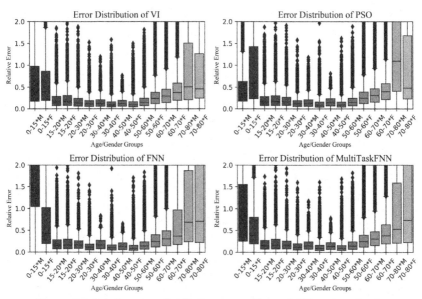

Figure 5.6 Relative error distribution comparison of different methods.

from the inferred users' demographic characteristics with the statistical data *"Survey on Time Use and Leisure Activities"* (conducted by the Statistics Bureau of Japan).

As Fig. 5.7 shows, the results of VI matched the government survey data better than other baselines, reaching a 0.78 r-square, while Multi-task FCN shows the worst matching with a 0.22 r-square. The results show that the inference result from VI well mined the life-pattern difference between different demographic groups.

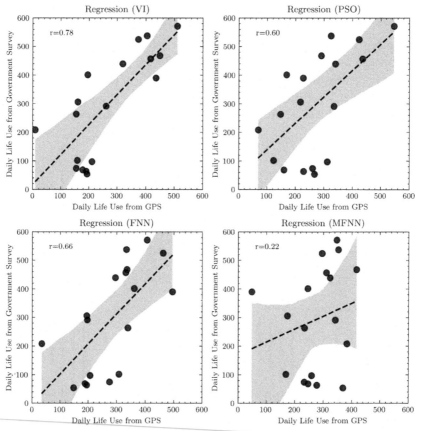

Figure 5.7 Daily time use regression between government survey and GPS trajectory data.

4.6 Evaluation by built environment demographics

In terms of the estimation results of built environment demographics, VI also shows superior performance to baselines. The MAPE of different methods is 0.23 for VI, 0.51 for Base, 0.40 for PSO, 0.30 for FCN, and 0.31 for multi-tasking FCN, meaning the MAPE is improved by 0.07 ~ 0.28. If we investigate the scatter graph between estimation and ground-truth, VI better performance could be observed, especially when estimating the minor demographic groups (Fig. 5.8).

5. Conclusion

This paper proposed a variation-inference-theory-based approach to perform the demographics inference sorely using GPS trajectory data and census data, which could serve as an effective way for trustworthy user demographic characteristics inference.

We demonstrated the feasibility of inferring demographics sorely by using GPS trajectory data and census data. The overall MAE between the inferred demographics and census demographics reached 0.0123. The

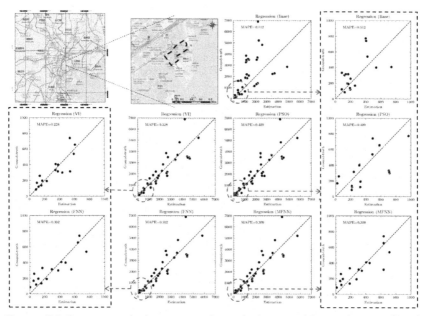

Figure 5.8 Scatter graph between estimated demographics and ground-truth demographics.

Pearson correlation coefficient between the estimated daily time use and the government survey data reached 0.78. Also, taking a region in Tokyo as a case study, we evaluated the estimation of built environment demographics: the MAPE obtained based on ground-truth data reached 0.23.

Further, we concluded the efficiency of our VI-based method in terms of the convergence rate—the VI method consumed less than half of the time to converge compared to the PSO method. Also, through different evaluation metrics, the VI method demonstrated a superior accuracy against other baselines—MAPE of built environment demographics estimation was improved by 0.07 ~ 0.28.

Despite the performance of our proposed VI method, several uncertainties that could further complicate the inference problem remain untreated in our experiment. This study only considered the proportion of different demographic groups instead of using a set of scaling factors to calculate the absolute population of different demographic groups. In addition, the generality of our method may be limited as we only selected a region of 23 wards in Tokyo to conduct the case study.

References

[1] M.N. Alverti, K. Themistocleous, P.C. Kyriakidis, D.G. Hadjimitsis, A study of the interaction of human smart characteristics with demographic dynamics and built environment: the case of Limassol, Cyprus, Smart Cities 3 (1) (February 2020) 48–73, [Online]. Available: https://www.mdpi.com/2624-6511/3/1/4/htm.

[2] Q. Zhang, J. Wu, M. Zanella, W. Yang, A.K. Bashir, W. Fornaciari, Sema-iiovt: Emergent Semantic-Based Trustworthy Information-Centric Fog System and Testbed for Intelligent Internet of Vehicles, IEEE Consumer Electronics Magazine, 2021.

[3] W.Z. Khan, Y. Xiang, M.Y. Aalsalem, Q. Arshad, Mobile phone sensing systems: a survey, IEEE Communications Surveys Tutorials 15 (1) (2013) 402–427.

[4] M. Thejaswini, P. Rajalakshmi, U.B. Desai, Novel sampling algorithm for human mobility-based mobile phone sensing, IEEE Internet of Things Journal 2 (3) (June 2015) 210–220, 1em plus 0.5em minus 0.4em Institute of Electrical and Electronics Engineers Inc.

[5] P. Li, et al., IIoT based Trustworthy Demographic Dynamics Tracking with Advanced Bayesian Learning, in, IEEE Transactions on Network Science and Engineering (n.d.), https://doi.org/10.1109/TNSE.2022.3145572.

[6] A. Solomon, A. Bar, C. Yanai, B. Shapira, L. Rokach, Predict demographic information using Word2vec on spatial trajectories, in: UMAP 2018—Proceedings of the 26th Conference on User Modeling, Adaptation and Personalization, vol 18, 1em plus 0.5em minus 0.4em Association for Computing Machinery, Inc, July 2018, pp. 331–339, [Online]. Available: https://doi.org/10.1145/3209219.3209249.

[7] Z. Yu, E. Xu, H. Du, B. Guo, L. Yao, Inferring user profile attributes from multidimensional mobile phone sensory data, IEEE Internet of Things Journal 6 (3) (June 2019) 5152–5162.

[8] F. Xu, Z. Lin, T. Xia, D. Guo, Y. Li, SUME: semantic-enhanced urban mobility network embedding for user demographic inference, Proceedings of the ACM on

Interactive, Mobile, Wearable and Ubiquitous Technologies 4 (3) (September 2020), [Online]. Available: https://doi.org/10.1145/3411807.

[9]   W. Li, et al., Metagraph-based Life Pattern Clustering with Big Human Mobility Data, in, IEEE Transactions on Big Data (n.d.), https://doi.org/10.1109/TBDATA.2022. 3155752.

[10] D.M. Blei, A. Kucukelbir, J.D. Mcauliffe, Variational inference: a review for statisticians, Journal of the American Statistical Association 112 (518) (2017) 859−877.

[11] A.Y. Zhang, H.H. Zhou, Theoretical and computational guarantees of mean field variational inference for community detection, Annals of Statistics 48 (5) (October 2020) 2575−2598, https://doi.org/10.1214/19-AOS1898 [Online]. Available:.

[12] A. Almaatouq, F. Prieto-Castrillo, A. Pentland, Mobile communication signatures of unemployment, LNCS, in: Lecture Notes in Computer Science (Including Subseries Lecture Notes in Artificial Intelligence and Lecture Notes in Bioinformatics), vol 100461em plus 0.5em minus 0.4em Springer Verlag, November 2016, pp. 407−418 [Online]. Available: https://link.springer.com/chapter/10.1007/978-3-319-47880-7_25.

[13] M. Clerc, Particle swarm optimization, Particle Swarm Optimization (2010) 1942−1948.

[14] Statistics Burea of Japan, Survey on Time Use and Leisure Activities, 2011, [Online]. Available: http://www.stat.go.jp/english/data/shakai/2011/gaiyo.html.

Further reading

[1]   X. Lu, E.I. Pas, Socio-demographics, activity participation and travel behavior, Transportation Research Part A: Policy and Practice 33A (1) (January 1999) 1−18.

[2]   F. Luo, G. Cao, K. Mulligan, X. Li, Explore spatiotemporal and demographic characteristics of human mobility via Twitter: a case study of Chicago, Applied Geography 70 (May 2016) 11−25.

[3]   P. Wang, F. Sun, D. Wang, J. Tao, X. Guan, A. Bifet, Inferring demographics and social networks of mobile device users on campus from ap-trajectories, in: 26th International World Wide Web Conference 2017, WWW 2017 Companion, 2017, pp. 139−147, [Online]. Available: https://doi.org/10.1145/3041021.3054140.

[4]   L. Wu, L. Yang, Z. Huang, Y. Wang, Y. Chai, X. Peng, Y. Liu, Inferring demographics from human trajectories and geographical context, Computers, Environment and Urban Systems 77 (September 2019) 101368.

[5]   A. Roy, E. Pebesma, A machine learning approach to demographic prediction using geohashes, in: Proceedings - 2017 2nd International Workshop on Social Sensing, SocialSens 2017 (Part of CPS Week), 2017, pp. 15−20.

[6]   J. Chen, J. Wu, H. Liang, S. Mumtaz, J. Li, K. Konstantin, A.K. Bashir, R. Nawaz, Collaborative trust blockchain based unbiased control transfer mechanism for industrial automation, IEEE Transactions on Industry Applications 56 (4) (2019) 4478−4488.

[7]   F. Qiao, J. Wu, J. Li, A.K. Bashir, S. Mumtaz, U. Tariq, Trustworthy Edge Storage Orchestration in Intelligent Transportation Systems Using Reinforcement Learning, IEEE Transactions on Intelligent Transportation Systems, 2020.

[8]   C. Kang, S. Gao, X. Lin, Y. Xiao, Y. Yuan, Y. Liu, X. Ma, Analyzing and geovisualizing individual human mobility patterns using mobile call records, in: 2010 18th International Conference on Geoinformatics, Geoinformatics 2010, 2010.

CHAPTER SIX

Generative model for human mobility

Dou Huang
Center for Spatial Information Science, The University of Tokyo, Kashiwa-shi, Chiba, Japan

1. Introduction

1.1 Background

Many big cities have grown, thanks to the rapid urbanization progress, which has modernized many people's lives but also engendered significant challenges [1]. Years ago, solving this kind of challenge seems impossible because of the complex and dynamic settings of cities. Nowadays, some impressive methods of locational datasets collection have shown an opportunity for human mobility applications. For example, human mobility in a city that occurs during some rare events like earthquakes was recorded. How can we use this data to evaluate the situation if the earthquake happened in another city? Although the usage of those kinds of datasets, which are owned by enterprises or government, can give us opportunities for some potential applications, they have some limitations twofold:

(1) it has the risk of privacy violation in some cases if used directly;

(2) it will contain some bias, or the sampling rate is low.

For some human mobility prediction problem that aims to predict human mobility in a target area, it is necessary to know the actual situation about the current human mobility. However, in reality, the provided data cannot reflect that actual situation if the data only contains 1% of the entire population in the real world. To tackle this kind of problem, we can develop a scaling factor for each trajectory sample by combining some information, such as population density, from other data sets.

The scaling factor can add more trajectories based on observed trajectories to approximate the actual situation of human mobility in a target area. However, its limitations are also apparent. It can only add some trajectories based on the existed observations. Thus, it is a lack of diversity as different people are assumed to behave somehow differently even though

Handbook of Mobility Data Mining, Volume 2
ISBN: 978-0-443-18424-6
https://doi.org/10.1016/B978-0-443-18424-6.00002-7

they may be in a similar situation. It is more reasonable to achieve a diversity of trajectories when reconstructing the actual human mobility patterns.

In general, a generative model is a model of the conditional probability of the observable X, given a target Y, symbolically, $P(X|Y = y)$ [2]. It can be used to generate random outcomes, either of observation and target (x, y), or of an observation x given a target value y. A generative model is not designed for transportation planning and applications directly. However, we can use this kind of model to improve the existing datasets to match the implementation of other applications. This kind of model can solve the limitations of the aforementioned scaling factor method.

First of all, a generative model can learn a low dimensional feature space that can infer the travelers' pattern from the complex redundant collected locational datasets. Then, we can utilize the learned feature space for transportation planning and applications. Furthermore, if necessary, we can resample from the learned low dimensional feature space to generate a fake dataset with a similar pattern to the real dataset for further use. There are two reasons for generating fake datasets:

(1) using generated fake datasets can avoid the risk of violation of customers' privacy;

(2) obtain enough data samples if the dataset is too small to be used.

Therefore, the problem of how to build a generative model that can capture the features from accurate human mobility trajectories is a fascinating topic. Nowadays, many deep learning methods have been investigated in image processing, natural language processing (NLP), and human mobility prediction, based on virtual neural networks. Many different neural networks have been proposed to solve different problems in various domains. Although different deep learning frameworks were proposed for solving the problems lying on very different implementations, we can still be inspired by those deep learning frameworks. Variational Autoencoders (VAE) [3] were proposed initially for image processing, and many applications using VAEs achieved an excellent performance. However, owing to the structure of VAEs, it can only be implemented in applications using nonsequential data.

To tackle problems of human mobility, which is a kind of sequential data, we need to use recurrent neural networks (RNN) to build our model. Since vanilla RNNs have difficulties with long-length sequence training due to vanishing gradient problems, long–short term memory (LSTM) and Gated Recurrent Unit have been designed and widely used when coming to the long-length sequence problem.

1.2 Problem definition

We were given a citywide human mobility trajectory data set, denoted as x, which contains complex multimodal information. That dynamic information about human mobility patterns is usually privacy-sensitive, so we want to find its corresponding latent space, denoted as z. The problem becomes to find the posterior distribution of $p(z|x)$, which can be calculated using Bayesian inference like:

$$p(z|x) = \frac{p(z, x)}{\int p(z, x) dz} \tag{6.1}$$

Fig. 6.1 illustrates the intuition about using the deep generative model to solve the above problem. We are able to build the citywide human mobility trajectory estimator if we can solve the equation. Moreover, by solving the above Eq. (6.1), we can know (1) the prior distribution of latent distribution of citywide human mobility $p(z)$, (2) the posterior distribution of latent distribution given observed human mobility $p(z|x)$, (3) the posterior distribution of human mobility $p(x|z)$, which is calculated by

$$p(x|z) = \frac{p(z|x)p(x)}{p(z)} \tag{6.2}$$

Then, if we sample some noise vector $z^\star$ in latent distribution, we can recover the human mobility trajectory $x^\star$.

1.3 Research objective

We aim to use a deep generative model to tackle this chapter's citywide human mobility generation problem. In the model architecture, we focus on learning the hidden space of the posterior distribution of human mobility. Then we can resample from the learned distribution and reconstruct the human mobility trajectories.

Our objective is as follows:

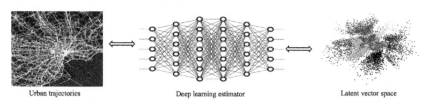

Urban trajectories   Deep learning estimator   Latent vector space

Figure 6.1 Intuition of citywide human mobility estimation using a generative model.

(1) Controlled generation. We want our proposed model architecture to allow us to generate more trajectories that follow the distribution of the learned human mobility pattern. Moreover, we can control the number of trajectories we want to generate.

(2) Diversity. We can obtain some reasonable virtual human mobility trajectories, which are not contained in the original data set, to achieve diversity.

(3) We will use some metrics to quantitatively evaluate the performance of the proposed model for trajectories of human mobility.

We use real navigation GPS data to experiment. The data we used is locational data containing trajectories of human mobility of entire Japan.

2. Methodology

2.1 Preliminary

We will use a variational inference method to solve Eq. (6.1) since its denominator is usually intractable due to the integral. Following the variational inference method, instead of directly finding the intractable posterior distribution $p(z|x)$, we select some approximate distribution, denoted by $q(z)$, from a family of variational distributions. To measure the gap between the selected approximate distribution and the actual intractable posterior distribution, we use Kullback-Leibler Divergence between these two distributions:

$$D_{KL}(q||p) = \int q(z)\log\frac{q(z)}{p(z|x)}\,dz \tag{6.3}$$

By minimizing the KL-divergence, we could find an approximate close distribution of the posterior distribution. In most cases, minimizing Eq. (6.3) is difficult since the KL-divergence contains the unknown posterior distribution $p(z|x)$. We rewrite the above equation as:

$$D_{KL}(q||p) = E_q\left[\log\frac{q(z)}{p(z|x)}\right] = E_q[\log q(z)] - E_q[\log p(z|x)]$$

$$= E_q[\log q(z)] - E_q[\log p(x,z)] + \log p(x) \tag{6.4}$$

Given an observation dataset, its logarithm of distribution $\log p(x)$ should be a constant. Therefore, we define an Evidence Lower Bound (ELBO) by:

$$ELBO(q) = -E_q[\log q(z)] + E_q[\log p(x,z)] \tag{6.5}$$

The ELBO is defined according to the following process:

$$\begin{aligned}
\log p(x) &= \log \int p(x,z)\,dz = \log \int \frac{p(x,z)q(z)}{q(z)}\,dz \\
&= \log E_q\left[\frac{p(x,z)}{q(z)}\right] \le E_q\left[\log\frac{p(x,z)}{q(z)}\right] \\
&= E_q[\log p(x,z)] - E_q[\log q(z)]
\end{aligned} \tag{6.6}$$

We use Jensen's inequality on the log probability of the observations here. Then, minimizing KL-divergence is equivalent to maximizing ELBO, which means that we are able to find an approximate posterior distribution.

Autoencoders have been widely used for generations before. However, its fundamental problem is that the latent space, constructed by the Autoencoder from learning the features of input data, may not be continuous or allow easy interpolation.

The purpose of building a generative model is that we want to randomly sample more data from the approximate latent space or generate variations on input data from a continuous latent space.

When the latent space constructed has discontinuities, the decoder will simply generate an unrealistic output if we sample or generate a variation from there. That is because the decoder cannot deal with that region of the latent space since it never saw such an encoded vector from that region of latent space during training.

One fundamentally unique property of VAEs, which separate them from vanilla Autoencoders, is that their latent space is designed to be continuous, allowing easy random sampling and interpolation. It is also this property that makes VAEs useful for generative modeling.

That property is achieved by making its encoder output two vectors of size n: a vector of means μ, and another vector of standard deviation σ, instead of just outputting one single encoding vector of size n.

These two encoding vectors then form the parameters of a vector of random variables of length n, with the i-th element of μ and σ being the mean and standard deviation of the i-th random variable x_i, from which we sample to obtain the sampled encoding, which we pass onward to the decoder.

This stochastic generation means that even for the same input. In contrast, the mean and standard deviations remain the same. The actual encoding will somewhat vary on every single pass simply due to sampling.

Intuitively, the main difference between a standard Autoencoder and a VAE is the constructed latent space. In the latent space of a VAE, the encoded mean vector μ and the standard deviation σ initialize a probability distribution. In contrast, the encoded vector of a standard Autoencoder is a direct encoding coordinate. In the case of training a VAE, encodings can be generated randomly from the probability distribution. Therefore, the decoder of a VAE can learn to reconstruct the output from a probability distribution rather than just a group of specific points in the latent space.

Kullback-Leibler divergence [4] is a measure of how one probability distribution diverges from a second, expected probability distribution. The most critical metric in information theory is Entropy which is to quantify the information in data. The definition of Entropy for a probability distribution $p(x)$ is:

$$H = -\sum_{i=1}^{N} p(x_i)\log p(x_j) \tag{6.7}$$

Based on the formula of entropy, the Kullback-Leibler divergence, which measures the difference between a probability distribution $p(x)$ and the approximating distribution $q(x)$ can be given:

$$D_{KL}(p\|q) = \sum_{i=1}^{N} p(x_i)(\log p(x_i) - \log q(x_i)) \tag{6.8}$$

With Kullback-Leibler divergence, we can calculate precisely how much information is lost when we approximate one probability distribution with another one. The encoder of a VAE is designed to convert the input data point x to a hidden representation z with weights and biases θ. Therefore, the encoder is denoted to be $q_\theta(z|x)$. The noisy values of hidden representation z are sampled from this distribution as the input of the decoder. The decoder of a VAE has weights and biases ϕ, denoted by $p_\phi(x|z)$. It gets the noisy values of the latent representation z as input and reconstructs the output data x.

The reconstruction log-likelihood $\log p_\phi(x|z)$ is used to measure the information lost in the procedure mentioned above. It also gives the efficiency of the decoder for reconstructing input data x given its latent representation z.

The loss function of the VAE is:

$$l_i(\theta, \phi) = -E_{z \sim q_\theta(z|x_i)}\Big[\log p_\phi(x_i|z)\Big] + KL(q_\theta(z|x_i)\|p(z)) \tag{6.9}$$

It contains two-part: (1) the first term is named to be reconstruction loss; (2) the second term is a Kullback-Leibler divergence between the probability distribution of encoder and a unit Gaussian distribution.

This loss function is well designed as we can also treat the second term to be a regularizer, just like many other loss functions. A reconstruction loss forces the model to give the output just as similar as possible compared with the input.

Meanwhile, the purpose of the second term is to make sure the latent space constructed in the training process is not complex. When the second term is small, we can use a simple latent space to approximate the real posterior distribution of latent space.

RNN are widely used in solving many sequential problems such as NLP tasks [5–7].

The main contribution of RNNs is that they can capture sequential information for use.

For instance, it is a good idea to obtain the previous location in which a data point is located before we predict the next location where the data point will be.

A typical RNN is shown in Fig. 6.2.

Input data is denoted by $x = (x_1, ..., x_{t-1}, x_t, x_{t+1}, ...)$. An observation x_t Indicates the observed data in step t. Corresponding to the input data, a hidden space is denoted by $s = (s_1, ..., s_{t-1}, s_t, s_{t+1}, ...)$. However, a hidden space is not only related to input data but also related to the previous hidden state: $s_t = f(Ux_t + Ws_{t-1})$. The function $f(\cdot)$ is nonlinear activation such as ReLU or tanh. A hidden state s_t can capture the information of current observation x_t and take the previous information captured by s_{t-1} into account. Then, the output $o = (o_1, ..., o_{t-1}, o_t, o_{t+1}, ...)$ can be calculated by $o_t = g(Vs_t)$, where function $g(\cdot)$ is another nonlinear activation.

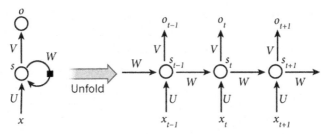

Figure 6.2 Architecture of recurrent neural network.

From Fig. 6.2, we notice that weights U, V, and W only be changed after a sequence is computed completely. Therefore, the total number of parameters of a RNN is not so big compared with other traditional deep neural networks. However, there is the main difference between a RNN and some other traditional deep neural networks, which is that the backpropagation algorithm is used for training traditional neural networks while it cannot be used for training a RNN. That is because the gradient at each output depends not only on the current step but also on previous steps. In that case, a specific backpropagation is designed for training a RNN, which is called Backpropagation Through Time (BPTT).

LSTM was designed to combat vanishing gradients through a gating mechanism [8].

How an LSTM calculates a hidden state s_t is shown as follows:

$$
\begin{cases}
i = \sigma\left(x_t U^i + s_{t-1} W^i\right) \\[2mm]
f = \sigma\left(x_t U^f + s_{t-1} W^f\right) \\[2mm]
o = \sigma\left(x_t U^o + s_{t-1} W^o\right) \\[2mm]
g = \tanh\left(x_t U^g + s_{t-1} W^g\right) \\[2mm]
c_t = c_{t-1} \circ f + g \circ f \\[2mm]
s_t = \tanh\left(c_t\right) \circ o
\end{cases}
\qquad (6.10)
$$

An LSTM layer, shown in Fig. 6.3, has three gates i, f, o. i is called the input gate, f is the output gate, and o is the output gate. The sigmoid function is used in these gates, which have values between 0 and 1. For example, if the value of a gate is 1, then it means that let all information pass toward, while if the value of a gate is 0, it means that no information shall be passed onwards. The function of different gates is different. The input gate i determines the quantity of information of current input to be passed onwards. The forget gate f determines the quantity of information from the previous state is passed onwards. The output gate o determines the quality of information of the internal state is passed onwards.

Besides, g is designed to be a kind of candidate hidden state which is also calculated based on the current input x_t and the previous output s_{t-1} just like

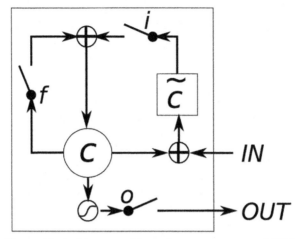

Figure 6.3 Architecture of long-short-term memory (LSTM).

the hidden state calculated in a vanilla RNN. However, this candidate hidden state is not the final hidden state calculated in a LSTM as it should be selected by the aforementioned input gate.

c_t a LSTM unit is internal memory. It is used to capture the information by combining the previous internal memory c_{t-1} with selected candidate hid state g. Using an internal memory, we can completely ignore the previous memory by setting the value of the forget gate to be 0 or completely ignore the new input by setting the value of the input gate to be 0. However, what we really want is the information between these two extremes.

Finally, we can compute the output hidden state s_t using the internal memory c_t. Since there is an output gate that controls the quantity of information to be passed onwards, the hidden state s_t could contain only partial information about the hidden internal state.

The ability to model long-term dependencies is improved in LSTMs, thanks to the gating mechanism.

2.2 Framework

Since urban trajectory data is a kind of sequence data, using LSTM networks is a natural choice. LSTM network is a kind of improved RNN that uses a gated mechanism designed to solve the vanishing gradient problems that happen in vanilla RNN networks. Here, we use two LSTMs to handle the urban trajectory dataset. One LSTM is used as an encoder which takes trajectory data as input and then gives compressed low dimensional vectors as output, while the other LSTM is used as a decoder which takes compressed vectors as input and then gives reconstructed trajectory as output. The model structure is shown in Fig. 6.4, which follows a VAE framework.

The training process of this model follows a semisupervised learning scheme, which means that the input and the output are the same. The loss function of this model is

$$l_i(\theta, \phi) = -E_{z \sim q_\theta(z|x_i)} \Big[\log p_\phi(x_i|z) \Big] + w * KL(q_\theta(z|x_i)||p(z)) \qquad (6.11)$$

where θ, ϕ are the parameters of decoder and encoder, respectively. The first term of the loss function is the reconstruction accuracy measurement, and Euclidean distance is often used to measure the reconstruction error. The second term is the KL-divergence of the approximate posterior distribution with a unit Gaussian Mixture. We assume the posterior distribution is a Gaussian distribution because we want to find a simple yet efficient latent space for real urban trajectories.

As discussed above, VAE can build a hidden space that follows Gaussian distribution to approximate the real distribution of the observed trajectories. The reason for constructing a hidden space that follows a Gaussian distribution is that by learning the parameters of the Gaussian distribution representing the observed input trajectories, we can sample from the distribution and generate new samples of trajectory.

The ability to construct hidden space following a Gaussian distribution is exactly what we want in the variational generative model. However, the VAE lacks the ability to tackle sequential data, which is the main limitation.

The seq2seq model framework usually uses several RNNs as encoders and decoders. Therefore, a seq2seq model can handle sequential data without difficulties, but the hidden space C is not well constructed.

We can regard the seq2seq model as a sequential Autoencoder. By doing that, it is natural to consider that if we combine VAE and seq2seq model, as Fig. 6.4 shows, we can combine their advantages. That means the variational generative model is a well-designed generative model for sequential data.

Let $x = (x_1, x_2, ..., x_t)$ Denote a high dimensional sequence, such as a trajectory of human mobility with t steps. We use an LSTM neural network

Figure 6.4 Architecture of variational generative model.

as a recurrent encoder to capture the information of the input trajectory x. Then we will obtain a series of the hidden state s_t, and a series of output o_t. In the actual case, what we really care about is the final output o rather than a sequence of output value o_t. Since we only keep the final output, we can obtain an intermediate nonsequential vector o to represent the information captured from the input sequence using this recurrent encoder.

After intermediate vector o is obtained, we treat this vector as the input of the VAE part. Then we can write the joint probability of the model as $p(o, z) = p(o|z)p(z)$. $p(z)$ is a prior latent distribution, and $p(o|z)$ is the likelihood. Then we need to calculate the posterior latent distribution $p(z|o)$ given observed data:

$$p(z|o) = \frac{p(o|z)p(z)}{p(o)} \qquad (6.12)$$

by marginalizing the latent distribution:

$$P(z|o) = \frac{p(o|z)p(z)}{\int p(o|z)p(z)dz} \qquad (6.13)$$

This is an exponential time-consuming process. Therefore, variational inference approximates the real posterior distribution with a family of distribution $q_\lambda(z|o)$. Usually, we choose q to follow a Gaussian distribution, then λ would be the mean and variance of the latent distribution $\lambda = (\mu, \sigma)$.

Kullback-Leibler divergence is used for measuring the information lost when using q to approximate p. The optimal approximate posterior is thus:

$$q_\lambda^*(z|o) = \underset{\lambda}{\mathrm{argmin}} KL(q_\lambda(z|o)||p(z|o)) \qquad (6.14)$$

In the VAE model, we parametrize approximate posterior $q_\theta(z|o)$ using an inference network, the approximate likelihood $p_\phi(o|z)$ using a generative network.

Then the loss of the model will be:

$$loss = -E_{q_\theta(z|o)}\left[\log p_\phi(o|z)\right] + KL(q_\theta(z|o)||p(z)) \qquad (6.15)$$

Finally, we use another LSTM neural network as a recurrent decoder to reconstruct the trajectories of human mobility, x from parameters in learned latent distribution.

3. Experiments

3.1 Descriptions of raw data

The data we used for this research is locational navigation data, which is collected when vehicles are using navigation applications. The coordinate system of this GPS data is WGS84, and the records of the locations cover all over Japan. However, owing to some reasons, such as privacy protection, we can only use 1-month records, which are from Oct 1, 2015, to Oct 31, 2015. Besides, the ID of the users was deleted, so privacy is protected well. We can only get the information of the ID of each navigation route to distinguish different trajectories.

Our data contains the information of:

1. Daily user ID: a random unique ID of a vehicle in a day;
2. Route ID: the unique ID of each navigation trip;
3. Timestep: the recorded time of current location;
4. Longitude and Latitude: the value of longitude and latitude after conducting map matching;
5. Sensor longitude and Sensor latitude: the value of raw records of longitude and latitude.

To get an intuitive image of the data we used, a visualization of the GPS data in the selected Tokyo area is given as follows:

Fig. 6.5 given is drawn using the recorded locational points. Since the records are dense and map matched, the points can shape lines and infer

Figure 6.5 Distribution of navigation GPS points.

the road map perfectly. Moreover, we can imagine intuitively that more vehicles drive on major roads than those drive on small roads. Thus we can see that the lines of major roads are thicker than on small roads.

In summary of the human mobility trajectory in the raw data set, we get a simple Table 6.1:

Table 6.1 Summary of daily statistics.

Total records	6,137,308,784
Total daily user IDs	1,168,592
Total route IDs	2,507,308
Average records	197,977,703/day
Average daily user IDs	38,632/day
Average route IDs	81,791/day

3.2 Data preprocessing

The navigation GPS data we used in this research is really big data and contains a wealth of sequential information. However, it is very difficult to handle such big data. We must do some data preprocessing for this raw data and then get a data set we want to utilize in our experiment. The aforementioned basic statistics of the navigation GPS data are all done by coding using python. Since the whole data is as huge as 1.2 terabytes, divided into 938 common-separated values (csv) files, conducting statistics on such big data is very hard, time-consuming work. To improve the efficiency of basic statistics, we use parallel computing to make full use of the central processing units of my machine. Thus, the computing time is reduced to one-sixth and saves lots of time. We use the "haversine" formula to calculate the great-circle distance between two points, which is the shortest distance over the earth's surface.

$$\begin{cases} a = \sin^2\left(\dfrac{\delta\phi}{2}\right) + \cos\phi_1 \cos\phi_2 \sin^2\left(\dfrac{\delta\gamma}{2}\right) \\ c = 2a\tan(\sqrt{a}\sqrt{1-a}) \\ d = Rc \end{cases} \tag{6.16}$$

where ϕ is latitude, γ is longitude, R is the earth's radius (mean radius is 6371 km).

Then, we get the distance delta between every two points using the above algorithm. By summarizing the distance delta of the same navigation trip, we can finally get the traveling distance of all trajectories in the navigation GPS data.

Another process is that we also compute the time interval between every two points. Although it is not used in the aforementioned basic statistics, it will be useful for the experiment.

The time interval of the raw data is not fixed, which means that it will lead to some potential difficulties to further use.

To simplify the data structure of the data which we will use in the experiment, we conduct a linear interpolation to the navigation GPS data to make the time interval of the records fixed. The reason for linear interpolation is twofold: (1) simplify the data structure; (2) obtain trajectories in a specific length. The navigation GPS data is not intuitive for those who are not familiar with trajectory data, so the visualization of the navigation GPS data is necessary. The visualization tool is called mob map, developed by Satoshi Ueyama, a researcher from our laboratory. In this paper, we use mobmap to visualize both the raw GPS data and the output results of our proposed model to make the data and results more intuitive.

For creating the data set used in our experiment, not all raw data is necessary as the size of the raw navigation GPS data is too big. Instead, we chose a selected Tokyo area, longitude from 135.5 to 139.9 and latitude from 35.5 to 35.8. Also, it is not necessary to use the whole month's GPS data since most navigation distance is shorter than 50,000 m and will be ended in one single day.

Since most navigation trips will last hours, it is natural to get 1 hour's data to conduct the experiment.

We select the records from 10 to 11 a.m. October 1, 2015. The data set contains more than 2000 trajectories, which has fixed time interval.

3.3 Experimental settings

We make a brief description of the general process of how to train the VAE model. The first step is preparing training data. The input data we used in the experiment is navigation GPS data which contains trip ID, longitude, latitude, and timestamp. However, the raw data should be preprocessed before the training process. The data preprocessing of linear interpolation is done to simplify the input data by forcing the trajectories to have a fixed timestamp. Therefore, the input only contains information about longitude and latitude but can still represent the dynamics of the trajectories.

We then use several LSTMs as a recurrent encoder which aims to capture the salient features of the sequential input data. LSTMs return an output in every step, which means that the output could also be a sequential output. However, in the VAE model, a nonsequential output, which we make an intermediate vector, is better. This intermediate vector captures the salient features of the input trajectories while keeping a nonsequential data structure. We want the intermediate vector to be nonsequential since the custom VAE has no ability to handle the sequential data.

After the intermediate vector is provided by the recurrent encoder, it will be the input of the custom VAE. This layer aims to build the latent space which can capture the features of the input and follow a Gaussian distribution at the same time. The output of this layer is mean and logarithm variance, which is used for constructing the latent space which follows the Gaussian distribution. The final output of this layer is sampled from this latent space, and it will be the input of the next recurrent decoder.

The latent vector should be repeated several times to match the length of the output trajectories. Then the recurrent decoder consisting of several LSTMs will reconstruct the output trajectories using the aforementioned latent vector. Reconstructed trajectories should be as similar as possible compared with original input trajectories by minimizing the loss function. At the same time, the latent Gaussian distribution should also be as simple as possible to make the VAE model robust.

We use the aforementioned data to conduct the experiment. Mean Distance Error (MDE) between real trajectories and generated trajectories is used for evaluating the performance of the VAE model with different parameter settings:

(1) Short sequence and long sequence, of which length is 6 and 20 respectively, as input of the VAE model to test the ability to tackle long sequence of the model;

(2) The dimensionality of hidden space is set to be 8, 12, and 16, respectively, to test the performance of the model for different dimensionality of hidden space;

(3) Three kinds of input (values of coordinate only, grid ID only, and combination input of values of coordinate and grid ID) are tested.

The results are given in the next section.

3.4 Results and visualization

We use two datasets as our training set for the VAE model. One dataset is 2000 trajectories of which length is all set to be 6, and the other one is 2000 trajectories of which length is all set to be 20. The two data sets are all chosen from the same raw dataset but with different lengths of every sequence. Respectively, we train the VAE model using these two datasets, changing the parameters which control the dimensionality of the constructed latent space and inputs.

The values of loss in different VAE models have been summarized in Table 6.2.

The values of the loss are calculated using the aforementioned formula (6.14):

The values in the table are given by the loss of the final step's training. The smaller the value is, the better the results the trained VAE should give theoretically.

Owing to the lackness of exited generative model for trajectories of human mobility, we evaluate our results just using the designed MDE.

$$E_j = \sum_{i=1}^{N} \frac{dis\left(l_{ij}, \widehat{l_{ij}}\right)}{N} \tag{6.17}$$

where $dis(a, b)$ calculate the distance between point a and point b using their coordinate values; l_{ij} is the ground truth, and $\widehat{l_{ij}}$ is the outputs of the VAE model.

In Fig. 6.6, we also give a visualization of four true trajectories chosen from ground truth and its corresponding reconstructed trajectory. From the figure, we can see that the driver moves from south-east to north-west in about 20 min. Therefore, the locations of the true record and

Table 6.2 VAE loss.

Loss	Both input	Coordinate input	Grid input
6 steps, 8 latent dimension	0.01731	0.0181	0.0174
20 steps, 8 latent dimension	0.0279	0.0293	0.0276
6 steps, 12 latent dimension	0.0175	0.0184	0.0173
20 steps, 12 latent dimension	0.0279	0.0307	0.0293
6 steps, 16 latent dimension	0.0172	0.0181	0.0178
20 steps, 16 latent dimension	0.0296	0.0312	0.0350

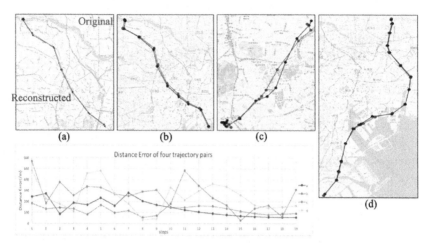

Figure 6.6 Reconstruction error of generated points (/meter). The reconstruction accuracy is acceptable.

reconstructed record every 5 min are given to show the accuracy of the results in an intuitive way.

Instead of just giving a visualization of the single trajectory, quantitative measurement is given by calculating the distance of two points in every step. The unit of the distance error is a meter. We will use this result to explain the limitation of the VAE model.

4. Conclusion

4.1 Discussion

Besides, it should be mentioned that training the VAE model using long sequences as inputs is more time-consuming. Therefore, the epochs of iterations should be carefully considered to reduce the computation. We set epochs of iterations to be 1,000, which make sure that the model is trained fully. By adding regularizers to our neural network layers, we can avoid overfitting.

Table 6.2 indicates three points: (1) in general, the loss values of training using both coordinate values and grid ID as input is the smallest, following training using grid ID as input and using coordinate values as input; (2) the loss values of higher dimensional latent space is often larger than those of lower-dimensional latent space; (3) the loss values of long sequences is larger than those of short sequences.

A reasonable explanation of the aforementioned phenomenon is that the loss function of this VAE model is designed as the combination of reconstruction errors and Kullback–Leibler divergence of approximated posterior distribution and unit Gaussian distribution.

Therefore, the phenomenon that the loss value of training long sequences with a higher dimensional latent space is larger than others can be easily explained. Since long sequences have 20 steps, it is likely that the sum of 20 small losses is greater than the sum of six small losses of short sequences, which have six steps. That will cause a greater reconstruction error of loss function when training long sequences. The situation for higher dimensional latent space is almost the same. Higher-dimensional latent space is likely to have greater values of Kullback–Leibler divergence, which is also a part of loss when training the VAE.

Since the approximated posterior distribution constructed in the latent space of the VAE model is aimed to capture as many features of input training data as possible while in a limited capacity, when the input data is very complex, then the capacity of the latent space should be larger to be able to learn the features. If the dimensionality of the latent space is limited to be small, then it will lead to the lackness of the ability to learn most of the features of training data. However, when we increase the dimensionality of latent space, the ability to learn features of the VAE model is increased indeed. But it could not always be the right strategy to increase the dimensionality of latent space since the information contained in training data is finite, which means a proper VAE model can learn most of the salient information contained in training data using a finite-dimensional latent space. Therefore, when the dimensionality of latent space is too high, the story becomes to be that part of the latent space capture the most salient features, and the rest of the latent space is used to deal with the redundant trivial information. In that case, a higher-dimensional latent space achieves a performance just like a lower-dimensional latent space or even worse.

A comparison of four individual trajectories and virtually generated trajectories is given in Fig. 6.6. Also, we calculate the distance error every 3 min, which is shown at the bottom of Fig. 6.6. The tendency of the distance error is reduced with time, which means that reconstructing a moving trajectory is harder than reconstructing a staying object.

In general, the results of evaluation using MDE show that the reconstruction error of the VAE model is smaller than 800 m. Considering that the selected experiment area is approximately $33,000m \times 36,000m$, we think that the accuracy of the results of the VAE model is enough to tackle the city-scale problems.

Actually, there is a trade-off between the accuracy of the reconstruction trajectories and the robustness of the ability to generate resampled trajectories. As mentioned before, the loss function of the VAE model consists of reconstruction error and Kullback-Leibler divergence. In the practical training process, minimizing the reconstruction error will increase the accuracy of reconstructing input trajectories, while minimizing the Kullback-Leibler divergence will reduce the complexity of learned latent space.

The goal of training the VAE model is to minimize both reconstruction error and Kullback-Leibler divergence. However, there can be a trade-off between them as we usually add weight, smaller than 1, to one of them. When we want our model to achieve higher accuracy in reconstructing trajectories, we add a small weight to the Kullback-Leibler divergence to reduce the contribution of the Kullback-Leibler divergence for the whole loss.

Therefore, the training process becomes that we care less about the complexity of the learned latent space and just make sure the output reconstructed trajectories are as accurate as possible. In that case, we can get a model which has a very good performance in reconstructing input trajectories but a very poor performance in generating resampled trajectories. On the other hand, if we add a big weight to Kullback-Leibler divergence, we aim to train a robust model in which latent space is as simple as possible.

Therefore, we are likely to get a robust model which has poor performance in reconstructing input trajectories. Both of the aforementioned models are not the ideal model we want. Overall, as discussed above, based on the evaluation and visualization of the results, we think our model is trained in a balanced way.

4.2 Limitations

We also want to make a brief discussion about the limitation of the current VAE model when handling the trajectories of human mobility. As shown in Fig. 6.6, a real trajectory and its corresponding reconstructed trajectory are given. The real trajectory is tortuous, while the reconstructed trajectory is smooth. Although the reconstruction error is small, the output reconstructed trajectories of the VAE model seem to be a smooth approximation of tortuous real trajectories.

The main limitation is that many points of reconstructed trajectories don't locate in the road network. Implementing map matching to the generated trajectories may solve the problem, but we believe a better choice is that change the current coordinate and grid-based model to a node-based model. Another idea for this problem is to change the current resampling from the Gaussian distribution strategy to resampling from historical trajectories.

References

[1] Y. Zheng, L. Capra, O. Wolfson, H. Yang, Urban computing: concepts, methodologies, and applications, ACM Transactions on Intelligent Systems and Technology (TIST) 5 (3) (2014) 1−55.
[2] S. Permission, Generative and Discriminative Classifiers: Naive Bayes and Logistic Regression, 2005.
[3] D.P. Kingma, M. Welling, Auto-encoding Variational Bayes, 2013 arXiv preprint arXiv:1312.6114.
[4] S. Kullback, R.A. Leibler, On information and sufficiency, The Annals of Mathematical Statistics 22 (1) (1951) 79−86.
[5] T. Mikolov, M. Karafiát, L. Burget, J. Černocký, S. Khudanpur, Recurrent neural network-based language model, Interspeech 2 (3) (September 2010) 1045−1048.
[6] T. Mikolov, S. Kombrink, L. Burget, J. Černocký, S. Khudanpur, Extensions of recurrent neural network language model, in: 2011 IEEE International Conference on Acoustics, Speech and Signal Processing (ICASSP), IEEE, May 2011, pp. 5528−5531.
[7] T. Mikolov, G. Zweig, Context dependent recurrent neural network language model, in: 2012 IEEE Spoken Language Technology Workshop (SLT), IEEE, December 2012, pp. 234−239.
[8] S. Hochreiter, J. Schmidhuber, Long short-term memory, Neural Computation 9 (8) (1997) 1735−1780.

Further Reading

[1] J. Mueller, D. Gifford, T. Jaakkola, Sequence to better sequence: continuous revision of combinatorial structures, in: International Conference on Machine Learning, PMLR, July 2017, pp. 2536−2544.
[2] M. Baratchi, N. Meratnia, P.J. Havinga, A.K. Skidmore, B.A. Toxopeus, A hierarchical hidden semi-markov model for modeling mobility data, in: Proceedings of the 2014 ACM International Joint Conference on Pervasive and Ubiquitous Computing, September 2014, pp. 401−412.
[3] K. Ouyang, R. Shokri, D.S. Rosenblum, W. Yang, A non-parametric generative model for human trajectories, in: IJCAI, July 2018, pp. 3812−3817.
[4] Q. Chen, X. Song, H. Yamada, R. Shibasaki, Learning deep representation from big and heterogeneous data for traffic accident inference, in: Thirtieth AAAI Conference on Artificial Intelligence, February 2016.
[5] M. Morikawa, Population density and efficiency in energy consumption: an empirical analysis of service establishments, Energy Economics 34 (5) (2012) 1617−1622.
[6] A.Y. Xue, R. Zhang, Y. Zheng, X. Xie, J. Huang, Z. Xu, Destination prediction by sub-trajectory synthesis and privacy protection against such prediction, in: 2013 IEEE 29th International Conference on Data Engineering (ICDE), IEEE, April 2013, pp. 254−265.

[7] Y. LeCun, Y. Bengio, G. Hinton, Deep learning, Nature 521 (7553) (2015) 436–444.

[8] A. Hess, K.A. Hummel, W.N. Gansterer, G. Haring, Data-driven human mobility modeling: a survey and engineering guidance for mobile networking, ACM Computing Surveys (CSUR) 48 (3) (2015) 1–39.

[9] S. Isaacman, R. Becker, R. Cáceres, M. Martonosi, J. Rowland, A. Varshavsky, W. Willinger, Human mobility modeling at metropolitan scales, in: Proceedings of the 10th International Conference on Mobile Systems, Applications, and Services, June 2012, pp. 239–252.

[10] R. Jiang, X. Song, Z. Fan, T. Xia, Q. Chen, Q. Chen, R. Shibasaki, Deep ROI-based modeling for urban human mobility prediction, Proceedings of the ACM on Interactive, Mobile, Wearable and Ubiquitous Technologies 2 (1) (2018) 1–29.

[11] Z. Fan, X. Song, R. Shibasaki, R. Adachi, Citymomentum: an online approach for crowd behavior prediction at a citywide level, in: Proceedings of the 2015 ACM International Joint Conference on Pervasive and Ubiquitous Computing, September 2015, pp. 559–569.

[12] C. Doersch, Tutorial on Variational Autoencoders, 2016 arXiv preprint arXiv: 1606.05908.

[13] M. Yin, M. Sheehan, S. Feygin, J.F. Paiement, A. Pozdnoukhov, A generative model of urban activities from cellular data, IEEE Transactions on Intelligent Transportation Systems 19 (6) (2017) 1682–1696.

CHAPTER SEVEN

Retrieval-based human trajectory generation

Dou Huang
Center for Spatial Information Science, The University of Tokyo, Kashiwa-shi, Chiba, Japan

1. Introduction

1.1 Background

We analyzed the advantages and disadvantages of generating human mobility data through a deep generative model directly in the previous chapter. The main limitation of directly using the deep generative model for trajectory generation is that the generated virtual human mobility trajectory data does not have geographic information restrictions. Therefore, although the newly generated virtual human mobility trajectory does not infringe on user privacy, it cannot be proven to be realistic in the real world, where the trajectory falls perfectly on the road grid. However, we have also tried some map matching methods to generate virtual human mobility trajectories with no geographic information constraints to the road network. As discussed in the previous chapter, directly using map matching as a postprocessing method will change the pattern similarity between ground truth human mobility trajectories and newly generated virtual trajectories. Based on the shortcomings of these previous practices, we consider the direction of improvement from the perspective of pursuing the authenticity of the trajectory.

Another issue worth considering is how we measure the authenticity of the virtual human mobility trajectory directly generated by the deep learning model. We realize that the authenticity of the human mobility trajectory is a more difficult indicator to quantify and measure than the similarity of the human mobility trajectory. Here we are taking the similarity of human mobility trajectories as an example. Many previous studies have put forward some quantitative measures. Their primary purpose is to establish whether different human mobility trajectories are similar to tackle the trajectory clustering problem. However, the authenticity of the virtual human mobility trajectory cannot be measured entirely by the trajectory

Handbook of Mobility Data Mining, Volume 2
ISBN: 978-0-443-18424-6
https://doi.org/10.1016/B978-0-443-18424-6.00004-0

similarity. It is because even if we assume that the virtual human mobility trajectory data generated by the deep learning model, which is similar to the ground truth human mobility trajectory, has a high authenticity. We cannot deny that generated virtual human mobility trajectory, which is not similar to the observed human mobility dataset, is not real. We must remember that the human mobility trajectory data we can access is usually a low sampling rate with sampling bias data. Therefore, we do not have enough evidence to deny that the human mobility trajectory that is not similar to the observations we get does not exist in this world.

Suppose we insist on taking the traditional measure of trajectory similarity to measure the authenticity of the newly generated virtual human mobility trajectory. In that case, an essential prerequisite is that we need to assume that the actual observed human mobility trajectory data we can currently obtain is sufficient and can reflect the flow of people in the real world. This assumption itself is untrue, and it is in contrast to the purpose of our work because under this assumption. In this case, we do not need to explore a suitable method of estimating the human mobility trajectory data to solve human mobility trajectory data which does not fully reflect the real-world human mobility pattern. Nevertheless, in any case, we hope that the new virtual trajectory generated by the deep learning model is realistic enough, so we should use another idea to solve this problem.

In order to avoid the authenticity problem of the generated virtual human mobility trajectory data and at the same time refer to enough research on the similarity of human mobility trajectory methods, we propose a retrieval-based human mobility trajectory generation method. Our method is still based on the deep learning method and uses the deep learning model to capture essential features in the human flow trajectory. Problem definition.

We refer to the traditional definition and method of similarity of human mobility trajectory before and convert the problem of directly generating virtual human flow trajectory into a problem of using a deep learning model to construct trajectory similarity. We define it as historical human mobility trajectory data for the entire human mobility trajectory data we can currently get. This historical human mobility trajectory data acts as a database. In this database, we only keep the trajectory data and delete all other information that may infringe on personal privacy. One of our assumptions here is that although we only have a small part of the real human flow trajectory data, we can still get a trajectory database with sufficient information if we continue to sample for a long time. Assuming that we already have a small part of the human mobility trajectory data observations, we need to generate more virtual human flow trajectories. We can use some of the trajectories in this historical trajectory database as supplementary trajectories. Therefore, we turn the problem into selecting a suitable supplementary trajectory from the historical trajectory database to make the small part of the observed human flow trajectory data more in line with the current real human flow pattern.

1.2 Research objective

In this chapter, our research objectives are as follows:

1) Conduct experiments to evaluate the change of citywide human mobility pattern when using map matching technique as postprocessing;
2) Propose a search-based method to generate human flow trajectory data to avoid the problem of imperfect authenticity encountered when directly generating virtual human flow trajectories;
3) We compare the human flow trajectory similarity method established by the proposed trajectory feature extraction method based on the Encoder-Decoder deep learning framework with the traditional method;
4) Carrying out numerical experiments to verify that our proposed method has obtained better results

2. Map-matching as postprocessing

This section aims to evaluate the human mobility pattern change between generated virtual trajectories and virtual trajectories after map-matching.

2.1 Framework

For simplification, we use a statistical method of the probability of migration for virtual trajectory generation, which can be written as the following equation [1]:

$$T_{ij} = T_i \frac{m_i n_j}{\left(m_i + s_{ij}\right)\left(m_i + n_j + s_{ij}\right)} \tag{7.1}$$

where T_i is the total number of commuters that start their trip from location i, which can be calculated by:

$$T_i = m_i \frac{N_c}{N} \tag{7.2}$$

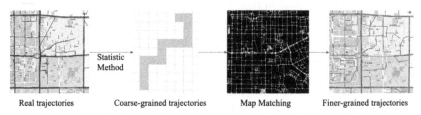

| Real trajectories | Coarse-grained trajectories | Map Matching | Finer-grained trajectories |

Figure 7.1 Framework of using shortest path algorithm with map matching technique as postprocessing of virtual human mobility trajectories.

where N_c is the total number of commuters and N is the total population of the city. Besides, m_i, n_j, s_{ij} Indicates the population of grid i, j, from grid i to j, respectively.

Therefore, the first step is to convert the real human mobility trajectories to grid-based sequences. By implementing the above equation, we got generated coarse-grained virtual trajectories. Then, we know that the generated coarse-grained trajectories should be processed using the Shortest path algorithm with a map matching technique to produce virtual finer-grained trajectories in the road network. The entire process of producing those virtual trajectories is shown in the Fig. 7.1. Our objective in this section is that we want to evaluate human mobility pattern changes after this process.

2.2 Experiments

We used a month's taxi navigation GPS track, and the data range is a rectangular area within a city that is roughly 8×8 km. The data collection interval we used is $2 \sim 4$ s, which shows that the data was initially high-quality trajectory data. At the same time, the original data points are all on the road network.

3. Metrics for assessment

Mean square error (MSE) and mean absolute error (MAE) are used in this section, which can be written as:

$$MSE = \frac{1}{m} \sum_{i=1}^{m} (y_i - \widehat{y}_i)^2 \tag{7.3}$$

$$MAE = \frac{1}{m} \sum_{i=1}^{m} |y_i - \widehat{y}_i| \tag{7.4}$$

We also use some trajectory similarity metrics proposed recently, shown in Fig. 7.2 [2].

3.1 Results

At first, we will show a visualization for comparison between ground truth trajectories used in this experiment and finer-grained virtual trajectories after processing of shortest path algorithm with the map matching technique.

We notice some differences between the two figures in Fig. 7.3: 1) the trajectories distribution is different, meaning there are some virtual trajectories in some places with no ground truth trajectories and 2) shortest path algorithm with map matching technique introduces some error in virtual finer-grained human mobility trajectories (Fig. 7.4).

Since the predicted trajectory and the real trajectory are equivalent to 1 hour in length, and there are only the starting point and the endpoint, and the trajectory information in the middle part is ignored, the trajectory is split for a more detailed trajectory evaluation. Split the trajectory for 20 and 30min, respectively (equivalent to sampling at 1/3, 1/2 of the trajectory grid list) to split the original trajectory into two or three subtrajectories, and then use these subtraces trajectories to evaluate the quality of the production (Fig. 7.5). The true value and predicted value are split in the same way.

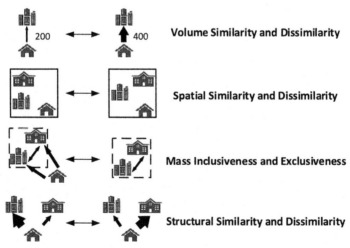

Figure 7.2 The above four figures give an illustration of four metrics of human mobility trajectory similarity.

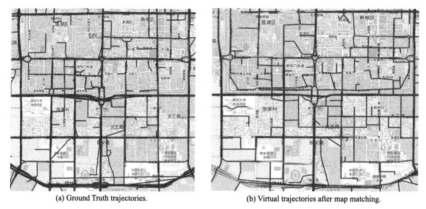

(a) Ground Truth trajectories.   (b) Virtual trajectories after map matching.

Figure 7.3 Visualization of ground truth trajectories and virtual trajectories after map matching.

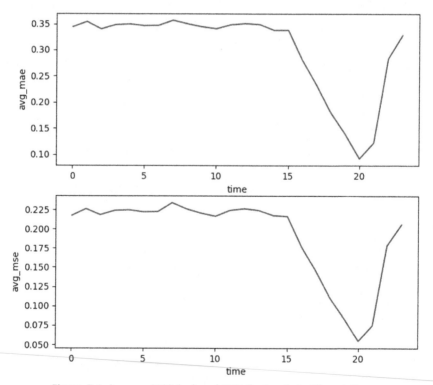

Figure 7.4 Average MAE (up) and MSE (bottom) at different times.

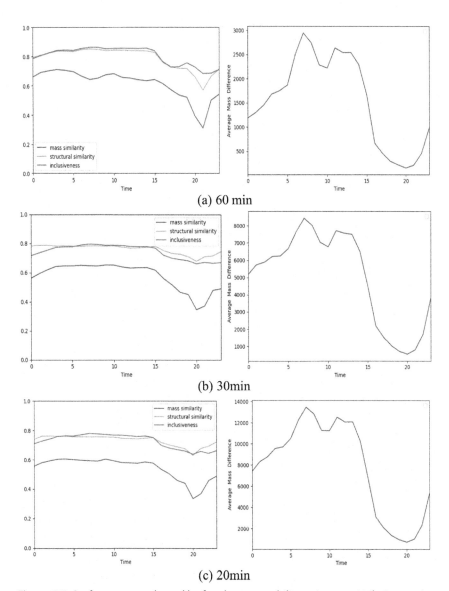

(a) 60 min

(b) 30min

(c) 20min

Figure 7.5 Performance evaluated by four human mobility trajectory similarity metrics.

In short, the conclusion is that the more refined the trajectory is split, the worse the effect displayed by the evaluation index, which is shown in Table 7.1.

Table 7.1 Performance of shortest path with map matching.

	Mass difference	Mass similarity	Inclusiveness	Structural similarity
60 min	1542.21	0.6131	0.8038	0.7872
30 min	4996.7	0.5748	0.7433	0.7608
20 min	7738.34	0.5414	0.7268	0.7314

3.2 Discussion

The data is a kind of navigation data of trips. People drive mainly to the core areas with large numbers of people or core residential areas in cities. At the same time, the time when the number of cars is the largest is about 7:00−16:00. According to the human migration formula, people are more inclined to go to the grid with more people. The probability is significantly reduced when the distance of the grid with many people is significant. So the reflected movement trend must be related to the number of cars in the grid (i.e, the predicted trend must be $A \rightarrow B$ if the movement of people who go to work in the morning is $A \rightarrow B$ when people drive a car to return home in the evening, $B \rightarrow A$ is required. The predicted value is still $A \rightarrow B$). This causes the number of cars to decrease, and the deviation of the predicted trajectory in the afternoon and evening of the return journey gradually increases.

Since the current map matching is based on the shortest path, the shortest path may not be reasonable in the actual situation. For cars, the data acquisition system will also consider it when planning the path. With actual traffic conditions, road conditions, and other information, it is entirely reasonable for a car to move a long distance to pursue the shortest time. So if the prediction is correct for the starting point and the endpoint, the result is correct without splitting the trajectory at this time. If the trajectory is split, it is likely to cause an error, which will result in a drop in the evaluation index. At the same time, the greater the number of trajectories split, the greater the number of erroneous trajectories, which leads to a further decline in the evaluation index. That is, if the transfer vector used for evaluation is correct when it is not split, it is possible that if it is split into two, then two transfer vectors will be wrong, and if split into three, three transfer vectors will be wrong, resulting in a decline in the evaluation index.

4. Retrieval-based model

4.1 Preliminary

4.1.1 Bidirectional long-short term memory

Deep neural networks, which are composited mainly feedforward fully connected neural networks, are powerful but not appropriate for sequence data such as time-series data or natural language. They are outstanding for mapping input data to discrete output or continuous variables but not sequence to sequence mapping. Sequence-to-sequence (seq2seq) model uses two Long Short-Term Memory (LSTM) models. One LSTM learns vector representation from the input sequence of fixed dimensionality, and another LSTM learns to decode from this input vector to the target sequence. LSTM is a variant of recurrent neural networks that solves long sequences using different gates. Seq2seq model was recently proposed and demonstrated the excellent result of Natural Language Processing (NLP) [3–5]. This model proved to be more effective than previous methods at NMT and is now used by Google Translate.

LSTM was designed to combat vanishing gradients through a gating mechanism by Hochreiter and Schmidhuber in 1997 [6]. The ability to model long-term dependencies is improved in LSTM, thanks to the gating mechanism. However, a single LSTM is insufficient to learn the context information because the hidden space is learned heavily depending on the input information before, while some future information is ignored. Schuster and Paliwal proposed a bidirectional recurrent neural network structure to learn the context information from both forward and backward directions in 1997 [7]. We use bidirectional LSTM to achieve spatiotemporal feature extraction of human mobility trajectory. Bidirectional LSTM can be mathematically described as:

$$\begin{cases} \overrightarrow{h}_t = H\left(W_{x\overrightarrow{h}}x_t + W_{\overrightarrow{h}\overrightarrow{h}}\overrightarrow{h}_{t-1} + b_{\overrightarrow{h}}\right) \\ \overrightarrow{h}_t = H\left(W_{x\overleftarrow{h}}x_t + W_{\overleftarrow{h}\overleftarrow{h}}\overleftarrow{h}_{t+1} + b_{\overleftarrow{h}}\right) \\ h_t = \left[\overleftarrow{h}_t, \overrightarrow{h}_t\right] \end{cases} \tag{7.5}$$

We extract the intermediate vector with the fixed dimension as the input of Variational Autoencoder to approximate the latent distribution of spatiotemporal features. Still, the raw GPS trajectories with different lengths are difficult for batch processing, and the LSTM model will go down with the length of the input sequence. Bearing these two concerns in mind, we slice the historical trajectories into a fixed length, the process of which can be written as:

$$\widehat{tr} = \{tr[i: i+L]|i = 0, L, ..., tr.length - L\} \tag{7.6}$$

where $tr[i : i+L]$ is the subsequence of tr with the indices j ranging from $i \leq j \leq i + L$.

5. K-dimensional tree

The k-dimensional tree, which is a multidimensional binary search tree, was invented by Jon Louis Bentley in 1975 [8]. Here we give a brief introduction to the k-d tree data structure. Let $P = \{p_1, ..., p_n\} \subset R^d$ be a finite data set with $p_i = (p_i^1, ..., p_i^d)^T \in R^d$ for $i = 1, ..., n$. A k-d tree for P is defined recursively. An empty tree or a tree with only one node which contains only one data point will be built if P is empty or contains only one data point, respectively. Otherwise, it is determined in which dimension $d' \in [d]$ the data set has the largest spread.

That is, d' is chosen such that there are two points p_i, p_j with $\left|p_i^{d'} - p_j^{d'}\right| \geq \left|p_l^{d''} - p_m^{d''}\right|$ for all $d'' \in [d]$, $l, m \in [n]$. For any number $n \in N$ of ordered points, we define the median to be the point with an index $\left[\frac{n}{2}\right]$.

Now, we should find the median of the points p_I according to a sorting along this dimension, i.e., $p_{i_1}^{d'} \leq ... \leq p_{i_{\frac{n}{2}}}^{d'} \leq ... \leq p_{i_n}^{d'}$, denoted by $q = p_{i_{\frac{n}{2}}}$. After finding the median, a hyperplane $H = \left\{x \in R^d \mid x^{d'} = p_{i_{\frac{n}{2}}}^{d'}\right\}$ is introduced, which splits the set P into two subsets:

$$\begin{cases} P_1 = \left\{p_{i_1}, ..., p_{i_{\frac{n}{2}-1}}\right\} \\ \\ P_2 = \left\{p_{i_{\frac{n}{2}+1}}, ..., p_{i_n}\right\} \end{cases} \tag{7.7}$$

with P_1 containing at most one point more than P_2. A node is created, holding q and H. The node is given the results of recursively processing P_1 and P_2 as children, and then it is returned.

5.1 Framework

The basic idea of building a retrieval-based trajectory generator is that we use Variaitonal AutoEncoder (VAE) as a feature extractor because we have shown its capability of learning the latent vector space from latent vector space causes some limitations mentioned above. We consider the posterior distribution parameterized by vectors corresponding to human trajectories as an index. Then, this index is used for retrieving more trajectories from the historical dataset in which the distance of the index is under a threshold with query trajectories.

A query trajectory dataset is arbitrarily selected, which consists of all human trajectories at the current time we may be interested in. From an information retrieval perspective, a historical trajectory dataset can be regarded as a knowledge base for providing some supportive information for a query trajectory. We define a query trajectory dataset as $traj^q$, and a historical trajectory dataset as $traj^h$. It should be mentioned that some query trajectories in $traj^q$ and some historical trajectories in $traj^h$ can be sliced from some long original trajectories, so they have more correspondence even if they are different in some GPS points.

Given a query trajectory dataset $traj^q$, which usually consist of only a small number of human trajectories, can hardly reflect the movement pattern, especially in some rural areas. For example, we may observe enough human trajectories in a high way to briefly estimate some statistics to describe the traffic situation on this highway. However, there are lots of small streets which we cannot ignore when a more fine-grained estimation is necessary. In such small streets, no observation can sometimes be found considering the low sampling rate of the dataset. For instance, at eight clocks, we observe five cars go through the street, while at nine clocks, we observe 0 cars. Assuming we know the low sampling rate of our trajectory dataset is 1%, we cannot conclude that there are 500 cars going through the street at eight clocks, while no single car at nine clocks. Therefore, we want a reasonable approach to recover a bigger dataset that has more reasonable trajectories given a small dataset.

We give a framework of our retrieval-based trajectory generator in Fig. 7.6. In the first step, we train a VAE model using a large historical

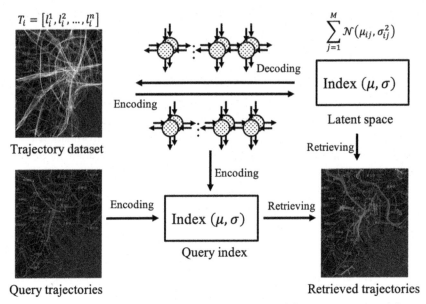

Figure 7.6 Framework of retrieval-based human mobility generation model.

trajectory dataset. Then, we regard this large trajectory dataset as a database in which every trajectory is indexed by its corresponding latent vector. It is also known that the latent vector of each trajectory forms a Gaussian mixture.

In the next step, our goal is to recover the large trajectory dataset given a small limited query trajectory dataset. We use the encoder of trained VAE to get its corresponding vector index of each query trajectory. Then we use the k-dimensional tree method to find some nearest points of query index in the historical dataset. Finally, we select those urban human trajectories using these nearest points to recover a large trajectory dataset.

6. Experiments

6.1 Data description

This study utilizes the navigation GPS dataset, a dataset of navigation route GPS records of different types of cars with user IDs intentionally deleted to preserve users' privacy. In this dataset, we can only recognize each navigation route's ID, so we cannot track the specific users in the long term, although 1-month data was provided. For each trajectory of a single navigation route, the location of each coordinate point is map matched to the road network, and its timestamp is just about 2 or 3 s. It is a very high-quality navigation GPS trajectory data. However, bearing the limited capacity of LSTMs, we decided to crop the trajectory data into a fixed 1-hour length, with the timestamp as 1 min, so the length of every single trajectory is 60 steps. To quantitatively experiment, we use the 1-hour length of trajectory dataset of which timestamp is 2015-10-31 11:00:00 as the query trajectory dataset and those trajectory datasets before as historical trajectory dataset.

Two straightforward representations exist for the trajectory cells, the one-hot representation and the coordinates of the GPS points. For the case of raw GPS records that contain random noise, an ingenious method of pretraining cell presentations was proposed to create the context for each cell instead of using the two representations mentioned above. However, in our experiment, we assume the coordinates of every GPS point are exactly correct since they were all matched to the road network. Under this assumption, we use coordinates of GPS points for the presentations of trajectory cells to reduce the complexity of the experiment since the coordinates of GPS points naturally encode the spatial proximity of the cells of trajectory.

6.2 Baseline methods and metrics

We compare our method with the previous t2vec method [9], which is a deep learning-based trajectory similarity method, and other four traditional trajectory similarity methods for measuring the trajectory similarity, namely, Dynamic Time Warping (DTW), Edit Distance on Real sequences (EDR), Edit Distance with Projections (EDwP), and Longest Common Subsequence (LCSS). Since we use map-matched GPS records of trajectories, we do not have to learn cell presentations through pretraining, so we use a simplified version of t2vec as a baseline method. Besides, we use LSTMs and bidirectional LSTMs to replace RNNs in t2vec as we need LSTMs' capacity to handle longer sequences.

The method of t2vec is the first solution based on deep learning for creating representations of trajectories that are used as a trajectory similarity method. This method is at least one order of magnitude faster than other traditional trajectory similarity methods and has higher accuracy. While DTW, EDR, EDwP, and LCSS are some very classic trajectory similarity measurements. DTW is first introduced to measure time-series data, including this method as a baseline method. Also, both LCSS and EDR are two of the most widely used methods for analyzing spatiotemporal data. EDwP is the state-of-the-art method for measuring the similarity of nonuniform and low sampling rate trajectories. Moreover, we compare with the LSTMs to show bidirectional LSTMs' ability to learn the spatio-temporal features of trajectories.

We provide three metrics for the assessment of different models for retrieving human mobility trajectory data to reconstruct the citywide human mobility pattern. CityEMD is defined as follows:

$$CityEMD(t) = \sum_o dist\left(p(d|o), \widehat{p}\left(\widehat{d}|0\right)\right) \tag{7.8}$$

where d, $\widehat{d}$ is ground truth, retrieved locations of subjects originated from o, respectively.

Another metric called hard match ratio is defined as the ratio of retrieved trajectories that share the same route ID with training data:

$$\sigma = P\left(\left\{B\middle|B^{ID} \subset \left\{A^{ID}\middle|A, H\right\}\right\}\right) \tag{7.9}$$

Because a complete trajectory of navigation has a unique route ID, if a sub-trajectory has the same route ID as another one, they are preprocessed from the same long complete trajectory. So if we can retrieve more of these kinds of trajectories, we consider our model has a better ability to reconstruct the dataset.

The other one is the recover ratio.

$$\xi = P(A|A - B, H + B) \tag{7.10}$$

We use a subset of the target trajectory dataset, which is $A-B$, and throw subset B into the historical dataset H, if we can retrieve more trajectories belonging to B from the historical dataset $H + B$, we consider our model has a better ability to recover the original dataset.

6.3 Results

Here we show some experimental results. Fig. 7.7 shows that the query trajectories (left figure) lack some details in rural areas in Tokyo, while the recovered trajectory (right figure) dataset has more details even in those areas. Since all retrieved trajectories are selected in a historical database, so it is very reasonable that these trajectories could be shared by someone else even though they are not captured by the collected dataset due to the low sampling rate.

We also give some quantitative comparisons with some baseline methods. The metrics of evaluation are CityEMD, hard match ratio, and

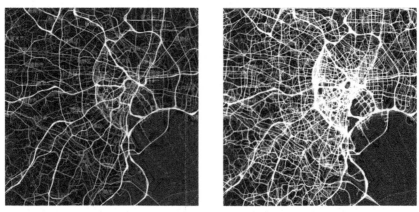

Figure 7.7 Visualization of ground truth human mobility (left) and retrieved human mobility (right).

recover ratio. CityEMD is a kind of distance proposed by the previous researcher that measures the similarity of large area human mobility patterns. The hard match ratio is the ratio of retrieved trajectories that share the same route ID with part of known training data. The recover ratio is the probability of recovering the known training dataset.

Figs. 7.8 and 7.9, and Table 7.2 show that our methods outperform other traditional trajectory similarity methods. It means that our retrieval-based trajectory generator has a better ability to construct a large trajectory dataset that is more similar to the real world.

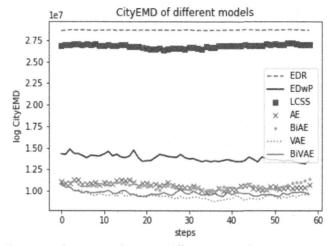

Figure 7.8 Comparison between different methods using CityEMD.

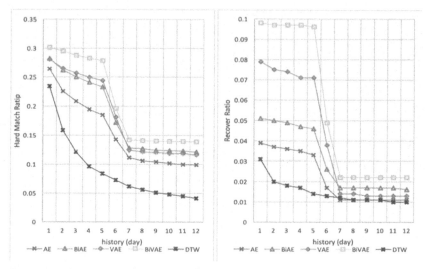

Figure 7.9 Comparison between different methods using HardMatchRatio and RecoverRatio.

Table 7.2 Comparison of different methods.

	DTW	EDR	EDwP	LCSS	AE	BiAE	VAE	BiVAE
CityEMD	—	17.1728	16.4438	17.1059	16.1798	16.1771	16.0617	16.0941
HMR	0.0615	0	0.058	0.0005	0.1115	0.128	0.124	0.142
Ratio	0.012	0	0.002	0	0.011	0.017	0.014	0.022

7. Conclusion

Retrieval-based trajectory generators indeed solved some limitations of a VAE generative model for generating urban trajectories. The reconstructed trajectories come from the historical dataset by latent index encoded by a trained generative model. While we also notice some limitations of the current retrieval-based trajectory generator, the first one is that we need a large historical trajectory dataset to achieve diversity of reconstructed trajectory datasets, which is not always possible in reality. The second one is that we are not able to determine the scaling factor for each query trajectory by setting a distance threshold since the historical dataset itself could be biased, so the retrieved large trajectory dataset will also be biased. Therefore, our next step is to reduce the bias of the trajectory dataset by incorporating information from other data sources, such as census data.

References

[1] F. Simini, M.C. González, A. Maritan, A.L. Barabási, A universal model for mobility and migration patterns, Nature 484 (7392) (2012) 96–100.

[2] Y. Yao, H. Zhang, J. Chen, W. Li, M. Shibasaki, R. Shibasaki, X. Song, Mobsimilarity: Vector Graph Optimization for Mobility Tableau Comparison, 2021 arXiv preprint arXiv:2104.13139.

[3] R.J. Weiss, J. Chorowski, N. Jaitly, Y. Wu, Z. Chen, Sequence-To-Sequence Models Can Directly Translate Foreign Speech, 2017 arXiv preprint arXiv:1703.08581.

[4] T. Liu, K. Wang, L. Sha, B. Chang, Z. Sui, Table-to-text generation by structure-aware seq2seq learning, in: Thirty-Second AAAI Conference on Artificial Intelligence, April 2018.

[5] S. Gu, F. Lang, A Chinese text corrector based on seq2seq model, in: 2017 International Conference on Cyber-Enabled Distributed Computing and Knowledge Discovery (CyberC), IEEE, October 2017, pp. 322–325.

[6] A. Graves, Long short-term memory, Supervised Sequence Labelling with Recurrent Neural Networks (2012) 37–45.

[7] M. Schuster, K.K. Paliwal, Bidirectional recurrent neural networks, IEEE Transactions on Signal Processing 45 (11) (1997) 2673–2681.

[8] J.L. Bentley, Multidimensional binary search trees used for associative searching, Communications of the ACM 18 (9) (1975) 509–517.

[9] X. Li, K. Zhao, G. Cong, C.S. Jensen, W. Wei, Deep representation learning for trajectory similarity computation, in: 2018 IEEE 34th International Conference on Data Engineering (ICDE), IEEE, April 2018, pp. 617–628.

Further reading

[1] Z. Fan, X. Song, R. Shibasaki, T. Li, H. Kaneda, CityCoupling: bridging intercity human mobility, in: Proceedings of the 2016 ACM International Joint Conference on Pervasive and Ubiquitous Computing, September 2016, pp. 718–728.

[2] Z. Yu, L. Yuan, W. Luo, L. Feng, G. Lv, Spatio-temporal constrained human trajectory generation from the PIR motion detector sensor network data: a geometric algebra approach, Sensors 16 (1) (2015) 43.

[3] D. Brockmann, L. Hufnagel, T. Geisel, The scaling laws of human travel, Nature 439 (7075) (2006) 462–465.

[4] M.C. Gonzalez, C.A. Hidalgo, A.L. Barabasi, Understanding individual human mobility patterns, Nature 453 (7196) (2008) 779–782.

[5] J. Yuan, Y. Zheng, X. Xie, Discovering regions of different functions in a city using human mobility and POIs, in: Proceedings of the 18th ACM SIGKDD International Conference on Knowledge Discovery and Data Mining, August 2012, pp. 186–194.

[6] Z. Zhu, X. Wang, S. Bai, C. Yao, X. Bai, Deep learning representation using autoencoder for 3D shape retrieval, Neurocomputing 204 (2016) 41–50.

CHAPTER EIGHT

Grid-based origin-destination matrix prediction: a deep learning method with vector graph transformation similarity loss function

Wenxiao Jiang
Center for Spatial Information Science, The University of Tokyo, Kashiwa-shi, Chiba, Japan

1. Introduction

Machine learning is a method of data analysis that encompasses automatic computing procedures based on logical or binary operations that learn a task from a series of examples [1]. Deep learning is a branch of machine learning. It allows computational models that are composed of multiple processing layers to learn representations of data with multiple levels of abstraction [2]. Deep learning algorithms are widely used in various fields. For example, in medicine, a study [3] shows that the use of deep learning to model temporal relations among events in electronic health records could improve model performance in initial diagnosis prediction of heart failure compared to conventional methods. In natural language processing, a deep learning architecture [4], a dynamic memory network, is introduced to process input sequences and questions, form episodic memories, and generates relevant answers. In image recognition, a deep network architecture [5] is introduced to dissect the image by finding prototypical parts and combining features from the parts to make an image classification. Their experiments show that the deep network architecture can achieve comparable accuracy. Moreover, in transportation, a deep learning architecture [6] is proposed to identify travelers' transportation modes. It can automatically extract relevant features from trajectories and exploit useful information in unlabeled data.

The research of Origin-Destination (OD) matrix prediction is an important part of the transportation field [7]. mentioned that the OD matrix

Handbook of Mobility Data Mining, Volume 2
ISBN: 978-0-443-18424-6
https://doi.org/10.1016/B978-0-443-18424-6.00010-6
135

contains two aspects of information: combinations of different OD and the number of travel demands for each OD combination. As an important part of the prediction model, loss functions are defined to measure the difference between the output value of the deep learning model and the given target value [8]. It can directly affect the performance of the model. There are numerous traditional error metrics that can be adopted as loss functions for solving the problems based on Origin-Destination (OD) matrices, such as Mean Square Error (MSE) [9], Mean Absolute Error (MAE) [10], Root Mean Square Error (RMSE) [11], Mean Absolute Percentage Error (MAPE) [12], and so on. Although these loss functions have simple mathematical formulations and are effective in deep learning models, they simply reflect the numerical similarity and ignore all other properties. As shown in Fig. 8.1, Fig. 8.1A and B are two pairs of examples that include an OD matrix and its corresponding target OD matrix. When using traditional error metrics like MSE, Fig. 8.1A and B have the same values. It indicates that traditional error metrics cannot distinguish the difference between Fig. 8.1A and B. However, from a spatial point of view, Fig. 8.1A is obviously closer to the target OD than Fig. 8.1B.

To solve this problem [13], firstly proposed a new quality measure called Structural SIMilarity (SSIM) index. Based on this study, a Mean Structural Similarity index (MSSIM) is presented by Ref. [14]. Furthermore [15], developed a geographical window-based structural similarity index (GSSI). Compared to traditional MSSIM, the GSSI is capable of preserving geographical integrity, comparing results with physical significance, and

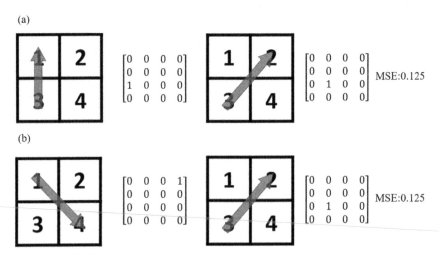

Figure 8.1 The examples of an OD matrix and target OD matrix.

capturing local travel patterns. Although many spatial metrics are proposed for OD matrices, there are rare studies that apply these metrics as the loss function for OD matrix prediction.

In this study, the vector graph transformation loss function is designed according to the study by Ref. [16]. It is used to measure the transformation cost from a vector graph to another vector graph, where the vector graph can be regarded as an OD matrix in their study. And an evaluation of the OD matrix prediction model with the novel loss function is proposed and discussed.

2. Origin-destination matrices

As the name indicates, Origin-Destination (OD) data represents human mobility through geographic space, from an origin (O) to a destination (D). It is always used to present travel demands in the transportation area. And it is an important factor in dynamic user equilibrium traffic assignment. The typical format that expresses OD data is named Origin-Destination matrices. The OD matrix is a matrix in that each cell of it represents the number of travel demands from the origin (row) to the destination (column). This matrix is always a square matrix because the number of origins and destinations is the same. It can be expressed as Eq. (8.1).

$$A = \begin{bmatrix} a_{1,1} & a_{1,2} & \cdots & a_{1,j-1} & a_{1,j} \\ a_{2,1} & a_{2,2} & \cdots & a_{2,j-1} & a_{2,j} \\ \vdots & \vdots & \ddots & \vdots & \vdots \\ a_{i-1,1} & a_{i-1,2} & \cdots & a_{i-1,j-1} & a_{i-1,j} \\ a_{i,1} & a_{i,2} & \cdots & a_{i,j-1} & a_{i,j} \end{bmatrix} \tag{8.1}$$

where A is an OD matrix; $a_{i,j}$ is a cell of the OD matrix; i, j are the number of origins and destinations.

There have been many studies focusing on the estimation of OD matrices since decades ago. Traditional methods of building OD matrices are based on roadside, household surveys, and traffic counts. The Generalized Least Squares (GLS) method, which is one of the classical methods, are suggested for estimating OD matrices by a number of authors [17,18]. Based on their research, a simple algorithm [19] is proposed to solve the GLS problem subject to inequality constraints. It is demonstrated that the algorithm can improve the accuracy of the GLS method by reducing errors in the input data. Moreover [20], used the gravity model to estimate the OD matrices in Bogor city, Indonesia. However, the roadside and household surveys for origin–destination involve expensive data collection and thereby have limited sample sizes and lower update frequencies. With the development of technology, tremendous location data such as GPS data and mobile phone CDR data can be obtained easily. Therefore, different methods for developing OD matrices are presented. A methodology [21] is proposed to develop OD matrices using mobile phone CDR data from 2.87 million users of Dhaka, Bangladesh, over a month and traffic counts from 13 key locations over 3 days of that month. Another method [22] is also presented to estimate OD trips from mobile phone CDR data of millions of anonymized users. These CDR data are converted into clustered locations, and the locations are inferred to be home, work, or other depending on observation frequency, day of the week, and time of day.

In this study, the OD matrix is built based on the trajectory data. Each cell of the OD matrix can be obtained by counting origins and destinations from trajectory data. The grids are used to divide the study area into appropriate sizes, as shown in Fig. 8.2, and each grid has its own unique number. The origins of trajectories in the same grid are regarded as the same origins. Similarly, the destinations of trajectories in the same grid are regarded as the same destinations. For instance, there are two trajectories in a study area, as red lines shown in Fig. 8.3. These two trajectories can be considered as the same OD because the origins of these two trajectories are Grid 1, and the destinations of these two trajectories are Grid 16. Except for $a_{1,16}$ is equal to two in the OD matrix. The others are all zero.

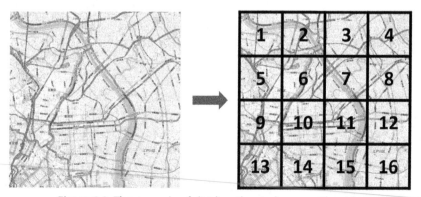

Figure 8.2 The example of dividing the study area with grids.

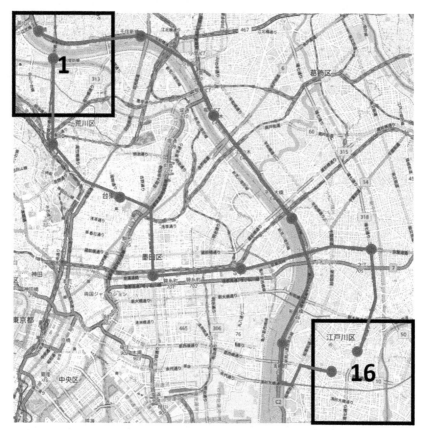

Figure 8.3 The example of building an OD matrix from two trajectories.

3. Methodology

3.1 Deep learning model-based vector graph transformation loss function

In their study [16], they proposed three basic operations for the vector graph transformation: add, shift, and delete.

Add means to add a new vector into the graph. The cost of the add operation is the Manhattan distance between the start point and end point of the added vector. It can be expressed as Eq. (8.2).

$$Cost_{add} = |d_x - o_x| + |d_y - o_y| \qquad (8.2)$$

where $Cost_{add}$ is the cost of the added operation. d_x, d_y are the x and y coordinates of the endpoint. o_x, o_y are the x, and y coordinates of the start point. For example, as shown in Fig. 8.4A, the red vector ((3,1), (3,3)) is added to the graph. And the cost of adding operation equals 2.

The shift represents shifting a vector from its position to a new position. The cost of the shift operation is calculated between the previous start point and end point and the new start point and end point. It can be defined as Eq. (8.3).

$$Cost_{shift} = |o_{x'} - o_x| + |o_{y'} - o_y| + |d_{x'} - d_x| + |d_{y'} - d_y| \qquad (8.3)$$

where $Cost_{shift}$ is the cost of the shift operation. x', y' are the x, and y co-ordinates of the previous position. x, y are the x, and y coordinates of the new position. As shown in Fig. 8.4B, the vector changed from ((1,2), (2,1)) to ((2,3), (3,2)). The cost of shift operation equals 4.

Delete denotes deleting a vector from the graph. The cost of the delete operation is the Manhattan distance between the start point and end point of the deleted vector. It can be described in Eq. (8.4), which is similar to Eq. (8.2).

$$Cost_{delete} = |d_x - o_x| + |d_y - o_y| \qquad (8.4)$$

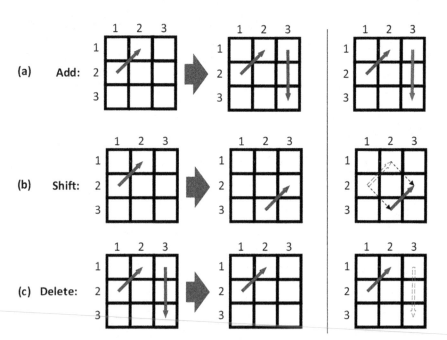

Figure 8.4 Basic operations for vector graph transformation [16].

where $Cost_{delete}$ is the cost of the delete operation. As shown in Fig. 8.4C, the vector ((3,1), (3,3)) is deleted from the graph. The cost of the delete operation equals 2.

The vector graph transformation loss function is defined as the least cost of a transformation from a vector graph to another vector graph based on the basic operations mentioned above. To achieve this goal, the Kuhn Munkres algorithm is adopted to find the minimum since there are many vectors in a vector graph.

However, the vector graph transformation loss function cannot be implanted as a loss function in a deep learning model because it is based on the Kuhn Munkres algorithm, which is not differentiable. To solve this problem, a deep learning model is proposed to approximate the vector graph transformation loss function, and big input data is needed to train the model. The flowchart for building the deep learning model-based vector graph transformation loss function is shown in Fig. 8.5. The first step is to generate OD matrix data. Since the difference between two OD matrices determines the value of the vector graph transformation loss function, instead of the value of the OD matrices, one matrix is set as a zero matrix. Another matrix is generated by random values, which can be positive or negative. The second step is to obtain the cost data by using the vector graph transformation loss function to calculate the difference between the generated OD matrices. Then, the next step is to take the generated OD matrix data as training data and the cost data as target data to train a deep learning model. Finally, the deep learning model-based vector graph transformation loss function is built.

The specific steps of the OD matrix generation are shown in Fig. 8.6. In order to make the generated OD matrices both reasonable and random, the OD number is set from 0 to 100. The OD number indicates how many pairs of OD are in the OD matrix. For each OD number, if the OD number is less than 2, all the OD matrices that match the OD number are built. Otherwise, a certain number of the OD matrices are built randomly, and then some values of the OD matrices are turned negative. Lastly, the OD matrices are scaled to range from −1 to one to make the deep learning model extract features easier.

The convolutional neural networks are adopted for developing the deep learning model-based vector graph transformation loss function because they have good performance when dealing with matrix data. The deep learning model structure is shown in Fig. 8.7. It consists of 2 2D convolutional layers, a flattened layer, and two fully connected layers. To find which

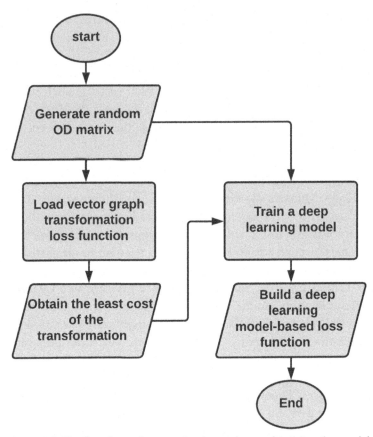

Figure 8.5 The flowchart of generating input data and training the model.

kernel size can make the deep learning model extract features better, seven models are built with the same structure but different kernel sizes of the first 2D convolution layer. Therefore, the output size of the first 2D convolution layer is different. It is represented by $128 \times m \times n$. The kernel size of the second 2D convolution layer is 1×1. The padding and the stride of the two convolution layers are 0 and 1, respectively. The flattened layer is used to reshape the output into a one-dimensional matrix that can be used as the input in fully connected layers. The two fully connected layers with output sizes 256 and one are adopted to obtain the final output. The epoch of the training deep learning model is 30.

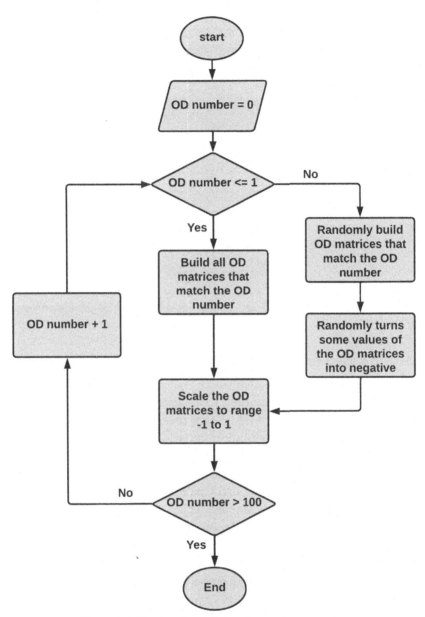

Figure 8.6 The flowchart of the OD matrix generation.

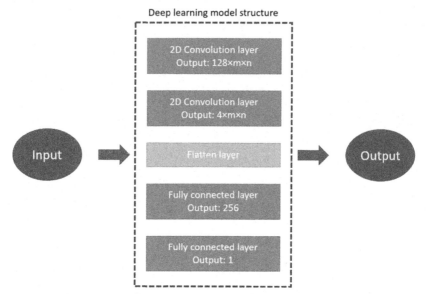

Figure 8.7 The structure of the deep learning model-based vector graph transformation loss function.

3.2 Grid-based origin-destination matrix prediction model

In this study, a CNN–LSTM architecture is adopted to predict the OD matrix because the input data are time series matrix data. The deep learning structure of the grid-based OD matrix prediction model is shown in Fig. 8.8. Firstly, two 2D convolution layers are adopted to extract spatial features from the input data. The 12 in the output size of 2D convolution layers mean the 12 OD matrices that are used to generate results. Then, two LSTM layers are applied to extract temporal features. Finally, the fully connected layers are used to produce the output data.

To show the performance of the proposed deep learning model-based vector graph transformation loss function (VGT), eight different loss functions are used. The loss functions used for OD matrix prediction are MSE, MAE, the proposed loss function, and the combination of MSE and the proposed loss function.

The first combination can be expressed as Eq. (8.5).

$$L_{plus} = L_{MSE} + \lambda \times L_{VGT} \tag{8.5}$$

where L_{plus} is the combination with plus. L_{MSE} is the MSE loss function. L_{VGT} is the deep learning model-based vector graph transformation loss

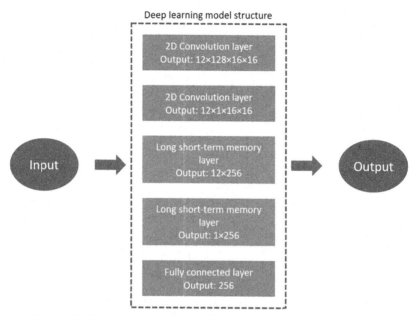

Figure 8.8 The structure of the grid-based OD matrix prediction model.

function. λ is a constant parameter to adjust the value of the combination loss function. 1, 0.1, 0.01, 0.001 are adopted in the combination loss function. The second combination can be described in Eq. (8.6).

$$L_{multiply} = L_{MSE} \times L_{VGT} \qquad (8.6)$$

where $L_{multiply}$ is the combination with multiply.

4. Data generation and study area

In this study, large amounts of input data are generated for the deep learning model-based vector graph transformation loss function. 3,955,000 pairs of OD matrices in the input data are training data, and 194,000 pairs of OD matrices are used as test data. The size of the OD matrix is 16 × 16, which is built to match the OD matrix prediction model.

For the grid-based OD matrix prediction model, the dataset used are the OD matrix data built based on the trajectory data that is provided by NTT Docomo from August 1st, 2012, to August 31st, 2012, in the center of Tokyo, as shown in Fig. 8.9. This study area is divided into 4 × 4 grids based on longitude and latitude. Therefore, there are 256 cells in the OD matrix.

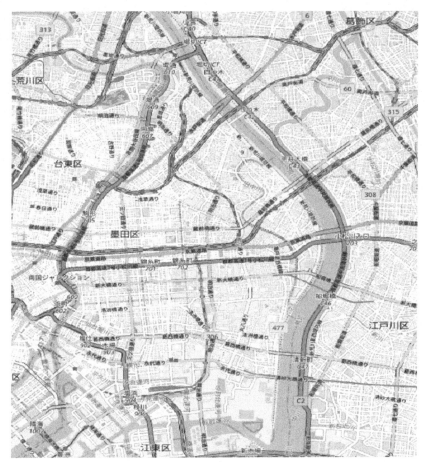

Figure 8.9 The study area of the grid-based origin-destination matrix prediction model.

The data from August 1st, 2012, to August 25th, 2012, are employed as training data, and the data from August 26th, 2012, to August 31st, 2012, are adopted as test data. Each OD matrix is collected from the trajectory data in a time range of 15 min. For example, the time range of the first OD matrix is 0—15 min, the time range of the second OD matrix is 15—30 min, and so on. Since there are only 1-month trajectory data, it is not enough to train a deep learning model well. To build more training data, the time range is staggered by 3 min 5 times. For example, the time range of the first OD matrix is changed to 3—18 min, the time range of the second OD matrix is changed to 18—33 min, and so on. Therefore, five times as much training data can be obtained. Moreover, in the deep learning model, the first 12 OD matrices are used to predict the 13th OD matrix.

5. Result and discussion

5.1 Result of deep learning model-based vector graph transformation loss function

The results of the deep learning model-based vector graph transformation loss function are shown in Table 8.1. In these seven deep learning models, the kernel size of the first 2D convolution layer is 1×1, 1×2, 2×2, 1×3, 3×3, 1×4, and 1×5, respectively.

The deep learning model with the best performance is the model with kernel size 1×3. The RMSE and the MAPE are 3.6099% and 14.2136%, respectively. And it is indicated that square kernels are inappropriate for the OD matrix prediction model. Since the row and column of each cell of the OD matrix represent the number of origins and destinations, the features extracted from square kernels have little spatial meaning. Conversely, the spatial features can be obtained from the cells in the same row of the OD matrix. Therefore, the models with kernel size one$\times$ n have relatively good performance.

To make the OD matrix prediction model have better performance, deep learning model-based vector graph transformation loss function with kernel size 1×3 is employed in the grid-based OD matrix prediction model in the next section.

Table 8.1 Seven deep learning models with different kernel sizes.

Kernel size	RMSE	MAPE (%)
1×1	3.7955	15.0016
1×2	3.6927	14.5878
2×2	3.6829	14.6523
1×3	3.6099	14.2136
3×3	3.7265	14.9701
1×4	3.6502	14.3977
1×5	3.7191	14.9058

5.2 Result of grid-based origin-destination matrix prediction model

As shown in Table 8.2, the error metrics RMSE and the value of the vector graph transformation loss function are employed to show the performance of eight different loss functions in the proposed OD matrix prediction model. The MSE and MAE loss functions are used as baselines. The VGT model is the deep learning model-based vector graph transformation loss function. The Plus means the loss function combination with plus, and the value of constant parameters is marked on the right side. The Multiply indicates the loss function combination with multiply.

The performance results indicate that the loss function combination with multiply has the best performance. Compared with the MSE loss function, the RMSE of the proposed loss function decreased by 1.12%. The VGT has been reduced by 2.85%. Compared with the MAE loss function, the RMSE of the proposed loss function decreased by 16.70%. The VGT has been reduced by 37.32%. However, when the deep learning model-based vector graph transformation loss function is used as the loss function, the performance is not good. The reason is that the deep learning model-based loss function is trained by using scaled input data. It cannot extract features well from input data that is not scaled, but the MSE loss function is appropriate to find the scale value. Therefore, the combination of MSE and the deep learning model-based loss function by multiplication has admirable performance. Furthermore, the loss function combination with plus only has a slight effect on the performance no matter what the constant parameter λ is, compared with the MSE loss function.

To show the performance of the proposed loss function is not limited to the CNN-LSTM architecture, three other deep learning structures are

Table 8.2 The performance of grid-based Origin-Destination matrix prediction model.

Loss function	RMSE	VGT
MSE	1.1175	118.14
MAE	1.2897	157.74
VGT model	1.5451	163.18
Plus $\lambda = 0.001$	1.1163	117.86
Plus $\lambda = 0.01$	1.1189	117.76
Plus $\lambda = 0.1$	1.1157	117.51
Plus $\lambda = 1$	1.1583	126.42
Multiply	1.1051	114.87

employed for comparison. In these four deep learning structures, including the proposed deep learning structure, the convolution layers are the same. Only the type of recurrent layers is changed. There are two types of recurrent layers: traditional RNN and LSTM. Each recurrent layer is divided into bidirectional and not bidirectional. The percentage decrease of RMSE and VGT from the MSE loss function to the proposed loss function in each deep learning structure is adopted as indicators. As shown in Fig. 8.10, the loss function combined with multiply can improve the performance in all these four deep learning structures, compared with the MSE loss function. For the deep learning model with traditional RNN, the percentage decrease of RMSE and VGT are only 0.61% and 1.01%, respectively. As the structure becomes more complex, the improvement becomes better. For the model with LSTM, the percentage decrease of RMSE and VGT are 1.06% and 1.76%, respectively. Also, the bidirectional recurrent layers can reduce the error metrics compared to normal recurrent layers.

6. Conclusion

In this study, a CNN–LSTM architecture-based OD matrix prediction model with a novel loss function is proposed. The loss function is built based on the vector graph transformation loss function, which is designed according to the study by Ref. [16]. It is used to measure the transformation cost from a vector graph to another vector graph, where the vector graph can be regarded as an OD matrix in their study. For appropriately adopting

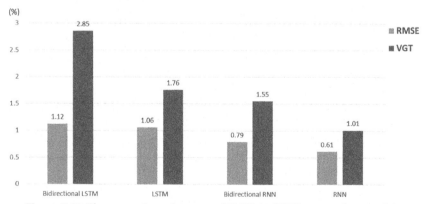

Figure 8.10 The percentage decrease of RMSE and VGT among four models.

the novel loss function into the deep learning-based OD matrix prediction model, a convolutional neural network-based model is developed to approximate the vector graph transformation loss function, and big input data is generated to train the model.

To find which deep learning model-based vector graph transformation loss function is better, seven models are developed with the same structure but different kernel sizes of the first 2D convolution layer. Besides, to show the performance of the proposed deep learning model-based vector graph transformation loss function, eight different loss functions are employed. The loss functions used for OD matrix prediction are MSE, MAE, the proposed loss function, and the combination of MSE and the proposed loss function. Moreover, to show the performance of the proposed loss function is not limited to the CNN-LSTM architecture, three other deep learning structures are adopted for comparison.

The result shows that the proposed loss function has a better performance compared with traditional loss functions. And as the structure of the deep learning model becomes more complex, the improvement becomes better.

References

[1] D. Michie, J. D, Machine Learning. Neural and Statistical Classification, Prentice Hall Inc, 1994.

[2] Y. LeCun, Y. Bengio, G. Hinton, Deep learning, Nature 521 (7553) (2015) 436–444.

[3] E. Choi, A. Schuetz, W.F. Stewart, J. Sun, Using recurrent neural network models for early detection of heart failure onset, Journal of the American Medical Informatics Association 24 (2) (2016) 361–370, 2016.

[4] A. Kumar, O. Irsoy, P. Ondruska, M. Iyyer, J. Bradbury, I. Gulrajani, V. Zhong, R. Paulus, R. Socher, Ask me anything: dynamic memory networks for natural language processing, in: ICML, 2016.

[5] C. Chen, O. Li, C. Tao, A.J. Barnett, J. Su, C. Rudin, This looks like that: deep learning for interpretable image recognition, in: Proceedings of the 33rd International Conference on Neural Information Processing Systems, 2019.

[6] S. Dabiri, C. Lu, C.K. Reddy, K.P. Heaslip, Semi-supervised deep learning approach for transportation mode identification using gps trajectory data, IEEE Transactions on Knowledge and Data Engineering 32 (5) (2020) 1010–1023.

[7] Y. Wang, H. Yin, H. Chen, T. Wo, J. Xu, K. Zheng, Origin-destination Matrix Prediction via Graph Convolution: A New Perspective of Passenger Demand Modeling, KDD, 2019, 2019.

[8] T. Qiu, X. Shi, J. Wang, Y. Li, S. Qu, Q. Cheng, T. Cui, S. Sui, Deep learning: a rapid and efficient route to automatic metasurface design, Advance Science 6 (2019) 1900128.

[9] A. Azzouni, G. Pujolle, NeuTM: a neural network-based framework for traffic matrix prediction in SDN, in: NOMS 2018-2018 IEEE/IFIP Network Operations and Management Symposium, April 2018, Taipei, Taiwan, 2018.

[10] P. Noursalehi, H.N. Koutsopoulos, J. Zhao, Dynamic Origin-Destination Prediction in Urban Rail Systems: A Multi-Resolution Spatio-Temporal Deep Learning Approach, TITS, 2021, 2021.

[11] J. Zhao, H. Qu, J. Zhao, D. Jiang, Spatiotemporal traffic matrix prediction: a deep learning approach with wavelet multiscale analysis, Transactions on Emerging Telecommunications Technologies 30 (12) (2019) e3640.

[12] X. Zou, S. Zhang, C. Zhang, J.J.Q. Yu, E. Chung, Long-term origin-destination demand prediction with graph deep learning, IEEE Transactions on Big Data (2021) 1—15, 2021.

[13] T. Djukic, S. Hoogendoorn, H. Van Lint, Reliability assessment of dynamic OD estimation methods based on structural similarity index, in: Transportation Research Board Annual Meeting, National Academies, Washington D.C., 2013, p. 13.

[14] T. Day-Pollard, T. Van Vuren, When are origin-destination matrices similar enough?, in: 94th Annual TRB Meeting, Washington DC, 2015.

[15] K.N. Behara, A. Bhaskar, E. Chung, Geographical Window-Based Structural Similarity Index for OD Matrices Comparison, Queensland University of Technology, 2019.

[16] Y. Yao, H. Zhang, J. Chen, W. Li, M. Shibasaki, R. Shibasaki, X. Song, Mobsimilarity: Vector Graph Optimization for Mobility Tableau Comparison, 2021 arXiv preprint arXiv:2104.13139 (2021).

[17] C. Hendrickson, S. McNeil, Matrix entry estimation errors, in: Proceedings of the Ninth International Symposium on Transportation and Traffic Theory, The Netherlands, Delft, July, 1984, pp. 413—430.

[18] E. Cascetta, Estimation of trip matrices from traffic counts and survey data: a generalised least squares estimator, Transportation Research 18B (1984) 289—299.

[19] M.G.H. Bell, The estimation of origin-destination matrices by constrained generalised least square, Transportation Research Part B: Methodological Journal 25 (1991) 13—22. Boston Metropolitan Planning Organization, 1991. 1991 Boston Household Travel Survey.

[20] I. Ekowicaksono, F. Bukhari, A. Aman, Estimating origin-destination matrix of bogor city using gravity model, in: IOP Conference Series: Earth and Environmental Science, vol 31, IOP Publishing, 2016, p. 012021.

[21] M.S. Iqbal, C.F. Choudhury, P. Wang, M.C. González, Development of origin-destination matrices using mobile phone call data, Transportation Research C 40 (2014) 63—74.

[22] L.P. Alexander, S. Jiang, M. Murga, M.C. González, Validation of origin-destination trips by purpose and time of day inferred from mobile phone data, Transportation Research Part C: Emerging Technologies 58 (2015) 240—250.

CHAPTER NINE

MetaTraj: meta-learning for cross-scene cross-object trajectory prediction

Xiaodan Shi

Center for Spatial Information Science, the University of Tokyo, Kashiwa-shi, Chiba, Japan

1. Introduction

Reasoning future pedestrian trajectories based on a short observation is highly valuable for safety driving of autonomous cars and navigation of social robots [1–3]. With the success of deep learning methods, a lot of research are proposed to address the problems of modeling social interactions, multimodality, and agent-to-scene interactions for trajectory prediction. However, the current performance of forecasting long-term trajectories is usually achieved when the training and testing data come from the same or similar scenes that contain the same types of objects. But in real-world applications, the scenes and objects will change over time. So it is critical to study cross-scene cross-object transfer learning for trajectory prediction.

In this paper, we explore to enable prediction models trained on source data to achieve good performance over target scenes and objects that are not accessible during training. We argue that the trajectory information from different scenes, such as static camera monitoring scenes and dynamic autonomous driving street scenes, are usually quite different due to different circumstance settings, such as walkable areas (e.g., roads, entries/exits etc.) and different objects, such as bicycles, scooters. The information is kept in trajectories, but not only the entire full-length trajectories, short observations will also provide some clues. Although target data are not accessible during training, the short observations of target trajectories can be firstly obtained during testing. Thus, we explore the use of short-term observation of new trajectories and quickly learn the prior trajectory information that is helpful to long-term prediction.

The current research usually utilizes two-dimensional offsets (location offset between two adjacent timesteps) to describe trajectories, to some

Handbook of Mobility Data Mining, Volume 2
ISBN: 978-0-443-18424-6
https://doi.org/10.1016/B978-0-443-18424-6.00001-5

extent which is stable to a certain type of object and can eliminate the effect of scene shift by compared to describe trajectories with absolute locations. However, the two-dimensional location offset on x-axis and y-axis represents the direction or trend of location offset sequence, which is still related to the circumstance setting and the types of objects and will cause the performance of a trained prediction model to degrade when used in other unseen scenes.

To address it, we propose a general meta-learning framework called MetaTraj (Fig. 9.1) that enables prediction models to quickly learn the information of trajectories from unseen scenes or objects. We creatively design two tasks, subtasks and meta-tasks of meta learning for trajectory prediction. Subtasks are a small set of dynamic-length sequence prediction tasks that can be generated from observations effortlessly, which helps the models learn prior information of trajectories, while meta-tasks ensure that the learned information is able to truly contribute to more accurate long-term future prediction.

Besides, we also design transformation approaches that are carefully designed for trajectories in the case that observed trajectory training data are limited. Transformation approaches are few in number but effectively simulate more circumstance setting and objects through some easy-to-use geometric functions. In this way, MetaTraj can obtain both scene generalization ability and trajectory-specific prior information that improve the performance of long-term prediction even when the training dataset is limited.

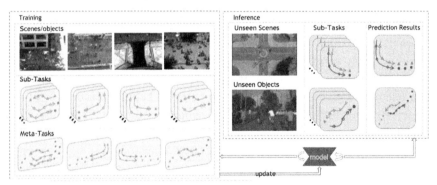

Figure 9.1 MetaTraj is a General Framework that Enables a Trajectory Prediction Model Transfer to Unseen Scenes/Objects. MetaTraj is Trained to Quickly Learn the Information of Trajectories Related to Scene/Objects from Carefully Designed Subtasks, Which then Contribute to Accurate Long-term Prediction (Meta-tasks).

2. Related works

2.1 Social interactions for trajectory prediction

Social LSTM introducing Social Pooling to learn a global feature of all nearby neighbors around an agent which is meant to represent common sense rules and social conventions, is a tipping point for data-driven long-term trajectory prediction. Many researches follow the way of Social LSTM [4] but with improvements. Attention mechanism is introduced to learn neighbors' weights on agent [5−8]. Instead of directly modeling hidden states of neighbors' motion, some research pool relative motion between agent and neighbors to model interactions [5,9,10]. Graph representation, specifically spatiotemporal graph (ST-graph) is well applied to illustrate human motion and their interactions [1,11−14].

2.2 Multimodality of trajectory prediction

Human motions under crowded scenes imply a multiplicity of modes. To capture the uncertainty of future path, some research apply generative adversarial network (GAN) to generate multiple possible paths [6,9]. Some research apply Mixture Density Network (MDN) to map the distribution of future trajectories [10,15,16]. There is also goal-based multitrajectory prediction [17−21]. Those models predict multiple futures based on hypothesis of goals. One kind of goal-based prediction models the trajectories based on the semantic destinations, such as turning right/left, going straight [17,19]. Another kind firstly forecasts multiple positional designations and then estimates futures matching the goal hypothesis [22].

2.3 Meta learning on trajectory prediction

Meta learning is also known as "learn to learn," which is one kind of transfer learning methods and mainly applied for few shot learning [23,24], multitasks learning [25], and reinforcement learning [26]. The goal of meta-learning is to train the model on a variety of learning tasks so that it can solve new learning tasks using only a small number of training samples [27]. Although transfer learning has been widely explored in image processing area, there is still rare research on transfer learning for pedestrian trajectory prediction. Current research mainly model trajectories using location offset instead of absolute location which helps to stabilize the training process and improve models' performance over new data [9,28]. But it still remains as a big challenge to transfer a prediction model to other circumstances and objects.

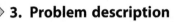

3. Problem description

We assume that all scenes are first preprocessed to obtain 2D spatial coordinates $(x^t, y^t) \ldots \in \mathbf{R}^2$ and 2D location offset $(u^t, v^t) \ldots \in \mathbf{R}^2$ of pedestrians at any time instance t. The observations of pedestrians are the past trajectories, which are represented as: $X^{0:\tau} = (x^t, y^t, u^t, v^t)\ t = 0, 1, 2, \ldots, \tau \ldots 1\}$ while the future trajectories are $Y^{\tau:T} = \{(x^t, y^t, u^t, v^t) \mid t = \tau, \ldots, T-1\}$. We assume data I are from source domain (training data) and data J are from unseen target domain (testing data) that contain unseen circumstance setting and objects. For a regular prediction model Φ, training data is denoted as $D_{tr} = \left(X_I^{0:\tau}, Y_I^{\tau:T} \right)$ the prediction process is denoted as follows:

$$\theta^* = \underset{\theta}{argmax} P\left(\theta | D_{tr}, \theta^0\right), \tag{9.1}$$

$$P\left(Y_J^{\tau:T}\right) = \Phi\left(X_J^{0\tau}; \theta^*\right), \tag{9.2}$$

where $P(\cdot)$ represents probability. Our goal is to make trajectory prediction models perform well even on unseen scenes and objects. To achieve this, we construct subtasks D^{sub} from observations of both training data and testing data, which help the models to quickly learn the prior information of trajectories from new circumstances or objects. The prediction process of MetaTraj is as follows:

$$D^{sub} \leftarrow X^{0\tau}, \tag{9.3}$$

$$\theta' = \underset{\theta}{argmax} P\left(\theta | D^{sub}, \theta^0\right), \tag{9.4}$$

$$P(Y_{\tau:T}) = \Phi\left(X^{0\tau}; \theta'\right), \tag{9.5}$$

The functions (9.3)–(9.5) are same for training and testing. For training, θ^0 are initialized parameters of a prediction model while for testing θ^0 are parameters from a trained model.

4. MetaTraj

4.1 Overall architecture

Trajectory prediction is formulated as a sequence generation problem given a short observation. As we mentioned before, trajectory sequence are quite relevant to circumstance setting and objects, which will reduce the performance of trajectory prediction models transferred to unseen scenarios.

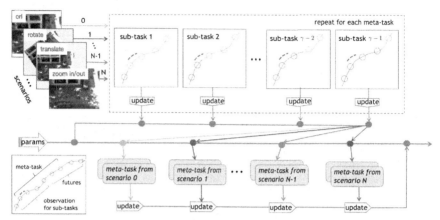

Figure 9.2 Framework of MetaTraj. The first row is training of subtasks while the second row is training of meta-tasks. The parameters of prediction models are first updated by each subtask of a meta-task. Then the meta task will update the network overall.

A possible solution to transfer learning for trajectory prediction task is to quickly learn the information of trajectories from the short observation. To this end, we introduce MetaTraj framework, as shown in Fig. 9.2, which intuitively creates trajectory-specific subtasks and meta-tasks. The subtasks and meta-tasks are naturally generated from trajectories and can be easily used for many prediction models. MetaTraj follows the basic idea of model-agnostic meta learning (MAML) [27] for training.

4.2 Subtasks and meta-tasks

Meta-learning aims to benefit the learning of a new task in a sample-efficient way, that is, to learn from small data by meta-training from meta-tasks [29]. Each meta-task should contain some samples (small samples) for meta-training. For example, meta-tasks for classification problem are usually classification tasks and the small samples used for meta-training belong to the same class. The task of trajectory prediction is a sequence generation problem without intuitive class labels. It is not suitable to use classification tasks as meta-tasks for trajectory prediction. In addition, it is also not appropriate to regard a scene as a meta-task because even trajectory sequence from the same scene might own different "rules" due to different exits/entries, velocity and type of objects. We consider the original prediction of a trajectory as a meta-task. However trajectory-specific long-term prediction itself couldn't be used as a meta-task. It usually doesn't have enough samples due to dynamically appearing scenes/objects, online predictions and limited trajectory lengths. So we construct subtasks from short observations as "small samples" of meta-tasks.

Algorithm 1. Training Process of MetaTraj.

Input: Trajectory $D = (D_{tr}, D_{val})$, $D_{tr/val} = \left(D_{tr/val}^{sub}, \, {}_{tr/val}^{meta} \right)$, batch B, learning rate q and/3, transformation functions $M = \{M_n \backslash n = 0,1,N\}$. Set p as "patience": number of times to observe worsening validation error before giving up;

1: Initialization: $\theta = \theta^0$, $j = 0$
2: $(\mathcal{D}_{tr/val}^{sub}, \mathcal{D}_{tr/val}^{meta}) = (X_{tr/val}^{0:t}, X_{tr/val}^{t:\gamma},$
$\quad X_{tr/val}^{0:\tau}, Y_{tr/val}^{\tau:T})$
3: **while** $j < p$ **do**
4:    **repeat**
5:       **for** $n = 0, 1, \cdots, N$ **do**
6:          $(\mathcal{D}_{tr}^{sub}, \mathcal{D}_{tr}^{meta})_{1:B}^n =$
$\quad\quad M_n((\mathcal{D}_{tr}^{sub}, \mathcal{D}_{tr}^{meta})_{1:B})$
7:          $t \leftarrow 1$
8:          **while** $t < \gamma$ **do**
9:             $(\hat{X}_{tr}^{t:\gamma})_{1:B}^n = \Phi_\theta((X_{tr}^{0:t})_{1:B}^n)$
10:         $L_{sub}^n \leftarrow \mathcal{L}_{sub}((\hat{X}_{tr}^{t:\gamma})_{1:B}^n,$
$\quad\quad (X_{tr}^{t:\gamma})_{1:B}^n)$
11:         update $\theta \leftarrow \theta - \alpha \nabla_\theta L_{sub}^n$
$\quad\quad t \leftarrow t + 1$
12:         **end while**
13:         $(\hat{Y}_{tr}^{\tau:T})_{1:B}^n = \Phi_\theta((X_{tr}^{0:\tau})_{1:B}^n)$
14:         $L_{meta}^n \leftarrow \mathcal{L}_{meta}((\hat{Y}_{tr}^{\tau:T})_{1:B}^n,$
$\quad\quad (Y_{tr}^{\tau:T})_{1:B}^n)$
15:         update $\theta \leftarrow \theta - \beta \nabla_\theta L_{meta}^n$
16:       **end for**
17:    **until** end of $\mathcal{D}_{tr}$
18:    Process of validation
19:    **repeat**
20:       $L_{val}^0 \leftarrow 10000 \quad\quad L_{val} \leftarrow 0$
21:       **for** $n = 0, 1, \cdots, N$ **do**
22:          $(\mathcal{D}_{val}^{sub}, \mathcal{D}_{val}^{meta})^n =$
$\quad\quad M_n((\mathcal{D}_{val}^{sub}, \mathcal{D}_{val}^{meta})_{1:B})$
23:          **for** $k = 1, \cdots, K$ **do**
24:             repeat line 7 $\sim$ line 12
25:          **end for**
26:          $(\hat{Y}_{val}^{\tau:T})_{1:B}^n = \Phi_\theta((X_{val}^{0:\tau})_{1:B}^n)$
27:          $L_{val} \leftarrow \mathcal{L}_{meta}((\hat{Y}_{val}^{\tau:T})_{1:B}^n,$
$\quad\quad (Y_{val}^{\tau:T})_{1:B}^n) + L_{val}$
28:       **end for**
29:       **if** $L_{val}/(N+1) > L_{val}^0$ **then**
30:          $j \leftarrow j + 1$
31:       **else**
32:          $L_{val}^0 \leftarrow L_{val}/(N+1)$
33:          $j \leftarrow 0$
34:       **end if**
35:    **until** end of $\mathcal{D}_{val}$
36: **end while**
37: **return** Φ_θ

The two levels of tasks, subtasks and meta-tasks are not scene-specific or class-specific but trajectory-specific. We argue that the potential information of a trajectory sequence is not only contained in the entire long-term sequence (unseen during inference) but also embodied by short-term observation. To this end, subtasks D^{sub} are designed based on short observations to learn trajectory-specific information. D^{sub} are naturally generated from observation $X^{0:t}$ without any further information or operation as follows:

$$D^{sub} = \left\{ \left(X^{0:t}, X^{t:\gamma} \right) | t = 1, 2, \cdots, \gamma - 1 \right\} \quad (9.6)$$

where $\gamma \leq \tau$, we observe $X^{0:t}$ and predict futures from t to τ. $\gamma^{t:\gamma}$ serves as ground truth for subtasks. D^{sub} is actually a set of prediction tasks with shorter observation and futures. To ensure the learned prior information of trajectories from D^{sub} helpful for final long-term prediction, we make meta-tasks as normal long-term prediction. We denote it as D^{meta}:

$$D^{meta} = \left(X^{0\tau}, Y^{\tau T} \right), \qquad (9.7)$$

The meta-tasks and subtasks are sequence prediction tasks of dynamic length, which limits the applications of MetaTraj to CNN-based prediction models that usually represent sequence length as preset channels and cannot handle flexible length of sequence. We argue that MetaTraj is suitable for recurrent models, such as RNNs-based models where an RNN unit is shared and repeated to encode dynamic-length trajectory sequence during training and testing. Currently, trajectory prediction models are mostly based on RNNs. These models store the information of sequence in the unit so that the information learned from subtasks is able to be fully used for meta-tasks.

4.3 MetaTraj training

In the training process of MetaTraj, subtasks D^{sub} and meta-tasks D^{meta} cooperate with each other and make meta-learners perform well on all meta-tasks from multiple scenes and objects. Worth noting that, each pair of subtasks and meta-tasks is from the same set of agents. In other words, each agent has its own subtasks and meta-tasks. For each batch training, as shown in Alg. 1, meta-learners firstly learn prior information from subtasks. Through meta-tasks, meta-learners check if the learned information helpful for long-term prediction and gradually improve their capabilities of learning from subtasks. To efficiently take use of short observation and learn useful features from it, we range t from one to seven to one during training, as shown in Alg. 1 line 8. During each iteration of training subtasks, we update parameters of the prediction model with learning rate a. After training the whole set of subtasks, we feed the meta-tasks into network to get the long-term prediction results and then update the model parameters overall with learning rate/3, as shown in Alg. line 13—15. Through this process, MetaTraj is able to quickly learn useful prior information of new trajectories. The learned prior information is firstly stored in the parameters of the model that are then set as initialized parameters of meta-tasks. By doing this, MetaTaj is able to help a prediction model get better results when transferred to other circumstances or objects.

4.4 Loss function

We discuss that various loss functions C (e.g., MSE loss and negative log-Likelihood loss etc.) suitable for trajectory prediction are able to be utilized for MetaTraj. Based on a minibatch $\left(X_{tr}^{0:t}, X_{tr}^{t:\gamma}, X_{tr}^{0:\tau}, Y_{tr}^{\tau:T}\right)_{1:B} \sim D_{tr}$ from source training data, where $\left(X_{tr}^{0:\tau}, Y_{tr}^{\tau:T}\right)_{1:B}$ serves for meta tasks and $\left(X_{tr}^{0:t}, X_{tr}^{t:\gamma}\right)_{1:B}$ serves for subtasks, we take use of transformation functions $\{M_n \mid n = 0,1, N\}$ where n = 0 denotes the original data, to map the minibatch data to $\left(X_{tr}^{0:t}, X_{tr}^{t:\gamma}, X_{tr}^{0:\tau}, Y_{tr}^{\tau:T}\right)_{1:B}$. MetaTraj firstly forecasts futures $(\widehat{X}_{tr}^{t:\gamma})^n_{1:B}$ of subtasks and calculate loss as shown Alg. 10. The parameters of network are updated for each subtask.

When training meta-tasks, we calculate meta loss of $N+1$ source data and then use meta loss to update the whole model respectively.

The testing and validation share the same process as shown in Alg. 1 line 19−34, which is similar to the process of training but different. First, the parameters of network are only updated with loss calculated from subtasks. Second, we repeat the process of training subtasks for K times during validation and testing as shown in Alg. 1 line 23. By using K, MetaTraj is able to learn more useful information for final long-term prediction. The validation loss of meta tasks serves as a signal of convergence of the whole training process. If validation loss doesn't decrease for p times, the model is considered to be converged.

4.5 Transformed trajectories

The quality of trajectory source data is critical to the effectiveness of a prediction model. However, in practice it is not easy to obtain enough real-world trajectories for training. To improve the generalization ability of MetaTraj, we expand the limited source data by applying a small set of transformation functions to let the training datasets cover a wide range of possible source domain. To augment the limited original source data to cover a wide range of possible scenes and objects while keeping the set of transformation functions small, we design translation, rotation, and zoom, totally six transformation functions for original source data, of which translation and rotation simulate various circumstances setting, and zoom simulates different objects. Transformation functions can be flexibly designed according to different motivations. But in this paper, we just randomly design some simple transformation functions. The details of transformation functions are shown in Appendix.

5. Experiments

To evaluate MetaTraj's performance when transferring to other scenes and objects, we test it on various prediction models over three publicly available datasets: UCY [30], ETH [31] and another large dataset ApolloScape [32]. Those datasets cover multiple scenes and objects. We also compare MetaTraj's performance against various baselines on these datasets.

Datasets. The ETH and UCY datasets contain five sets, which are UCY-zara01, UCY-zara02, UCY-univ, ETH-hotel, ETH-eth in four crowded scenes with totally 1536 pedestrian trajectories. We firstly preprocess those two datasets by resampling them as 2.5 fps and transforming the coordinates of people to world coordinates in meters.

ApolloScape is a large-scale dataset collected from urban streets in Beijing, China. With a sample rate of 2 Hz, the ApolloScape trajectory dataset consists of 53 min of training sequences and 50 min of testing sequences, which covers 8083 different traffic scenes. There are five different types of objects contained in this dataset, that is, vehicles, pedestrians, motorcyclists and bicyclists, and other.

Implementation Details. The experiments are implemented using Pytorch under Ubuntu 16.04 LTS with a GTX 1080 GPU. For opensource models, we utilize their code and follow original parameter settings for training and testing MetaTraj. For models we implemented, the size of hidden states of LSTM is set to 128. The embedding layers are composed of a fully connected layer with size 128. The batch size is set to 8. We clip the gradients of LSTM with a maximum threshold of 10 to stabilize the training process. The learning rates a and 0 for MetaTraj on LSTM are set to 0.001 and 0.01, and for MetaTraj on other models are set to 0.0003 and 0.003 respectively.

Evaluation Approach. For ETH and UCY datasets, we follow the same training and testing strategy, leave-one-out strategy as the baselines: trained on four sets and tested on the remaining set. We observe the trajectories for eight timesteps (3.2 s) and show prediction results for 12 timesteps (4.8 s). To evaluate the performance, we compare our method with other state-of-the-art models on two generally used metrics:1. Average displacement error (ADE): average L2 distance over all prediction results and ground truth; 2. Final displacement error (FDE): distance between prediction result and ground truth at final timestep.

For ApolloScape trajectory dataset, we also follow the same evaluation methods as its baselines. We observe six timesteps (3 s) and predict futures for six timesteps. To compare MetaTraj with baselines, we use the metrics: weighted sum of ADE (WSADE) and weighted sum of FDE (WSFDE) which consider different weights for vehicles, bicyclists and pedestrians. Besides, we also calculate ADEv/FDEv, ADEp/FDEp and ADEb/FDEb respectively for vehicles, pedestrians and bicycles. You may refer to ApolloScape official website (http://apolloscape.auto/trajectory.html) for more details about the metrics. All the results of metrics are obtained from online evaluation of ApolloScape (please refer to the official website).

Baselines. For ETH and UCY datasets, a few state-of-the-art baselines are used: 1. LSTM. An LSTM based encoder-decoder model taking offset as input and output, L2 as loss function [28]; 2. Social LSTM. This method models human interactions by pooling hidden states of spatially proximal motion sequences [4]. 3. SR-LSTM. This method proposes a state refinement LSTM and also considers social interactions. 4. Sophie. This is a GAN-based model which takes into account both social and physical constraints to predict multiple plausible futures [6]; 5. Social GAN. This approach contains an RNN based encoder-decoder generator and an RNN-based encoder discriminator to capture the multimodality of futures [9]; 6. Social BiGAT. This method uses a generator, two discriminators and a latent noise encoder to construct a reversible mapping between predicted paths and learned latent features of trajectories [33]; 7. Social STGCNN. The method substitutes aggregation methods by modeling the interactions as a graph [12]. 8. Att-LSTM. The method follows the idea of social LSTM (with negative log-Likelihood loss) and pools relative motion of pedestrians in a circle neighborhood setting (radius is 4m) with attention mechanism, which are common used in previous studies [5,9,10].

For ApolloScape, we compare MetaTraj with the following baselines on the ApolloScape leaderboard that have been published: 1. TrafficPredict. It is proposed by the official, which uses instance and category layers to predict trajectories [32]; 2. StarNet: StarNet has a star topology that includes a hub network and multiple host networks. The StarNet is the best method in the CVPR2019 trajectory prediction challenge [11]; 3. GRIP++. GRIP++ is a graph-based trajectory prediction approach that combines GCNs with a GRU-based encoder-decoder [34]. We also train LSTM, Att-LSTM, Social GAN exactly the same as Table 9.1 with ApolloScape trajectory data as three baselines.

Table 9.1 Quantitative results of baselines versus our method across ETH&UCY datasets for predicting 12 future timesteps(4.8 s) given eight timesteps observations(3.2 s) (lower is better). The results of Social LSTM, Social GAN are from Ref. [9], the results of Sophie, Social BiGAT, Social STGCNN, SR-LSTM are from Refs. [5,6,12,33] respectively. MetaTraj on SR-LSTM and on Social GAN are developed based on their source code(SR-LSTM: https://github.com/zhangpur/SR-LSTM; Social GAN: https://github.com/agrimgupta92/sgan).

Method	Note	Evaluation (ADE(m)/FDE(m))					
		ETH-eth	ETH-hotel	UCY-univ	UCY-zara01	UCY-zara02	Avg
LSTM	Offset as input	0.71/1.40	1.15/2.09	0.72/1.49	0.48/0.98	0.38/0.77	0.69/1.35
Social LSTM	Social interactions	1.09/2.35	0.79/1.76	0.67/1.40	0.47/1.00	0.56/1.17	0.72/1.54
SR–LSTM	W/o samples	0.63/1.25	0.37/0.74	0.41/0.90	0.32/0.70	0.51/1.10	0.45/0.94
Sophie	20 samples	0.70/1.43	0.76/1.67	0.54/1.24	0.30/0.63	0.38/0.78	0.54/1.15
Social GAN	20 samples	0.72/1.29	0.48/1.01	0.56/1.18	0.34/0.69	0.31/0.65	0.48/0.96
Social BiGAT	20 samples	0.69/1.29	0.49/1.01	0.55/1.32	0.30/0.62	0.36/0.75	0.48/1.00
Social STGCNN	20 samples	0.64/1.11	0.49/0.85	0.44/**0.79**	0.34/0.53	0.30/0.48	0.44/0.75
Att-LSTM	20 sample	0.56/1.15	0.27/0.59	0.58/1.25	0.39/0.85	0.32/0.73	0.42/0.91
trajectron++	20 sample	0.69/1.21	0.20/0.31	0.30/0.54	0.25/0.41	0.20/0.33	0.33/0.56
MetaTraj on LSTM	W/o samples	0.58/1.19	0.25/0.51	0.62/1.27	0.46/0.98	0.36/0.76	0.45/0.94
MetaTraj on Att–LSTM	20 samples	**0.48/1.00**	0.21/0.43	0.49/1.09	0.35/0.72	0.30/0.64	0.37/0.78
MetaTraj on SR–LSTM	W/o samples	0.50/1.19	0.33/0.64	**0.35**/0.80	0.30/0.68	0.40/0.87	0.38/0.84
MetaTraj on social GAN	20 samples	0.61/1.34	**0.19/0.34**	0.51/1.11	**0.30/0.48**	**0.25/0.45**	**0.37/0.74**
MetaTraj on trajectron++	20 sample	0.50/1.00	0.15/0.25	0.30/0.45	0.21/0.38	0.15/0.29	0.26/0.47

5.1 Quantitative evaluation

ETH and **UCY.** We compare MetaTraj on various prediction models to multiple baselines over two datasets ETH and UCY in Table 9.1. To better evaluate the generalization performance of MetaTraj on various trajectory prediction models, we also perform an ablation study of MetaTraj that are described as: 1. MetaTraj on LSTM; 2. MetaTraj on Att-LSTM. 3. MetaTraj on SR-LSTM. 4. MetaTraj on Social GAN. We design the same subtasks (Y is set to 8) and meta-tasks for all the prediction models. Because Social GAN contains a discriminator and a generator, we repeat the discriminator twice and generator once for each subtask, which follows the same training strategy of the original Social GAN. To make the comparison fair, MetaTraj here doesn't take use of transformation functions. The experiments over ETH-eth, ETH-hotel, UCY-univ are exactly tested on unseen scenes because of leave-one-out strategy for training and testing. We argue that the good performance of baselines over unseen scenes in ETH and UCY datasets benefit from: 1. they use offset as input, which are stable for an ordinary pedestrian across datasets; 2. the scenes of ETH and UCY are both static camera surveillance scenes and quite similar.

By comparing original basic models and MetaTraj on those models, we can easily see that MetaTraj is able to improve the performance of prediction models to a large extent especially over unseen scenes ETH-eth, ETH-hotel. The most inspiring thing is that MetaTraj on LSTM, the most basic prediction model, achieves better results than the baselines Social GAN, Social BiGAT, and Sophie overall. Those baselines show the best result of 20 samples and also consider social interactions. The performance gain of MetaTraj on multiple prediction models demonstrate generalization of the proposed design of subtasks and meta-tasks and its efficiency in unseen scenes.

ApolloScape. To further investigate the MetaTraj's ability to transfer to much different unseen scenes and objects, we test it over ApolloScape trajectories as shown in Table 9.2 where "Sub" means subtasks and "Meta" means meta training. ApolloScape collects trajectories from 8083 different traffic scenes and five objects, which makes it a good dataset to test MetaTraj's transferability. MetaTraj on LSTM, Att-LSTM, Social GAN is also implemented to further verify the efficiency and generalizability of MetaTraj. Although Social GAN on ApolloScape dataset doesn't obtain satisfactory results, its performance is still consistent with that of other research [35].

To better explore the performance of MetaTraj and how it is able to transfer to unseen scenes and objects, we train MetaTraj with ETH and

Table 9.2 Quantitative results of baselines versus our method across ApolloScape datasets for predicting six future timesteps (3.0 s) given six timesteps observations (3.0 s) (lower is better). The results of MetaTraj and baselines are reported on ApolloScape leaderboard.

Method	Components						Evaluation (m)							
	Apollo	ETH-eth	ETH&UCY	Sub	Trans.	Meta	WSADE	ADEv	ADEp	ADEb	WSFDE	FDEv	FDEp	FDEb
Traffic Predict	✓						8.59	7.95	7.18	12.88	24.23	12.78	11.12	22.79
StarNet	✓						1.34	**0.79**	2.39	**1.86**	2.50	**1.52**	4.29	**3.46**
GRIP++	✓						**1.29**	2.24	**0.73**	1.88	**2.41**	4.04	**1.39**	3.58
LSTM	✓						1.33	2.42	0.74	1.88	2.48	4.36	1.44	3.51
Social GAN	✓						1.96	3.32	1.26	2.57	3.69	6.05	2.43	4.87
Att-LSTM	✓						1.45	2.69	0.80	2.03	2.71	4.89	1.54	3.82
MetaTraj on LSTM	✓			✓	✓	✓	**1.29**	2.28	0.74	**1.86**	**2.41**	4.11	1.42	3.48
MetaTraj on social GAN	✓			✓	✓	✓	1.71	3.08	1.00	2.32	3.14	5.40	1.90	4.35
MetaTraj on Att-LSTM	✓			✓	✓	✓	1.37	2.34	0.80	1.99	2.57	4.20	1.56	3.75
MetaTraj-mini1		✓					3.21	7.15	1.32	4.61	6.07	13.17	2.63	8.69
MetaTraj-mini2		✓			✓	✓	1.87	3.50	0.92	2.88	3.55	6.50	1.80	5.50
MetaTraj-mini3		✓		✓		✓	1.70	2.75	1.05	2.43	3.28	5.02	2.19	4.59
MetaTraj-mini4		✓		✓	✓	✓	1.64	2.71	0.98	2.40	3.15	4.94	2.00	4.57
MetaTraj-mini5		✓					3.24	7.22	1.29	4.74	6.16	13.34	2.61	8.99
MetaTraj-larg1			✓				2.77	6.40	1.04	4.03	5.26	11.87	2.05	7.74
MetaTraj-larg2			✓		✓	✓	1.74	3.24	0.92	2.52	3.27	5.92	1.79	4.77
MetaTraj-larg3			✓	✓		✓	1.64	2.64	1.02	2.38	3.20	4.78	2.14	4.54
MetaTraj-larg4			✓	✓	✓	✓	1.63	2.69	0.99	2.35	3.14	4.88	2.05	4.43
MetaTraj-larg5			✓				2.84	6.58	1.06	4.13	5.38	12.20	2.08	7.88

UCY datasets and test it with ApolloScape trajectory data. ETH and UCY datasets contain four static camera surveillance scenes that are quite different from ApolloScape. More specifically, we train four versions of MetaTraj with a mini-dataset (i.e., ETH- eth) and a large dataset (i.e., ETH and UCY), respectively. We choose the most classic, simple LSTM as the basic model so that the transferring performance of MetaTraj can be demonstrated well. Overall, although MetaTraj trained with ETH and UCY doesn't outperform StarNet, GRIP++ and original LSTM etc., it still achieves amazing results because it is trained with data that are very different from target data. By comparing MetaTraj-mini1 and MetaTraj-mini2/3, MetaTraj-larg1 and MetaTraj-larg2/3, we can easily see that both the proposed sub/meta-tasks and transformation functions are able to improve the performance of the model to a large extent. Sub/meta-tasks help the model gain more than the transformation functions, especially over unseen objects vehicles and bicycles, which has largely proved that subtasks and meta-tasks are more predominant than transformation functions and help the model to get more accurate results. Transformation functions are beneficial to the model because they provide more diverse trajectories with flexible velocities and walking directions. MetaTraj-mini5 and MetaTraj-larg5 are trained with sub- and meta-tasks but not meta-trained. By comparing MetaTraj-mini3 and MetaTraj-mini5, MetaTraj-larg3 and MetaTraj-larg5, we can tell the performance of MetaTraj is not gained from the increase of training data, that is, the addition of training subtasks, but from the meta-settings. By comparing MetaTraj-mini3 and MetaTraj-mini4, MetaTraj-larg3 and MetaTraj-larg4, we can tell that in the case of applying subtasks and meta-tasks, transformation functions are more useful when only a small set of real observations is obtained. It is interesting that MetaTraj-mini4 achieves almost the same results with MetaTraj-larg4, which demonstrates that the proposed MetaTraj can also be efficiently trained through a small set of real observations.

5.2 Ablation studies

Ablation Study on Sub-Tasks. The elements of subtask set are subject to Y in Eq. (9.6). Seven not only controls the number of subtasks but also governs the observation and prediction length of each subtask. To test the impact of seven on MetaTraj performance, we ablate seven from two to eight to train MetaTraj on LSTM with ApolloScape trajectory data and

Table 9.3 Sensitivity of γ of subtasks (Eq. 9.6) to MetaTraj's performance. Evaluation (ADE(m)/FDE(m))

γ	ETH-eth	ETH-hotel	UCY-univ	UCY-zara01	UCY-zara02	ApolloScape
2	0.91/1.82	0.56/0.79	0.81/1.81	0.69/0.98	0.69/0.98	1.69/3.22
3	0.80/1.67	0.44/0.64	0.76/1.54	0.55/0.81	0.49/0.85	1.80/3.38
4	0.69/1.47	0.30/0.45	0.64/1.29	0.41/0.59	0.36/0.61	1.66/3.13
5	0.64/1.39	0.24/0.39	0.58/1.21	0.35/0.54	0.30/0.52	1.64/3.12
6	0.63/1.37	0.21/0.36	0.55/1.17	0.32/0.50	0.28/0.50	**1.63/3.10**
7	0.62/1.35	0.19/0.35	0.52/1.13	0.31/0.49	0.26/0.47	–
8	**0.61/1.34**	**0.19/0.34**	**0.51/1.11**	**0.30/0.48**	**0.25/0.45**	–

MetaTraj on Social GAN with ETH&UCY data respectively. The results are shown in Table 9.3. It is easy to see that the performance of MetaTraj gains most when seven becomes four and then stabilizes with the increase of 7.

Ablation Study on Transformation Functions. The proposed transformation functions have a large impact on the transferability of MetaTraj when sub-tasks and meta-tasks are not used. To test how transformation functions (i.e., zoom, rotation, translation) helps the model, we retrain MetaTraj-mini2 with ETH & UCY data and show its results in Table 9.4. By comparing to the original MetaTraj-mini2, it is not difficult to find that transformation functions of zoom are the most critical to the model's performance, especially for unseen object vehicles and bicycles. Zoom helps the model transfer to unseen objects by taking into account more trajectories with flexible velocities.

Sensitivity of K. To test how K shown in Alg. 1 line 23 affects the performance of MetaTraj, we show the testing accuracy of MetaTaj on Att-LSTM over ETH&UCY, MetaTaj on LSTM over ApolloScape with K ranging from 1 to 19 in Table 9.5. As we can see, the testing accuracy

Table 9.4 Sensitivity of transformation functions to MetaTraj's performance. Evaluation (m)

Trans.	WSADE	ADEv	ADEp	ADEb	WSFDE	FDEv	FDEp	FDEb
Whole	**1.87**	**3.50**	**0.92**	**2.88**	**3.55**	**6.50**	**1.80**	**5.50**
W/o zoom	2.52	5.80	0.97	3.61	4.85	10.96	1.91	7.02
W/o rotate	1.98	3.82	1.01	2.86	3.78	7.08	2.01	5.43
W/o translate	1.93	3.58	0.95	3.02	3.67	6.62	1.86	5.74

Table 9.5 Sensitivity of K (Alg. 1 line 23) to the performance of testing. Evaluation (ADE(m)/FDE(m))

K	ETH-eth	ETH-hotel	UCY-univ	UCY-zara01	UCY-zara02	ApolloScape
1	0.58/1.16	0.26/0.55	0.54/1.12	0.41/0.79	0.37/0.72	1.70/3.25
4	0.52/1.05	0.23/0.48	0.50/1.07	0.36/0.71	0.34/0.70	1.60/3.06
7	0.50/1.04	0.21/0.43	0.50/1.09	0.37/0.75	0.34/0.71	**1.57/3.00**
10	**0.48/1.00**	0.21/0.43	0.49/1.09	0.35/0.72	0.30/0.64	1.63/3.14
13	0.49/1.03	0.22/0.46	0.48/1.09	**0.33/0.68**	0.32/0.68	1.65/3.18
16	0.50/1.06	0.22/0.48	0.48/1.10	0.34/0.71	0.35/0.74	1.67/3.24
19	0.49/1.04	**0.21/0.42**	**0.48/1.08**	0.34/0.69	**0.30/0.65**	1.69/3.28

over all datasets doesn't always decrease as K increases. However, MetaTraj with bigger K (K > 7) shows a tendency of obtaining better and stable testing results than iterating the process of learning D^{sub} for only few times (K < 4) overall.

Sensitivity of K. To test how K shown in Alg. One line 23 affects the performance of MetaTraj, we show the testing accuracy of MetaTaj on Att-LSTM over ETH&UCY, MetaTaj on LSTM over ApolloScape with K ranging from 1 to 19 in Table 9.5. As we can see, the testing accuracy over all datasets doesn't always decrease as K increases. However, MetaTraj with bigger K (K > 7) shows a tendency of obtaining better and stable testing results than iterating the process of learning D^{sub} for only few times (K < 4) overall.

5.3 Qualitative evaluation

To further illustrate MetaTraj's performance, we visualize four scenes where people are walking in groups and socially interacting with each other to compare MetaTraj with its original models, Att-LSTM and Social GAN, as shown in Fig. 9.3. (a) shows group walking, (b) (c) depicts social interactions and (d) shows people are turning. Att-LSTM and Social GAN are easy to forecast futures of inaccurate walking direction, especially when the pedestrians potentially have multiple possible walking directions or the pedestrians are turning. MetaTraj is able to learn prior information of trajectories and outperforms its original models by better capturing heading direction of futures and walking speed in those scenes, which also demonstrate Meta-Traj's effectiveness.

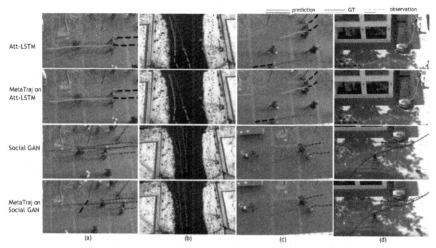

Figure 9.3 Visualization of Best Result of 20 Samples from Att-LSTM, Social GAN, and MetaTraj Over Four Scenes from ETH and UCY.

6. Conclusion

We proposed MetaTraj, a general framework of meta learning for trajectory prediction, which can transfer a prediction model to unseen scenes and objects. MetaTraj designs specific subtasks and meta-tasks for trajectories to quickly learn useful prior information of trajectories that are related to scenes and objects, which then contribute to accurate long-term prediction. The subtasks and meta-tasks are sets of trajectory prediction tasks of various length, which are able to be generated from original trajectory sequence effortlessly. Experiments over three trajectory prediction benchmarks, ETH, UCY and ApolloScape demonstrate that MetaTraj is able to be used for various RNN-based prediction models and perform well over unseen scenes and objects by comparing to baselines. Future work will focus on using MetaTraj on more prediction models and improve its performance over more unseen objects.

References

[1] V. Karasev, A. Ayvaci, B. Heisele, S. Soatto, Intent-aware long-term prediction of pedestrian motion, in: 2016 IEEE International Conference on Robotics and Automation (ICRA), IEEE, 2016, pp. 2543–2549.

[2] Q. Liu, S. Wu, L. Wang, T. Tan, Predicting the next location: a recurrent model with spatial and temporal contexts, in: Thirtieth AAAI Conference on Artificial Intelligence, 2016.

[3] N. Lee, W. Choi, V. Paul, C.B. Choy, P.H.S. Torr, M. Chandraker, Desire: distant future prediction in dynamic scenes with interacting agents, in: Proceedings of the IEEE Conference on Computer Vision and Pattern Recognition, 2017, pp. 336–345.

[4] A. Alexandre, K. Goel, V. Ramanathan, A. Robicquet, L. Fei-Fei, S. Savarese, Social lstm: human trajectory prediction in crowded spaces, in: Proceedings of the IEEE Conference on Computer Vision and Pattern Recognition, 2016, pp. 961–971.

[5] P. Zhang, W. Ouyang, P. Zhang, J. Xue, N. Zheng, Sr- lstm: state refinement for lstm towards pedestrian trajectory prediction, in: Proceedings of the IEEE Conference on Computer Vision and Pattern Recognition, 2019, pp. 12085–12094.

[6] A. Sadeghian, V. Kosaraju, S. Ali, N. Hirose, R. Hamid, S. Savarese, Sophie: an attentive gan for predicting paths compliant to social and physical constraints, in: Proceedings of the IEEE Conference on Computer Vision and Pattern Recognition, 2019, pp. 1349–1358.

[7] T. Fernando, S. Denman, S. Sridharan, C. Fookes, Soft+ hardwired attention: an lstm framework for human trajectory prediction and ab- normal event detection, Neural Networks 108 (2018) 466–478.

[8] Y. Yuan, X. Weng, Y. Ou, K. Kitani, Agentformer: Agent-Aware Transformers for Socio-Temporal Multi-Agent Forecasting Supplementary Material.

[9] A. Gupta, J. Johnson, L. Fei-Fei, S. Savarese, A. Alexandre, Social gan: socially acceptable trajectories with generative adversarial networks, in: Proceedings of the IEEE Conference on Computer Vision and Pattern Recognition, 2018, pp. 2255–2264.

[10] X. Shi, X. Shao, Z. Fan, R. Jiang, H. Zhang, Z. Guo, G. Wu, W. Yuan, R. Shibasaki, Multimodal interaction-aware trajectory prediction in crowded space, in: AAAI, 2020, pp. 11982–11989.

[11] Y. Zhu, D. Qian, D. Ren, H. Xia, Starnet: pedestrian trajectory prediction using deep neural network in star topology, in: 2019 IEEE/RSJ International Conference on Intelligent Robots and Systems (IROS), IEEE, 2019, pp. 8075–8080.

[12] A. Mohamed, K. Qian, M. Elhoseiny, C. Claudel, Social-stgcnn: a social spatio-temporal graph convolutional neural network for human trajectory prediction, in: Proceedings of the IEEE/CVF Conference on Computer Vision and Pattern Recognition, 2020, pp. 14424–14432.

[13] C. Yu, M. Xiao, J. Ren, H. Zhao, S. Yi, Spatio-temporal graph transformer networks for pedestrian trajectory prediction, in: European Conference on Computer Vision, Springer, 2020, pp. 507–523.

[14] Y. Peng, G. Zhang, X. Li, L. Zheng, STIRNet: a spatial- temporal interaction-aware recursive network for human trajectory prediction, in: Proceedings of the IEEE/CVF International Conference on Computer Vision, 2021, pp. 2285–2293.

[15] C.M. Bishop, Mixture Density Networks, 1994.

[16] O. Makansi, I. Eddy, O. Cicek, T. Brox, Overcoming limitations of mixture density networks: a sampling and fitting framework for multimodal future prediction, in: Proceedings of the IEEE Conference on Computer Vision and Pattern Recognition, 2019, pp. 7144–7153.

[17] C. Tang, R.R. Salakhutdinov, Multiple futures prediction, Advances in Neural Information Processing Systems 32 (2019) 15424–15434.

[18] K. Mangalam, H. Girase, S. Agarwal, K.-H. Lee, E. Adeli, J. Malik, A. Gaidon, It is not the journey but the destination: endpoint conditioned trajectory prediction, in: European Conference on Computer Vision, Springer, 2020, pp. 759–776.

[19] J. Li, Y. Fan, M. Tomizuka, C. Choi, Evolvegraph: Het- Erogeneous Multi-Agent Multi-Modal Trajectory Prediction with Evolving Interaction Graphs vol 2, 2020, p. 13921. ArXiv, abs/2003.

[20] J. Gu, C. Sun, H. Zhao, Densetnt: end-to-end trajectory prediction from dense goal sets, in: Proceedings of the IEEE/CVF International Conference on Computer Vision, 2021, pp. 15303—15312.

[21] Z. He, R.P. Wildes, Where are you heading? dynamic trajectory pre- diction with expert goal examples, in: Proceedings of the IEEE/CVF International Conference on Computer Vision, 2021, pp. 7629—7638.

[22] P. Dendorfer, A. Osep, L. Leal-Taixe, Goal-gan: multimodal trajectory prediction based on goal position estimation, in: Proceedings of the Asian Conference on Computer Vision, 2020.

[23] M. Ren, E. Triantafillou, S. Ravi, J. Snell, S. Kevin, J. B Tenenbaum, H. Larochelle, R.S. Zemel, Meta-learning for Semi- Supervised Few-Shot Classification, 2018 *arXiv preprint arXiv:1803.00676*.

[24] Q. Sun, Y. Liu, T.-S. Chua, B. Schiele, Meta-transfer learning for few-shot learning, in: Proceedings of the IEEE/CVF Conference on Computer Vision and Pattern Recognition, 2019, pp. 403—412.

[25] T. Yu, D. Quillen, Z. He, J. Ryan, K. Hausman, C. Finn, S. Levine, Meta-world: a benchmark and evaluation for multi- task and meta reinforcement learning, in: Conference on Robot Learning, PMLR, 2020, pp. 1094—1100.

[26] J.X. Wang, Z. Kurth-Nelson, D. Kumaran, D. Tirumala, H. Soyer, J.Z. Leibo, D. Hassabis, M. Botvinick, Prefrontal cortex as a meta-reinforcement learning system, Nature Neuroscience 21 (6) (2018) 860—868.

[27] C. Finn, P. Abbeel, S. Levine, Model-agnostic meta-learning for fast adaptation of deep networks, in: International Conference on Machine Learning, PMLR, 2017, pp. 1126—1135.

[28] S. Becker, R. Hug, W. Hübner, M. Arens, An Evaluation of Trajectory Prediction Approaches and Notes on the Trajnet Benchmark, 2018 *arXiv preprint arXiv: 1805.07663*.

[29] H. Yao, Y. Wang, W. Ying, P. Zhao, M. Mahdavi, D. Lian, C. Finn, Meta-learning with an adaptive task scheduler, Advances in Neural Information Processing Systems 34 (2021).

[30] A. Lerner, Y. Chrysanthou, D. Lischinski, Crowds by example, in: Computer Graphics Forum, vol 26, Wiley Online Library, 2007, pp. 655—664.

[31] S. Pellegrini, A. Ess, K. Schindler, L. Van Gool, You'll never walk alone: modeling social behavior for multi-target tracking, in: 2009 IEEE 12th International Conference on Computer Vision, IEEE, 2009, pp. 261—268.

[32] Y. Ma, X. Zhu, S. Zhang, R. Yang, W. Wang, D. Manocha, Trafficpredict: trajectory prediction for heterogeneous traffic-agents, in: Proceedings of the AAAI Conference on Artificial Intelligence, vol 33, 2019, pp. 6120—6127.

[33] V. Kosaraju, A. Sadeghian, R. Martín-Martín, I. Reid, R. Hamid, S. Savarese, Social-bigat: multimodal trajectory forecasting using bicycle-gan and graph attention networks, in: Advances in Neural Information Processing Systems, 2019, pp. 137—146.

[34] X. Li, X. Ying, M.C. Chuah, Grip++: Enhanced Graph-Based Interaction-Aware Trajectory Prediction for Autonomous Driving, 2019 *arXiv preprint arXiv:1907.07792*.

[35] L. Fang, Q. Jiang, J. Shi, B. Zhou, Tpnet: trajectory proposal network for motion prediction, in: Proceedings of the IEEE/CVF Conference on Computer Vision and Pattern Recognition, 2020, pp. 6797—6806.

CHAPTER TEN

Social-DPF: socially acceptable distribution prediction of futures

Xiaodan Shi[1], Xiaowei Shao[1,2], Guangming Wu[1], Haoran Zhang[4], Zhiling Guo[1], Renhe Jiang[3], Ryosuke Shibasaki[1]

[1]Center for Spatial Information Science, The University of Tokyo, Kashiwa-shi, Chiba, Japan
[2]Earth Observation Data Integration and Fusion Research Initiative, The University of Tokyo, Kashiwa-shi, Chiba, Japan
[3]Information Technology Center, The University of Tokyo, Kashiwa-shi, Chiba, Japan
[4]School of Urban Planning and Design, Peking University, Shenzhen, China

1. Introduction

The ability to predict long-term futures accurately lies at the heart of autonomous driving and social robots navigation [1—6] where autonomous driving cars and social robots share the same ecosystem with humans. They adjust their paths by anticipating human movements, specifically, avoiding collisions or maintaining a safe distance from other people. Modeling human interactions is a challenging aspect of trajectory prediction task. Although humans can intuitively know how to interact with other people in crowds, it is not easy for machines to learn those interaction rules owing to the complexities and uncertainties of human crowds (Fig. 10.1).

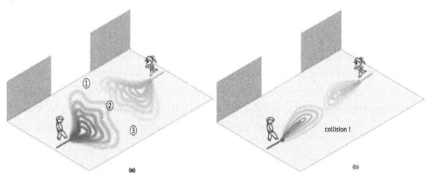

Figure 10.1 Objective of this Study is to Forecast Socially Acceptable Distributions of Futures. There are multiple plausible forthcoming paths in an interactive and dynamic scenario (for example, the boy walks to 1 and the girl walks to 2 or 3). The result of (b) is not socially acceptable owing to the collisions between them.

Handbook of Mobility Data Mining, Volume 2
ISBN: 978-0-443-18424-6
https://doi.org/10.1016/B978-0-443-18424-6.00003-9

Since the success of recurrent neural network (RNN) on sequence modeling, RNN-based models have been well developed for use in trajectory prediction.

Social LSTM which introduces social pooling to calculate the global representations for interactions by aggregating the latent states of spatially proximal pedestrians, is an important development for real-world paths forecasting [7]. The existing research follow the way of Social LSTM but with improvements. The research [8,9,14]; utilize spatiotemporal graph representations to describe motion dynamics over time and space. By modeling the topography of graphs, the models can naturally model social interactions and the movement of people. By contrast, generative adversarial network (GAN)-based models are investigated to model the uncertainty of futures [10–12]. GAN-based models usually contains social mechanisms in the generators and forecast multiple plausible trajectories instead of a single future path. The distributions of futures can be plotted through samples from the generators. The existing methods usually predict a single future path or distributions of the futures by minimizing (or a combination of) L_2 loss, adversarial loss or maximizing the lower bound of the log-likelihood function between the distributions of estimated futures and the distributions of ground truth.

However, predicting socially acceptable trajectories still remains as an issue. First, the existing research usually use "pooling" as an aggregation mechanism which is limited to model dynamic interactions and also leaky in information [13,14]. They either use a Euclidean-distance based ordering structure to select a fixed number of neighbors or use Max/Average functions for pooling, where the former is not rational for use in dynamic real-world scenarios and the latter loses individual uniqueness [12]. Although it can be optimized by introducing attention mechanism [15–17], it still can't model interactions accurately [11,17]. Second, although the existing research design architectures containing social mechanisms, their loss functions only access the accuracy of estimated distributions or locations are without considering social constraints, particularly collision avoidance, leading to a poor performance in terms of modeling social constraints.

To address the above limitations, we develop a trajectory prediction model named Social DPF for predicting socially acceptable multimodal distributions of futures. To deal with dynamic social interactions, we propose a new aggregation mechanism by capturing the inter-related dynamics between multiple motion sequences over space and time. The new aggregation mechanism selectively incorporates the latent states of concurrent movements in a shared environment through two message passing gates and generates social states that reveals how people interact in crowds. To further generate socially plausible distributions of futures, we propose a loss function that not only accesses how the predictions meet the ground truth but also measures if the interactive futures collide. Training maximizes the lower bound on the log-likelihood of the data. Social-DPF further uses mixture density functions to describe human path and learns to model multimodal futures jointly for all pedestrians.

2. Related works

2.1 Social compliant trajectory prediction

Since Social LSTM was proposed, many research have started investigating socially constrained RNN-based trajectory prediction models. Attention mechanisms were firstly utilized to improve Social LSTM by learning different weights of neighbors on an agent [11,16,17]. Some research embedded relative motion (e.g., the relative location and velocity) between pedestrians, followed by pooling the embeddings to generate a global feature for interactions, which is more intuitively than aggregating latent states of the RNNs directly [18,19]. Instead of setting a neighborhood size, some research took into account all people in a scenario or followed a radial basis function to select a certain number of people [12,20].

2.1.1 Spatiotemporal graphs for trajectory prediction

Structural RNN [21], combining high-level spatiotemporal graphs (ST-graphs) with sequence modeling success of RNN, has made significant improvements on problem of human motion modeling. Hence, there are many research following this direction [8,14]. ST-graphs for trajectory prediction are characterized with element points, spatial edges, and temporal edges that represent pedestrians, social interactions, and the temporal transition of trajectories, respectively. ST-graphs make it easy to illustrate the topography of human motion and their interactions and provide a more direct and natural way to model long-term path forecasting by modeling different elements using RNNs.

2.1.2 Multimodal trajectory prediction

Human motions under crowded scenarios imply a multiplicity of modes. Given the observation, there are multiple plausible future paths. Some studies have combined GAN and RNNs to capture the uncertainty of long-term future paths [10–12,22]. They usually contain an RNN-based encoder-decoder generator and an RNN- based decoder discriminator. Some research have applied mixture density network (MDN) to map the distributions of future trajectories [23,24]. The article [23], based on MDN, proposed a two-stage strategy that first predicted several samples of future with winner-take-all loss and then iteratively grouped the samples to multiple modes.

2.1.3 Loss functions for trajectory prediction

The existing models can be classified as deterministic or stochastic models [22]. Some deterministic models utilizes L_2 loss function to predict a single path of future [18,25]. The others, such as MDN-based methods modeling the trajectories as a mixture model of bivariate Gaussian models, are trained by minimizing the negative log-likelihood function over the modes [7,23,24]. The stochastic models, by contrast, are based on GAN and usually trained by minimizing the loss functions containing an L_2 loss and an adversarial loss L_{gan} [10,11]. To truly learn multimodality, Social BiGAT designed a loss function containing additional items to map the latent noise to an output trajectory [12]. However, the existing research have only accessed how ac-curate the estimated futures are. They haven't considered social interactions in loss functions.

3. Problem formulation

We assume that each scenario is first preprocessed to obtain 2D spatial coordinates $\left(x_i^t, y_i^t\right) \in \mathbf{R}$ and 2D walking speed $\left(u_i^t, v_i^t\right) \in \mathbf{R}$ of any pedestrian i at any time instant t. The observation of pedestrian i is the past trajectory, which is represented as: $X_i^{1:\tau-1} = \left\{\left(x_i^t, y_i^t, u_i^t, v_i^t\right) \mid t = 1, 2, \cdots, \tau - 1\right\}$ 1g while the future trajectory is $Y_i^{\tau:T} = \left\{\left(x_i^t, y_i^t\right) \mid t = \tau, \cdots, T\right\}$. We assume there are N agents in the scenario, $i = 1, 2, \ldots, N$.

Our goal is to learn socially acceptable posterior distribution $p\left(Y_i^{\tau:T} \mid X_i^{1:\tau-1}, X_{1:N\backslash i}^{1:\tau-1}\right)$. To this end, we jointly model multiple ego-trajectories and their interactions with.

Φ. Therefore, the distribution of futures is denoted as follows:

$$p\left(Y_i^{\tau T} \mid X_i^{1:\tau-1}, X_{\textit{t}N\backslash i}^{1:\tau-1}\right) = \Phi\left(X_i^{1:\tau-1}, X_{\textit{t}N\backslash i}^{1:\tau-1}; w^*\right) \qquad (10.1)$$

where w^* are the parameters of the model we aim to learn. We denote the predicted future paths as $\widehat{Y}_i^{\tau:T}$ which are generated from the distributions.

4. Methodology

4.1 Overall architecture

Social DPF is an encoder-decoder model using two sets of LSTMs (LSTMs in the same set share weights) to represent the movement of agents and their interactions in a scene, as shown in Fig. 10.2. Our model utilizes spatiotemporal graphs to represent human motions and their interactions. At any time instant, point elements of a graph are individuals characterized with location and velocity while the lines between two points are spatial edges representing their current interactions. We construct Social Memory, as depicted in Fig. 10.3, which not only can capture the current interactions among people, it can also model how interactions change over time. The Social Memory takes use of LSTMs and are recurrent over time. The Social Memory takes hidden states from single person's LSTM as input and selectively integrate the inter-related hidden states through two gates to generate social states. Then social states storing interaction information are fed into single person's LSTM to generate latent features. Based on the latent features, our model directly outputs the parameters of the distributions of future

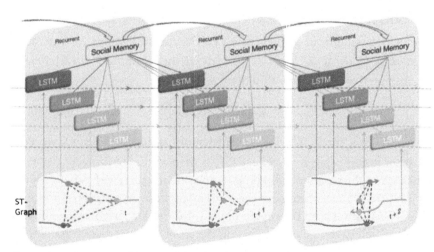

Figure 10.2 Overview of Our Model Architecture. We utilize two LSTMs to capture the spatial and temporal cues, specifically one LSTM for single person's trajectories, and one LSTM for social memory which selectively integrates the latent states coming from the single person's LSTM. The details of social memory are illustrated in Fig. 10.3.

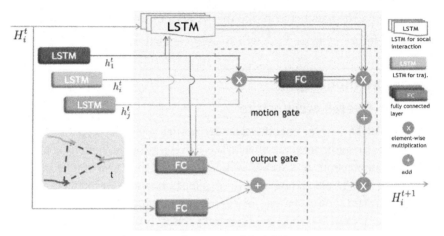

Figure 10.3 Illustration of Social Memory.

trajectories through MDN combining a multilayer perception with Gaussian mixture models (GMMs). For the loss function, we use $\mathcal{L}_{mode}$ to estimate how closely the predicted distribution matches the distribution of target variables in the training data, whereas $\mathcal{L}_{collision1}$ and $\mathcal{L}_{collision2}$ achieve access if the estimated futures of agents collide with each other. Our loss function is based on Winner-Takes-All (WTA) loss which can prevent the model from collapsing into a single mode [23].

4.2 Social memory

The hidden states from single person's LSTM at time instant $t - 1$ are represented as $\{h_i^{t-1} | i = 1, \cdots, N\}$ which are the input for Social Memory. We assume that a person with index i is the agent.

$$\tilde{h}_j^t = \psi_1\left(H_i^{t-1}, h_i^{t-1}; w_H^*\right) \tag{10.2}$$

where $\psi_1(\cdot)$ is the LSTM for Social Memory and its weights w_H^* are also shared among people in a scene, H_i^{t-1} is the social state of agent i at $t-1$ which stores the representation on how an agent interacts with other people, $j \in \{1, \cdots, N\}\backslash i$. To connect the current motions, we design a motion gate. The motion gate selectively obtains the motion information among people which have a genuine effect on the agent's path and contributes to a candidate social state.

$$d_j^{t-1} = \phi_1\left(h_i^{t-1} \cup h_j^{t-1}; w_1^*\right)$$

$$\gamma_i^t = \sum_{j=1}^{N\backslash i} d_j^{t-1} \odot h_j^t \tag{10.3}$$

where ϕ_1 $(\cdot)$ is a fully connected layer that connects an agent and other people, which are depicted as purple lines on ST-graph in Fig. 10.2. Here, γ_i^t is the candidate social state from the motion gate, representing the interaction information between an agent and neighbors. We then construct out-put gate. The output gate learns the role of the neighbors in the agent's social interactions, which controls the extent to which social interactions remains in the social states.

$$g_j^{t-1} = \phi_2\left(h_j^{t-1}; w_2^*\right)$$

$$o_j^{t-1} = \sum_{j=1}^{N\backslash i} g_j^{t-1} + \phi_3\left(H_i^{t-1}; w_3^*\right)$$ (10.4)

where o_j^{t-1} is the feature from output gate, ϕ_2 $(\cdot)$ and ϕ_3 $(\cdot)$ are fully connected layers with *dropout* $= 0.50$, ϕ_2 $(\cdot)$ is with Sigmoid nonlinearity, w_2^* and w_3^* are their weights respectively.

$$H_i^t = \gamma_j^t \odot o_j^{t-1}$$ (10.5)

where H_i^t is the social states which are then concatenated with the agent's current states for predicting the distributions of futures. The Social Memory is recurrent, thus H_i^t is also fed into the Social Memory in the next time step.

4.3 Path forecasting

As mentioned in Section 3, the agent i at time instant t is characterized with location (x_i^t, y_i^t) and velocity (u_i^t, v_i^t). We embed them respectively to obtain the input for single person's LSTM.

$$f_i^t = \left[\phi_4\left((x_i^t, y_i^t); w_4^*\right), \phi_5\left((u_i^t, v_i^t); w_5^*\right)\right]$$ (10.6)

where ϕ_4 $(\cdot)$ and ϕ_5 $(\cdot)$ are fully connected layers with ReLU nonlinearity and w_4^* and w_5^* are the embedding weights. We get the social states H_i^t of agent i at time t and concatenate it with f_i^t to predict the next state of the agent.

$$h_i^t = \psi_2\left(h_i^{t-1}, \left[f_i^t, H_i^t\right]; w_h^*\right)$$ (10.7)

Here, ψ_2 $(\cdot)$ is single person's LSTM and its weights w^*_h are shared between all people in a scenario. To capture the multi-modality of future paths, we utilize MDN which combines a multilayer perception with GMMs. The next location of agent are given by the following:

$$\widehat{\gamma}_i^{t+1} \sim N_2\left(\alpha_i^t, \mu_i^t, \sigma_i^t\right)$$ (10.8)

where priors α_i^t means μ_i^t and standard deviation σ_i^t are the output Gaussian mixture components of pedestrian i at)t. $\alpha_i^t = \left\{ \left(\alpha_g\right)_i^t | g = 1, ..., M \right\}$, $\mu^t = \left\{ \left(\mu_g\right)_i^t | g = 1, ..., M \right\}$, $\sigma_i^t = \left\{ \left(\sigma_g\right)_i^t | g = 1, ..., M \right\}$ and $\mu_g = \left(\mu_x, \mu_y\right)$, $\sigma_g = \left(\sigma_x, \sigma_y\right)$ is the number of Gaussian models of MDN. Each Gaussian model is a bivariate Gaussian model. The probability density function of the next location conditioned on h_i^t is denoted as follows:

$$p\left(\widehat{\gamma}_i^{t+1} | h_i^t\right) = \alpha_i^t p\left(\widehat{\gamma}_i^{t+1} | \mu_i^t, \sigma_i^t\right) \tag{10.9}$$

We learn the mixing coefficients μ_i^t, σ_i^t and α_i^t through the network. To constrain α_i^t to lie within the range [0, 1] and to sum to unity, we use the *softmax* function. Function *exp()* is used to avoid standard deviation σ_i^t smaller than or equal to zero.

$$\alpha_g = \frac{exp\left(a_g\right)}{\sum\limits_{k=1}^{M} exp(a_k)}$$

$$\mu_g = u_g \tag{10.10}$$

$$\sigma_g = exp\left(z_g\right)$$

where $\{a_g | g = 1, ... , M\}$, $\{u_g | g = 1, ... , M\}$ and $\{z_g | g = 1, ... , M\}$ is obtained through fully connected layers $\phi_\alpha\left(h_i^t\right)$, $\phi_\mu\left(h_i^t\right)$ and $\phi_\sigma\left(h_i^t\right)$, respectively.

4.4 Loss function

To avoid collisions and truly learn the multi-modality of human motion, we design the loss function as indicated Eq. (10.11), which combines three items for predicting the socially acceptable future trajectories for pedestrians.

$$\mathcal{L} = \mathcal{L}_{mode} + \lambda_1 \mathcal{L}_{collision1} + \lambda_2 \mathcal{L}_{collision2} \tag{10.11}$$

where L_{mode} is used to assess how accurate the estimated distributions are in predicting the future trajectories. In addition, $L_{collision1}$ and $L_{Collision2}$ are introduced to prevent pedestrians colliding in crowds. To avoid collisions with others, the estimated distribution of the agent should first uncover the future locations of other people. We utilize $L_{collision1}$ to capture this effect. Moreover, the estimated distributions at each time instant should be differ from each other. We use $L_{collision2}$ to measure the different probability distributions of one person from others.

For L_{mode}, instead of computing the negative log-likelihood function over all components of a mixture model, which easily collapses the model into a single mode, we always base the winner selection on the probability of the mixture model and multiply the winner probability with the learned weight as follows:

$$\mathscr{L}_{mode} = -\frac{1}{N} \sum_{t=\tau}^{T-1} \sum_{i=1}^{N} log\left(\alpha_i^t \, p\left(\widehat{Y}_i^{t+1} \middle| \mu_i^t, \sigma_i^t\right)\right) \tag{10.12}$$

where, $\alpha_i^t = (\alpha_g)_i^t$, $\mu_i^t = (\mu_g)_i^t$, $\sigma_i^t = (\sigma_g)_i^t$ and $g = $ arg $\max\limits_{g} p\left(\widehat{Y}^{t+1} \middle| \mu_g^t, \sigma_g^t\right)$. We assume that the predicted future path would be exactly the same as the ground truth and the neighbors are not supposed to lie within the estimated distribution of an agent. To achieve this effect, we introduced $\swarrow_{collision1}$ as follows:

$$\mathscr{L}_{collision1} = -\frac{1}{N^*(N-1)} \sum_{t=\tau}^{T-1} \sum_{i=1}^{N} \sum_{j=1}^{N\backslash i} log\left(1 - \alpha_i^t p\left(Y_j^{t+1} \middle| \mu_i^t, \sigma_i^t\right)\right)$$

$$\tag{10.13}$$

where, α_i^t, μ_i^t, σ_i^t are the same as in Eq. (10.12). When neighbors don't lie within the probability distribution of an agent, $L_{collision1}$ tends to be zero which has no effect on the entire loss function. Here, $C_{collision2}$ measures the amount of overlap between the predicted distributions of the pedestrians. If two predicted distributions can't be separate, the pedestrians tend to collide. We utilized Bhattacharyya distance to establish $L_{collision2}$ as follows:

$$\mathscr{L}_{collision2} = \frac{1}{N^*(N-1)} \sum_{t=\tau}^{T-1} \sum_{i=1}^{N} \sum_{j=1}^{N\backslash i} log\left(\int_z \alpha_i^t \sqrt{q_i^t(z)q_j^t(z)}\,dz\right)$$

$$\tag{10.14}$$

where, $q_i^t(z) = N_2\left(z \middle| \mu_i^t, \sigma_i^t\right), q_j^t(z) = \left(z \middle| \mu_j^t, \sigma_j^t\right)$. A smaller $\swarrow_{collision2}$ means that there is less overlap between two predicted distributions.

5. Experiments

In this section, the proposed model is evaluated on two publicly available datasets: UCY [26] and ETH [27]. The two datasets contain five sets, which are UCY-zara01, UCY-zara02, UCY-univ, ETH-hotel, ETH-eth in four crowded scenarios with totally 1536 trajectories. We firstly preprocess those two datasets by resampling them at 2.5 fps and transforming the coordinates of people into world coordinates in meters.

Implementation Details. Our model is trained end-to-end by minimizing the proposed loss function (Eq. 10.11). The experiments are implemented using Pytorch under Ubuntu.

16.04 LTS using a GTX 1080 GPU. The size of the hidden states of all LSTMs is set to 128. The embedding layers are composed of a fully connected layer with size 64 for Eq. 6 and 128 for the others. The batch size is set to eight and all the methods are trained for 200 epochs. The optimizer RM- Sprop is used to train the proposed model with a learning rate 0.001. We clip the gradients of the LSTM with a maximum threshold of 10 to stabilize the training process. We set Ai and A_2 in Eq. (10.11) as 0.1. The model outputs GMMs with three components.

Evaluation Approach. The proposed model is trained and tested on the two datasets with leave-one-out approach: trained on four sets and tested on the remaining set. We observe the trajectory for eight timesteps (3.2 s) and show the prediction results for 12 timesteps (4.8 s). To evaluate the performance, we compare our method with other state-of- the-art models on two generally used matrices.

1. Average displacement error (ADE): average L2 distance over all the prediction results and the ground truth.
2. Final displacement error (FDE): distance between prediction results and ground truth at the final timestep.

Baselines. The proposed model is compared with the following baselines.

1. Linear method. The second order Kalman Filter uses the position, velocity, acceleration.
2. LSTM. Human motion is modeled without considering human interactions. Offset is used as the input.
3. Social LSTM. It pools all hidden states of LSTMs for social interactions.
4. Social GAN. GAN-based model which considers social interactions and predicts multiple plausible futures.
5. Sophie. GAN-based model which considers both social and physical interactions to make more realistic predictions.
6. Social-BiGAT. This method uses a generator, local/global discriminators, and a latent noise encoder to construct a reversible mapping between predicted paths and learned latent features of trajectories.
7. Social STGCNN: The method substitutes aggregation methods by modeling the interactions as a graph.

Ablation Study To describe how our model works, we also represent the results of various versions of our model Social DPF in an ablation setting using $L_k G_m$. Here, L_k signifies which loss the model is trained with (where $k = 1,2,3$ indicates $\pounds_{mode}$, $L_{collisioni}$ and $L_{collision2}$, respectively.). In addition, G_m signifies which gate the model contains (where m = 1, 2 indicate the motion gate and output gate, respectively). For entire Social DPF, we also test two versions in a setting by: V_1 uses the means of the distributions with maximum weights for testing; V_2 draw 20 samples from the entire distributions for testing. We conducts three sets of ablation studies: set 1 containing $\checkmark_{1,2,3}\square_m$ (m = 1, 2), set 2 containing $\checkmark_k\square_{1,2}$ (k = 1,2,3), set 3 containing $\checkmark_{1,2,3}\square_{1t2}$-$\mathbf{\tilde{Z}}_n$(n = 1,2) that is the entire model of Social DPF.

5.1 Quantitative evaluation

ETH and UCY. We compare our model to various baselines in Table 10.1, reporting the ADE and final displacement error (FDE) for 12 timesteps of human movements. In general, the linear method performs worse than the other methods because it is limited to modeling the social context or multi-modality of human motion. Social LSTM only achieves an accuracy similar to that of LSTM, although it is trained with synthetic data and then fine-tuned on the benchmarks [10]. LSTM use offset as the input, which stabilizes the learning process and improves the performance. Sophie, Social GAN, Social BiGAT, and Social STGCNN capturing the uncertainty of long-term movement all achieve better results than Social LSTM and basic LSTM.

The first set of our models tests how the motion gate and output gate perform with Social DPF. The models $L_{1,2,3}G_1$ and $L_{1,2,3}\ G_2$ solely modeling human interactions with motion gate and output gate, respectively, made a poor performance. By comparing the first and the third sets, we can easily find that motion gate and output gate together help Social DPF to better capture the long-term interactions among people. Interestingly, the motion gate seems to have a larger effect than output gate, which also reveals the importance of connecting inter-related dynamics. The second set of our models test the performance of each item of our loss function. As expected, $L_{1,2}\ G_{1,2}$ and $L_{1,3}\ G_{1,2}$ achieve better results than $L_1\ G_{1,2}$ on most of the datasets, which demonstrates that collision loss is able to help our model performs better. Interestingly, $L_{1,3}\ G_{1,2}$ performs slightly better than $\pounds_{1,2}\pounds_{1,2}$, which potentially implying $\pounds_{collision2}$ is more helpful than $L_{collision1}$. On the other hand, $L_1\ \pounds_{1,2}$ solely utilizing the proposed new aggregation

Table 10.1 Quantitative results of baselines versus our method across datasets for predicting 12 future timesteps(4.8 s) given eight timesteps observations(3.2 s) (lower is better). The results of Social LSTM, Social GAN are from Ref. [10], the results of Sophie, Social BiGAT, Social STGCNN are from Refs. [11,12,14], respectively.

Method	Note	Evaluation (ADE(m)/FDE(m))					
		ETH-eth	ETH-hotel	UCY-univ	UCY-zara01	UCY-zara02	Avg
Linear	Kalman filter	1.65/2.84	0.99/1.70	0.86/1.51	0.83/1.44	0.54/0.96	0.97/1.69
LSTM	Offset is input	0.71/1.40	1.15/2.09	0.72/1.49	0.48/0.98	0.38/0.77	0.69/1.35
Social LSTM	Social pooling	1.09/2.35	0.79/1.76	0.67/1.40	0.47/1.00	0.56/1.17	0.72/1.54
Sophie	20 samples	0.70/1.43	0.76/1.67	0.54/1.24	**0.30**/0.63	0.38/0.78	0.54/1.15
Social GAN	20 samples	0.72/1.29	0.48/1.01	0.56/1.18	0.34/0.69	0.31/0.65	0.48/0.96
Social BiGAT	20 samples	0.69/1.29	0.49/1.01	0.55/1.32	**0.30**/0.62	0.36/0.75	0.48/1.00
Social STGCNN	20 samples	0.64/1.11	0.49/0.85	**0.44**/0.79	0.34/**0.53**	**0.30**/0.48	0.44/0.75
S-DPF-$\lambda_{1,2,3}\square_1$	set1, G_1, 20 samples	0.89/1.16	0.53/0.95	0.82/1.30	0.49/0.74	0.59/0.90	0.66/1.01
S-DPF-$\lambda_{1,2,3}\square_2$	set1, G_2,20 samples	0.76/0.96	1.24/1.26	0.94/1.32	0.88/1.12	0.81/1.01	0.93/1.13
S-DPF-$\lambda_1\square_{1,2}$	set2,L_1, 20 samples	0.71/0.95	0.35/0.54	0.62/0.78	0.40/0.65	0.45/0.57	0.51/0.70
S-DPF-$\lambda_{1,2}\square_{1,2}$	set2, $L_{1,2}$,20 samples	0.66/0.94	0.42/0.58	0.59/0.74	0.37/0.64	0.41/0.51	0.49/0.68
S-DPF-$\lambda_{1,3}\square_{1,2}$	set2, $L_{1,3}$,20 samples	**0.61/0.91**	0.40/0.54	0.57/0.75	0.36/0.63	0.39/0.49	0.47/0.66
S-DPF-$\lambda_{1,2,3}\square_1$	set3, entire model,1 sample	0.69/1.35	0.39/0.84	0.61/1.00	0.40/0.89	0.39/0.84	0.50/0.98
S-DPF-$\lambda_{1,2,3}\square_2$	set3, entire model, 20 samples	0.66/0.92	**0.34/0.50**	0.50/**0.69**	0.34/0.59	0.32/**0.45**	**0.43/0.63**

mechanism for the social context performs well on average, which also demonstrates the ability of the proposed aggregation mechanism to model long-term social interactions. To further illustrate that collision loss can help to generate socially acceptable results, we also qualitatively compare the results of $L_1 \pounds_{1,2}$ and $L_{1,2,3}\pounds_{1,2}$ in the next section (Qualitative Evaluation). The final model, $L_{1,2,3}\pounds_{1,2}$, consisting of collision loss and two gates, outperforms the previous models, suggesting that combining both collision loss and new aggregation mechanism allows for robust predictions.

Collision Avoidance. To better understand our model's ability to produce socially acceptable futures, we also utilize another evaluation metric that reflects the percentage of near-collisions as in Ref. [11]. We consider two pedestrians to have collided if they come closer than 0.20 m to each other. The average percentages of pedestrian collisions in ETH and UCY datasets are calculated as shown in Table 10.2 (average percentage of pedestrian collisions is the average of 20 samples from estimated distributions). Social DPF consistently outperforms other baselines in term of collision avoidance.

5.2 Qualitative evaluation

To investigate the ability of social DPF to forecast socially acceptable futures distributions, we visualize three sets of scenarios from ETH-hotel and UCY-zara02 and compare the predictions of two state-of-the-art models, Social GAN and Social STGCNN, to that of our model (Fig. 10.4). To compare their distributions more intuitively, we plot the entire distributions Social DPF predicted. In scenarios (a) where the walking pedestrians should adjust their courses to overtake people standing in front of them. Social GAN and Social STGCNN forecasted the futures distributions implying an incorrect walking direction or velocity, which further lead to collisions among people.

Table 10.2 Average % of colliding people each frame in ETH & UCY. Two pedestrians are considered collided if their Euclidean distance is less than 0.2 m.

	Collision evaluation (colliding persons per frame(%))				
Datasets	GT	Linear	S-GAN	S-STGCNN	S-DPF
ETH-eth	0.037	0.202	0.397	0.783	**0.030**
ETH-hotel	0.000	0.187	0.738	1.443	**0.012**
UCY-univ	0.304	2.408	2.519	3.741	**0.512**
UCY-zara01	0.000	0.523	0.186	1.100	**0.039**
UCY-zara02	0.044	0.833	0.904	3.100	**0.114**

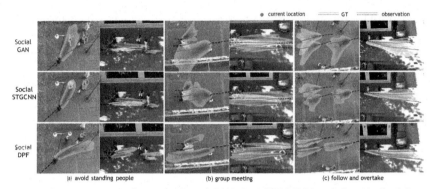

Figure 10.4 Comparison between Social GAN, Social STGCNN and Our Method Over Three Sets of Scenarios.

Scenarios (b) depict groups meeting where collisions would also happen if pedestrians maintained their momentum. Social DPF jointly models the dynamics between movements and better aligns the predictions to social constraints than Social GAN and Social STGCNN. Scenarios (c) illustrate people following and overtaking in which Social DPF outperformed Social GAN and Social STGCNN by better predicting the walking speed, directions, and avoidance behaviors.

To further illustrate that Social DPF is able to forecast multiple plausible distributions of futures, we also show three real-scenarios: overtaking, avoiding standing people, and two-groups meeting where people have to alter their course to avoid collisions, as shown in Fig. 10.5. In each scenario, two possible distributions (distributions of each agent with maximum and second maximum weights) of futures associated with velocity, walking

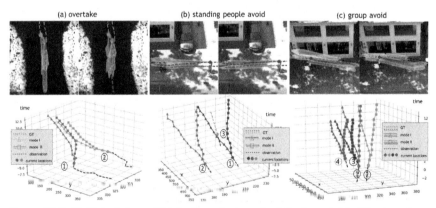

Figure 10.5 Multiple Futures Distributions that are Socially Acceptable. We show two sets of possible futures under each scenario where intense social interactions occur. The dynamics of people walking are shown in the 3D figures(we plot the average location of the distributions). Time is the z-axis and the same marker denote the same mode.

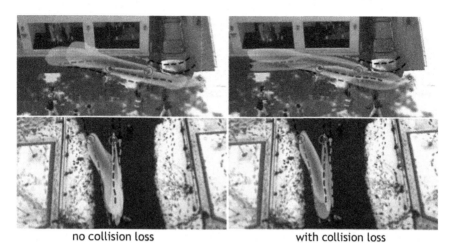

no collision loss   with collision loss

Figure 10.6 Comparison of Collision Loss.

direction are illustrated to show how people interact and navigate. In (a), the agent 1 will behave either in a mild way (I) or in an aggressive way (II) to overtake agent2. In (b), the agent 1 will collide with the standing pedestrian if he/she doesn't change walking direction. The agent 1 will overtake the standing people on the right or on the left. In (c), two groups meet in front of Zara store, and the results show multiple plausible interactions between them. The pedestrians' distributions of the same mode seem to show a global coherency and conformity to social norms which also help Social DPF to predict socially acceptable results for pedestrians in a scene.

We also consider two real-world scenarios from ETH-eth and UCY-zara02 where intense social interactions occur to investigate how collision loss perform with Social DPF, as shown in Fig. 10.6. In scenario1, two groups meet in a corner. Collision will happen if the agents doesn't change the walking course. In scenario2, the agent is merging into a group. Although Social DPF without collision loss is able to forecast the distributions of futures by adjusting walking direction or speed, $L_{collision1}$ and $L_{collision2}$ prevent the agent from colliding with others which can help the model to predict socially acceptable results better.

6. Conclusion

We propose a trajectory prediction framework Social DPF, which jointly takes into account multiple interacting movements and predicts multimodal socially acceptable distributions of futures. We introduce a novel aggregation mechanism called Social Memory to learn the long-term dynamic representations among pedestrians in a shared environment. Social Memory selectively integrates and stores the interaction information through two gates, motion gate, and output gate. To better model the social constraints, we introduce collision loss to alleviate collision on futures distributions. Social DPF outperforms other state-of-the-art models over a number of publicly available datasets. We also demonstrate that it is able to provide more socially acceptable distributions by qualitatively analyzing the performance of Social DPF under scenarios such as group meeting, collision avoidance comparing to other baselines. Our model forecasting distributions of the same mode tend to show a global coherency and conformity to social norms. Future work will continue to explore it and extend our model to forecast all possible future modes of an interacting group. We also intend to consider multiple objects, such as bicycles, cars, and test the model performance with more benchmarks.

References

[1] K.M. Kitani, B.D. Ziebart, J.A. Bagnell, M. Hebert, Activity forecasting, in: European Conference on Computer Vision, Springer, 2012, pp. 201–214.

[2] V. Karasev, A. Ayvaci, B. Heisele, S. Soatto, Intent-aware long-term prediction of pedestrian motion, in: 2016 IEEE International Conference on Robotics and Automation (ICRA), 2016, pp. 2543–2549.

[3] Q. Liu, S. Wu, L. Wang, T. Tan, Predicting the next location: a recurrent model with spatial and temporal contexts, in: Thirtieth AAAI Conference on Artificial Intelligence, 2016.

[4] N. Lee, W. Choi, P. Vernaza, C.B. Choy, P.H. Torr, M. Chandraker, Desire: distant future prediction in dynamic scenes with interacting agents, in: Proceedings of the IEEE Conference on Computer Vision and Pattern Recognition, 2017, pp. 336–345.

[5] H. Su, J. Zhu, Y. Dong, B. Zhang, Forecast the plausible paths in crowd scenes, IJCAI 1 (2017) 2.

[6] J. Liang, L. Jiang, J.C. Niebles, A.G. Hauptmann, L. Fei-Fei, Peeking into the future: predicting future person activities and locations in videos, in: Proceedings of the IEEE Conference on Computer Vision and Pattern Recognition, 2019, pp. 5725–5734.

[7] A. Alahi, K. Goel, V. Ramanathan, A. Robicquet, L. Fei-Fei, S. Savarese, Social lstm: human trajectory prediction in crowded spaces, in: Proceedings of the IEEE Conference on Computer Vision and Pattern Recognition, 2016, pp. 961–971.

[8] Y. Huang, H. Bi, Z. Li, T. Mao, Z. Wang, Stgat: modeling spatial-temporal interactions for human trajectory prediction, in: Proceedings of the IEEE International Conference on Computer Vision, 2019, pp. 6272–6281.

[9] J. Li, H. Ma, Z. Zhang, M. Tomizuka, Social- Wagdat: Interaction-Aware Trajectory Prediction via Wasser- Stein Graph Double-Attention Network, 2020 *arXiv preprint arXiv:2002.06241*.

[10] A. Gupta, J. Johnson, L. Fei-Fei, S. Savarese, A. Alahi, Social gan: socially acceptable trajectories with generative adversarial networks, in: Proceedings of the IEEE Conference on Computer Vision and Pattern Recognition, 2018, pp. 2255–2264.

[11] A. Sadeghian, V. Kosaraju, A. Sadeghian, N. Hirose, H. Rezatofighi, S. Savarese, Sophie: an attentive gan for predicting paths compliant to social and physi- cal constraints, in: Proceedings of the IEEE Conference on Computer Vision and Pattern Recognition, 2019, pp. 1349–1358.

[12] V. Kosaraju, A. Sadeghian, R. Martín-Martín, I. Reid, H. Rezatofighi, S. Savarese, Social-bigat: multimodal trajectory forecasting using bicycle-gan and graph attention networks, in: Advances in Neural Information Processing Systems, 2019, pp. 137–146.

[13] T. Williams, R. Li, Wavelet pooling for convolutional neural networks, in: International Conference on Learning Representations, 2018.

[14] A. Mohamed, K. Qian, M. Elhoseiny, C. Claudel, Social-STGCNN: a social spatiotemporal graph convolutional neural network for human trajectory prediction, in: Proceedings of the IEEE/CVF Conference on Computer Vision and Pattern Recognition, 2020, pp. 14424–14432.

[15] M.-T. Luong, H. Pham, C.D. Manning, Effective approaches to attention-based neural machine translation, arXiv preprint arXiv:1508.04025 (2015).

[16] T. Fernando, S. Denman, S. Sridharan, C. Fookes, Soft+ hardwired attention: an lstm framework for human trajectory prediction and abnormal event detection, Neural Networks 108 (2018) 466–478.

[17] P. Zhang, W. Ouyang, P. Zhang, J. Xue, N. Zheng, Sr-lstm: state refinement for lstm towards pedestrian trajectory prediction, in: Proceedings of the IEEE Conference on Computer Vision and Pattern Recognition, 2019, pp. 12085–12094.

[18] S. Becker, R. Hug, W. Hubner, M. Arens, An evaluation of trajectory prediction approaches and notes on the trajnet benchmark, arXiv preprint arXiv:1805.07663 (2018).

[19] X. Shi, X. Shao, Z. Guo, G. Wu, H. Zhang, R. Shibasaki, Pedestrian trajectory prediction in extremely crowded scenarios, Sensors 19 (5) (2019) 1223.

[20] C. Tang, R.R. Salakhutdinov, Multiple futures prediction, Advances in Neural Information Processing Systems (2019) 15424–15434.

[21] A. Jain, A.R. Zamir, S. Savarese, A. Saxena, Structural-rnn: deep learning on spatiotemporal graphs, in: Proceedings of the IEEE Conference on Computer Vision and Pattern Recognition, 2016, pp. 5308–5317.

[22] J. Amirian, J.-B. Hayet, J. Pettré, Social ways: learning multi-modal distributions of pedestrian trajectories with gans, in: Proceedings of the IEEE Conference on Computer Vision and Pattern Recognition Workshops, 2019.

[23] O. Makansi, E. Ilg, O. Cicek, T. Brox, Over- coming limitations of mixture density networks: a sampling and fitting framework for multimodal future prediction, in: Proceedings of the IEEE Conference on Computer Vision and Pattern Recognition, 2019, pp. 7144–7153.

[24] X. Shi, X. Shao, Z. Fan, R. Jiang, H. Zhang, Z. Guo, G. Wu, W. Yuan, R. Shibasaki, Multimodal interaction-aware trajectory prediction in crowded space, in: AAAI, 2020, pp. 11982–11989.

[25] H. Xue, D.Q. Huynh, M. Reynolds, SS-LSTM: a hierarchical LSTM model for pedestrian trajectory prediction, in: 2018 IEEE Winter Conference on Applications of Computer Vision (WACV), 2018, pp. 1186–1194.

[26] A. Lerner, Y. Chrysanthou, D. Lischinski, Crowds by example, in: Computer Graphics Forum, vol 26, Wiley Online Library, 2007, pp. 655–664.

[27] S. Pellegrini, A. Ess, K. Schindler, L. Van Gool, You'll never walk alone: modeling social behavior for multi- target tracking, in: 2009 IEEE 12th International Conference on Computer Vision, 2009, pp. 261–268.

Index

Note: 'Page numbers followed by "*f*" indicate figures and "*t*" indicate tables.'

Printed in the United States
by Baker & Taylor Publisher Services